Effective Frontline Fundraising

A Guide for Non-Profits, Political Candidates, and Advocacy Groups

Jeffrey David Stauch

Apress®

Effective Frontline Fundraising: A Guide for Non-Profits, Political Candidates, and Advocacy Groups

ISBN-13 (pbk): 978-1-4302-3900-0

ISBN-13 (electronic): 978-1-4302-3901-7

Trademarked names, logos, and images may appear in this book. Rather than use a trademark symbol with every occurrence of a trademarked name, logo, or image we use the names, logos, and images only in an editorial fashion and to the benefit of the trademark owner, with no intention of infringement of the trademark.

The use in this publication of trade names, trademarks, service marks, and similar terms, even if they are not identified as such, is not to be taken as an expression of opinion as to whether or not they are subject to proprietary rights.

President and Publisher: Paul Manning
Lead Editor: Jeff Olson
Editorial Board: Steve Anglin, Mark Beckner, Ewan Buckingham, Gary Cornell, Morgan Ertel, Jonathan Gennick, Jonathan Hassell, Robert Hutchinson, Michelle Lowman, James Markham, Matthew Moodie, Jeff Olson, Jeffrey Pepper, Douglas Pundick, Ben Renow-Clarke, Dominic Shakeshaft, Gwenan Spearing, Matt Wade, Tom Welsh
Coordinating Editor: Adam Heath
Copy Editor: Chandra Clarke
Compositor: Mary Sudul
Indexer: BIM Indexing & Proofreading Services
Cover Designer: Anna Ishchenko

Distributed to the book trade worldwide by Springer Science+Business Media, LLC., 233 Spring Street, 6th Floor, New York, NY 10013. Phone 1-800-SPRINGER, fax (201) 348-4505, e-mail orders-ny@springer-sbm.com, or visit www.springeronline.com.

For information on translations, please e-mail rights@apress.com, or visit www.apress.com.

Apress and friends of ED books may be purchased in bulk for academic, corporate, or promotional use. eBook versions and licenses are also available for most titles. For more information, reference our Special Bulk Sales–eBook Licensing web page at www.apress.com/bulk-sales.

To my teachers.
—JDS

Contents

About the Author

Photo Credit: Alex Roca Sala

Jeffrey David Stauch received his BA in political science at Middlebury College and his MA in social sciences at the University of Chicago. He started his career in fundraising in Boston with Grassroots Campaigns, Inc., and Telefund, Inc. Jeffrey is currently the assistant director of principal gifts at a small, elite liberal arts college. He is also the volunteer giving officer for Betasab (www.betasab.org), a home for orphaned children in Ethiopia. When not at work, he runs, coaches youth hockey, trains in the martial art of Aikido, and writes creative non-fiction. He has a pet rabbit.

Acknowledgments

I would like to begin by acknowledging the team at Apress, specifically Jeff Olson and Adam Heath for their guidance and patience while this book came together. Chandra Clarke made us all look good with her expedient and thorough copyediting. Special thanks to Jeff for trusting that we could pull this off in the first place, and for giving me the opportunity to put my thoughts to paper.

I would also like to thank my mentors past and present—Lisa, AJ, Hyam, Mama Duck, Stephanie, Matt, Meghan, Mike, and Sue K (twice now!)—for being generous with their time and wisdom over the years. Much of what is expressed in this book is owed to the lessons that I learned under these very talented fundraisers.

And, of course, thanks to all those donors who support the important work of the nonprofits out there.

Introduction

There's No Such Thing as Luck

My first job as a fundraiser was not glorious. I was working for a for-profit company that contracted with progressive nonprofits that had opted to outsource their fundraising operations. While the job was far from glamorous, it was a great training ground, and I was fortunate to meet many people dedicated to what we called internally *the movement*, or *the left-wing conspiracy*.

My first year, I was put in charge of directing the street canvassing office in Boston, in the lead-up to the mid-term US elections. Our client at the time, not surprisingly, was the Democratic National Committee (DNC). I worked six to seven days a week, averaging more than 60 hours a week (and oftentimes pushing 80). Three or four of those days, I was out with my crew, clipboard in hand in a bright blue DNC t-shirt, waving down pedestrians with a smile and a question along the lines of, "Do you have a minute for the Democrats?" or "Have a second to talk about the mid-terms?"

The work was grueling, and there were certainly moments when I questioned what I was doing. Back at the office, the saying went: "The hours are long, and the work is thankless, but at least the pay sucks."

One of the first lessons I learned, direct from the mouth of one of the vice presidents of the company, let's call him Stan, during our week of intense training in Newton, Massachusetts, was *there's no such thing as luck*. It was an interesting thought, and just counterintuitive enough to make all the young, starry-eyed liberals in the room pause for a second to internalize what exactly that meant.

Stan's point was that becoming an effective fundraiser is about developing a skill set, just as in any other job. His conviction proved true first in my job canvassing on the streets of Boston, then down the hall as I grew the call center of the canvassing company's sister organization, and now, at a small college in New England, soliciting six- and seven-figure gifts and coordinating eight-figure solicitations in collaboration with the college administration.

We often get into fundraising by accident; that was certainly the case for me. I was fresh out of graduate school, and I took the first job I was offered. Despite the long hours and lackluster paycheck, I was fortunate to have a solid training program and great supervisors who were goal driven and checked in weekly on how my staff was doing (or more frequently if performance was down). In most of the nonprofit world, this type of diligence and attention to quantitative data, at least with respect to the development shop, is rare.

Granted, this organization was a *for-profit*, whose sole duty was to raise money for nonprofits. The fact that nonprofits are outsourcing, however, is a sign that they aren't terribly good at doing the development work themselves. This can bring with it a number of problems, especially as an organization first turns toward making its fundraising department a professional "shop." Many clients that this company brought on were quite large: the American Civil Liberties Union (ACLU), the Sierra Club, Save the Children, the Democratic National Committee. All of these organizations were able to make that investment to outsource significant components of their development operations to a third party.

Smaller, younger nonprofits do not have that luxury. First, you might not have the money to spend to pay the vendor. Second, and more important, it is unlikely that you would be taken on as a client. The company I worked for operates on a profit motive, so it wants to concentrate on clients that already have name recognition, nonprofits readily recognizable to the average passerby on the street as canvassers like me tried day after day to flag someone down. Name recognition matters. In fact, the company I used to work for is now turning away business. So instead, young, protean nonprofits are left to their own devices when it comes to fundraising.

Even if it were financially viable for your organization to consider outsourcing, I would recommend against it. As you'll read later on, when I discuss messaging in Chapter 7, when you outsource your fundraising operations, you are also sacrificing a certain degree of quality control. You risk your message getting convoluted by a profit incentive as opposed to a sincere dedication to the mission that your nonprofit represents.

This book is intended to guide you through the steps of setting up a professional development shop, to help you come up with ambitious but achievable annual goals, to make you aware of the important behind-the-scenes aspects of the shop that are essential to moving your operations forward, and, of course, to provide you with the necessary tools to solicit gifts ranging from a one-time donation of $25 to a five-year commitment of $1 million— or more.

You should walk away from reading this book with the confidence to approach your nonprofit's top decision makers with a strong case for why you need to develop and staff a fundraising shop, and why it is a wise (and necessary) investment in the organization you represent. You should also be able to recruit, train, and manage a top-notch development team; come up with a strong annual plan; craft effective messaging; and follow it up with solid stewardship, which in turn prepares you to resolicit your donor base all over again.

Another lesson, which I learned in my second fundraising post working with a college's "Young Alumni" program was this: *You are not responsible for the outcome of the conversation, but you are responsible for the preparation going into that conversation.*

To that end, this book will also teach you how to plan a great fundraising trip, how to provide your prospects with meaningful follow-up, and how to shine in your face-to-face meetings with prospects small and large. This book will also provide you with lessons on how to solicit by phone and e-mail, which will in turn help you to train volunteers to do so. In short, you will learn how to ensure your organization has an impact on society for decades to come.

Before we get into the details, however, let's first look at philanthropy within the context of the nonprofit world.

Nonprofits, Cash Flow, and Philanthropy

Fitting the Puzzle Pieces Together

The aim of this book is to provide you with the tools necessary to expand and improve your nonprofit's fundraising operations. There are many reasons that make the effort worthwhile. Most importantly, more money empowers your organization to do more of what it's designed to do.

What you'll learn is that there's a lot of work that goes into an individual solicitation, whether for $100 or $1,000,000. Preparation and follow-up is a big part of what we do as fundraisers. The actual execution (i.e., the solicitation) is a small, small part of a much larger process.

The Road Ahead

This chapter will ease us into the wide, wide world of philanthropy. I'll begin with a broad sketch of nonprofits in the United States and where cash flow and philanthropy intersect. I'll then talk briefly about philanthropy, both in the United States and abroad. We'll end the chapter with a road map and preview of the path that your fundraising shop might follow.

Nonprofits in the US

The best way to explain how philanthropy fits into the nonprofit world is with an example. One with which I'm most familiar involves my current employer, a small liberal arts college in the heart of New England.

Like almost every college and university in the United States, it has three main sources of revenue. The first and most visible source of revenue is tuition. Every parent of a college-aged child knows about this one, as does every student graduating with thousands of dollars of college debt.

For many small, liberal arts colleges, a full-paying family will spend over $40,000 to send a son or daughter to college for one year. While a hefty price tag, to be sure, this amount does not even cover the entire cost of educating, housing, and feeding a student while at college, plus the costs of extracurricular activities, such as sports, speaking engagements, social events, etc. In many cases, the total cost is closer to $80,000 per year.

So, in the "best" of circumstances (i.e., when you have a full-paying student), there is still a gap of tens of thousands of dollars between tuition and the actual cost of obtaining an education. Also, since upwards of 40 percent of students receive some sort of financial aid (the average grant at many colleges is about $30,000), the gap between a student's family's financial contribution and the cost of educating that student is even greater. Financial aid can represent 15–20 percent of a top college's expenditures, usually second only to what it spends on instruction.

How do such colleges make up the difference between the true cost of education and the tuition charged? Many colleges and universities have endowments that help to alleviate some of the cost. The endowment is invested (in global equities, private equity, alternative assets, etc.) and grows over time. Small colleges and universities have endowments ranging from hundreds of millions to a few billion dollars (larger universities have endowments in the multi-billion dollar range). An average "spend-rate" for a college's endowment is 5 percent,[1] and the hope is that the endowment grows at a rate faster than 5 percent. In 2008–2009, the desired rate of growth was not achieved, which got a lot of institutions of higher education into some pretty troubled waters.

---

[1] Institutions of higher education are not taxed on these endowments, so long as they're actually spending the money. Some institutions have actually gotten into trouble, or almost gotten into trouble, because their endowments had grown to such proportions that they were only spending 2 percent.

Even with expensive tuitions and large endowments pushing $1 billion, these elite colleges *still* rely on philanthropic support in the millions, each year, from alumni, parents, and friends.

Many schools in this category will, for example, raise $15–20 million each year in expendable support (i.e., money that is spent immediately) and upwards of $20 million in endowed funds each year (i.e., money that is reinvested into the endowment and spent at the 5 percent spend rate).

This financial model is the industry standard for independent, private liberal arts colleges and universities, insofar as there is an industry standard. Some colleges rely more heavily on tuition than others, but philanthropy always plays a role in keeping educational institutions afloat.

The college that I represent now, and the nonprofits on whose behalf I canvassed in Boston, are relatively affluent. When I was working as a canvasser in Massachusetts, I was under contract with nonprofits that were large enough to outsource their fundraising—large in the sense that they had the money to spend on outsourcing and also in the sense that they had name recognition. Some of the nonprofits that my organization represented were ACLU, the Sierra Club, Save the Children, the Democratic National Committee, Amnesty International, Human Rights Campaign, People for the American Way, and even political candidates. There was a time, in the heat of the 2008 presidential elections, that my organization had to turn away business because it did not have enough staff to meet the demand for services.

Some of these very well-recognized nonprofits that outsource certain aspects their fundraising also have in-house operations. Arguably, this ability to invest in fundraising gives these nonprofits a distinct advantage over smaller nonprofits. One of the ways for smaller nonprofits to compete (and survive) is to invest in their own development shops. Outsourcing fundraising operations raises standards concerns and quality-control issues that can be avoided if the fundraising staff is on a nonprofit's payroll.

My own experience observing and managing canvassers that were fundraising for multiple clients at a time revealed several problems. Some of those were tied to pay structure, while other problems arose due to the fact that the canvassers were only indirectly working for the client. A good number of canvassers were there solely for the paycheck, and they lacked devotion to the cause of the nonprofit that they were representing. This problem can be avoided by making the investment to pay professional fundraisers to represent the nonprofits directly.

Whether protecting women's rights, saving the rainforest, eradicating poverty, or sustaining the local soccer organization, many nonprofits find themselves in similar situations: they are fiscally solvent, but are held back from expanding programming because they are just making ends meet every year. These nonprofits need someone to manage their fundraising programs, so that they can worry about advancing their main goals.

You can bring your nonprofit to new heights if you make the leap of faith that investing in a fundraising shop is a good idea.

Nonprofits Need Cash

Let's face it: asking for money can make people uncomfortable. Often, when I explain to friends or new acquaintances what I do for a living, the immediate response is "Oh, I could never do that!" My initial reaction is "Yes, fundraising is not for everyone," but I think that this mindset is little more than a mental barrier that must be overcome if you want to succeed in the nonprofit world.

Think about it: You asked your parents for an allowance. You negotiated a raise. You negotiated the price of a new car. While not exactly the same thing as asking someone for money to support a nonprofit, the skill set, I would argue, is quite similar. You just have to begin to see it that way.

Sometimes, asking for money makes people feel somewhat ashamed, much like asking for help with something that they should be able to take care of by themselves. This mindset must be abandoned if you are to be an effective fundraiser. This book will help you do just that.

It is also easy to start perceiving money, or those with money, as dirty, impure, and compromising to your mission. This outlook is perilous. Money, like it or not, is critical to your mission. The more quickly you can accept this truth, the more quickly you can set your sights on doing a good job soliciting people for money.

One of the most disarming questions a new fundraiser can face is, ironically, the most basic one. The question can come in many different forms, but usually is something along the lines of the following:

- Are you asking me for money?
- What do you need from me?
- What's the bottom line?

We'll get to how to respond to questions like these later on, but for now, know that your prospects, particularly the savvy ones, are going to be asking you these kinds of question every day, so you better have good answers at the ready. While that inquiry can sometimes come off as combative or confrontational, it is, in all actuality, an invitation for you to make your pitch.

The overarching point here is that all nonprofits—hospitals, women's shelters, soup kitchens, private (not-for-profit) schools, food shelves, local environmental groups, etc.—need cash. So do political candidates and advocacy groups. The bad news is that fundraising takes you away from your nonprofit's mission—unless you devote staffers to the task. The good news is that professional fundraising is a growing industry, meaning that there are more qualified people to hire. The better news is that there are plenty of people out there looking to give their money to your cause.

Wealth: Where Is It?

With an unbecoming frequency, when we think about where there's money to be had, expendable income to be given away, we turn our sights towards the financial sector, toward Wall Street. There is certainly *plenty* of money there, make no mistake; however, to stop your search there is to be fatally myopic.

You may not immediately become an expert on wealth and where the money is, but you should at least begin to think creatively about where to look for money. You can start with conventional wisdom, but then be sure to push past it. For example, major gift officers often have working knowledge of the wealthier zip codes in the regions and neighborhoods that they cover. To fail to search beyond those wealth zones, however, can be a costly mistake.

Think, for example, about the recession of 2008–2009. Almost every sector of the economy got hit. We know that Wall Street got slammed, that real estate wealth plummeted, etc., but not every industry got hit evenly. The artisanal chocolate business, for example, continued to thrive throughout the recession. I tell you this fact in an effort to drive home the point that there is *always* money somewhere, at all times, despite what headlines tell you. It is up to you to put negative messages aside and go bravely in search of the money. Turn over enough stones, and you *will* find buried treasure.

If you become your own detective, you'll soon learn where and how to look for wealth. Sometimes it's obvious; for example, the CEO of a large clothing company that distributes its product internationally. Sometimes, it's more of a surprise: someone inherits the family fortune of a meat-packing dynasty. If you look hard enough and think hard enough, you'll be able to find traces of wealth anywhere.

Our consumer-based economy provides you with ample clues. Anytime you go to the supermarket and buy chicken, or soda, or peanut butter, you are building the wealth of a company that put those products on the shelf. Not just the poultry company or the soda company or the peanut butter company, but also the trucking company that transports the goods, the bottling companies that packaged the soda and the peanut butter, and the supermarket itself. There is someone at the top of each of those companies, each one of them with lots of money which they, thanks to our tax code, are incentivized to give away.

When on your search for expendable wealth, one tip that seems simple, but is easy to overlook is *never, under any circumstances, judge a book by its cover*. Someone who looks wealthy may not be. It also means that someone who doesn't look wealthy may in fact be sitting on top of a fortune. One of my favorite prospects (as well as one of my most generous) drives a pickup truck and shows up to meetings unshaven in blue jeans and sandals. During those meetings, however, we're having discussions about six- and seven-figure gifts.

Get curious, and engage people on your search. You'll be surprised by how quickly networks begin to overlap and how soon you've stumbled upon someone with a huge family foundation, or at least someone who can write you a check for $2,000. We'll learn later on about the power of having events and engaging volunteers and donors to do your reconnaissance work; but, for now, just understand that there is wealth hidden everywhere and part of your job will be to uncover it.

Philanthropy in the US

The United States is uncharacteristically philanthropic. American citizens, as a population, simply give away more money than most other nations. There are plenty of historical and political reasons that this is the case. The historical reasons have largely to do with a relatively decentralized system of governance and a populace that was reticent to have the government involved with certain aspects of society. Out of this system rose voluntary associations. Alexis de Tocqueville noted as early as the eighteenth century that this phenomenon of voluntary associations, of citizens grouping together to change something in society, was distinct from European culture. At the time of Tocqueville's writing, in France one usually looked to the government to solve certain societal problems. In the United States, however, voluntary associations were formed.

Voluntary associations were the precursor to what we today call nonprofits. Each one focused on a mission and carried it out with help from volunteers, paid staff members, and, yes, patrons or philanthropists. Much like today, these associations had costs, and those costs were offset by dues, sales, and charitable donations.

Not only is there a history of philanthropic behavior in the United States, but charity is also encouraged by the tax code. Charitable giving is rewarded in this country by a generous tax-deduction policy. To give you an idea of just how incentivized charitable giving is, consider the following regulations: in 2011 and 2012, individuals have the ability to give away up to $5 million to recognized nonprofits without paying any gift taxes. In 2013, the amount will revert back to $1 million, unless Congress extends this window, but $1 million is still a pretty significant amount.

Granted, not all gifts are tax-deductible. Gifts to political parties, candidates and Political Action Committees (PACs), or groups that lobby are not. However, the exemptions still leave a good number of organizations that accept tax-deductible donations. Tax deduction is often a big selling point for prospective donors who are on the fence. Many Americans don't enjoy paying taxes, and if they are able instead to give what would be taxed to a cause in which they believe, they will.

A quick word on tax deduction: A nonprofit must apply for tax exempt status with the IRS. If an organization is not registered as a 501(c)(3) organization in the Internal Revenue Code, contributions made to it will not be tax-deductible. You can learn more by visiting the IRS's website: http://www.irs.gov/pub/irs-pdf/p4220.pdf.

To give you an idea of how much Americans give away in a year, let's look at some data from the Giving USA Foundation (www.aafrc.org). In 2010, approximately $291 billion in philanthropic contributions from private sources were made to this organization. All from big foundations, right? Wrong; 73 percent of that was from individuals. Fourteen percent came from foundations, and only 5 percent from corporations (another 8 percent came from bequests). To put $291 billion in perspective, consider that the amount is equal to 2 percent of the United States' entire GDP.

The numbers are a bit fuzzier when we get into how many Americans give money each year. Estimates range from 65 percent to 85 percent.[2] Either way, that's a lot of individuals giving money away. At the low range of that es-

---

[2] Arthur C. Brooks, "Giving Makes You Rich," http://www.portfolio.com/views/columns/2007/10/15/Charity-Makes-Wealth/index.html, 2007.

timate, that's about 195 million people making *some* type of charitable donation—that's the populations of the United Kingdom, Portugal, France, and Spain combined giving something away each year—and that's at the low range of that estimate!

Despite the economic uncertainty over the last few years, philanthropy either remained constant or increased; in 2010, the amount of philanthropic dollars increased in most sectors. While the United States is still not back at the levels of philanthropy that we saw in the mid-2000s, there has been a steady increase (with dips, of course) in giving since the 1970s: from just over $100 billion in 1970 to nearly $300 billion today.

So, Americans are generous. They give away money at a comparatively higher rate than other people in the world. This generosity is a good thing for your nonprofit. This largesse presents a separate problem, though: competition. In this country, there are a number of very worthy nonprofits that need money: public radio, the local hospital, your alma mater—the list goes on . . . and on and on. The Internal Revenue Service (IRS) reports each year on the number of nonprofit, charitable organizations registered under Section 501(c)(3) of the Internal Revenue Code. In 2001, there were 865,096 such organizations. In 2010, there were 1,280,739.[3]

If you've ever made a gift to one of these organizations, you probably get mail, e-mail, or phone calls from them annually asking you to renew your support. The challenge for a nonprofit then is to stick out in the crowd. How does a nonprofit create the most compelling message, the most inspiring case, so that at the end of the day, a donor, who is deciding between three different nonprofits, chooses to write the biggest check to yours? We'll get to that soon. Here, I want simply to highlight that while there is no dearth of generosity in the United States, there are an abundance of nonprofits, many with stated missions not too dissimilar from your nonprofit, which are competing for charitable contributions.

Philanthropy Around the World

Once you leave the United States, the philanthropic landscape changes drastically. Historically speaking, other nations just do not have a culture of giving money away like we do. The United Kingdom is often cited as having a somewhat philanthropic citizenry (there is, for example, the Prince's Chari-

---

[3] The Center on Philanthropy at Indiana University, "Giving USA 2011: Executive Summary," http://www.givingusareports.org/products/GivingUSA_2011_ExecSummary_Print.pdf, 2011.

ties, which is a group of 20 not-for-profit organizations of which HRH The Prince of Wales is Patron or President), but for the most part, philanthropy, on the scale that we see it here in the United States, is quite literally a foreign concept (even in the United Kingdom, the tax incentive for individual giving just isn't as lucrative as it is in the United States). The one notable exception to this rule is religion. Religious institutions and causes do tend to receive a good amount of charitable contributions.

In 2010, I had the pleasure of visiting friends in France. At that point in my career, I was a major gift officer. As such, my job was to cover the Midwest, Texas, Upstate New York, Pennsylvania, and Eastern Canada, and to manage a prospect pool of about 250 individuals who had the capacity to donate anywhere from $100,000 to $1 million over a five-year period. When I was explaining to my French friends what I did, they found the very concept of my job strange. To pay someone to travel to meet people to ask for large donations just didn't make sense to them.

This global attitude and awareness towards philanthropy is beginning to change, however, and some cultures are becoming more philanthropically inclined. This change is happening partially out of necessity, notably in Western Europe: the traditional welfare state, which has historically provided publicly for citizens such goods and services as health care, education, and more, is under a huge strain. The reasons are numerous: an aging population that no longer works is not only exhausting the resources drawn from taxes, but also living longer; families are getting smaller and fewer people are entering the work force, thereby eroding the tax base; stringent immigration policies also make it difficult for foreign workers to fill jobs, which would help to offset that eroding tax base; and yet, unemployment remains high.

These factors have all forced heretofore generous welfare states to cut certain services and to reduce the budget for others, or to increase the number of hours employees are asked to work each week. If a public school's budget is cut, how is it to make up the difference? The answer is to turn to alumni.

The situation described is exactly what has happened in France with the school at which I studied during my year abroad. The school is now allowed to raise money, and two-thirds of the value of the gift is tax-deductible for the donor. I now get solicited by them via e-mail and by mail, and once I even had the pleasure of being called at 7 a.m. to be solicited; the caller had neglected to account for the time difference.

It is an amateur shop, to be sure. The campaign has the feel of a small, scrappy shop when, in reality, the school is one of the more prestigious schools in France. It feels that way because it has no experience fundraising—

and it shows. In a video that features the president of the school, the lighting is poor, the classroom in which the video is shot is messy, and the message isn't all that clear (and that isn't just because my French is no longer that good, I promise). Interestingly, in that video, the school president explains that France is behind the curve on fundraising efforts and cites the United States and the United Kingdom as examples that must be followed, given the new economic landscape.

You don't have to go overseas to see the differences in cultures, however. You only have to cross the border into Canada to confirm that philanthropy in the United States is something unique. My work in Canada has been particularly challenging, as there does not appear to be as robust a culture or a history of giving, much less to an American institution such as the school I represent. While we are making headway there, and the tax code is favorable to charitable giving, it is still an uphill battle to educate Canadian prospects on the importance of philanthropy.

I include this section not to discourage those fundraisers who have shops outside the United States. There is still plenty to be optimistic about. As noted, the current economy and an aging population are putting a strain on governmental resources across the globe, so private charity will be playing a bigger role than ever. In many ways, nonprofit employees are in a great position to be ahead of the curve if they are on the ground outside of the United States. A peer I met at a conference, who was my age with similar experience, was already the director of major gifts at a nonprofit in France because he had taken his skills and experience in fundraising with him from the United States. One of the websites that I often cite in this book and refer peers to continually, the Showcase of Fundraising Inspiration and Innovation (www.sofii.org), is actually a British organization. The United States, while it is culturally well developed in terms of its philanthropy relative to other nations in terms of its philanthropic behavior, is *not* the only place in the world where private support plays a major role in the nonprofit world. The United States might be a trendsetter, but for all of you international fundraisers, instead of despairing, take full advantage of the robust set of practices that have evolved in the United States over time.

The Evolution and Development of a Fundraising Shop

Before we get into the nitty-gritty of the book, let's take a quick second here to set some realistic expectations for traveling the road toward a professional fundraising shop. It's a long one, with many potholes and potential detours (or, worse, road closures!), so it makes sense to start off with a clear idea of what lies ahead for you.

If you're reading this book, you may be part of a small or medium nonprofit that has little or no systematic fundraising operations. You might send out an appeal annually, have one phonathon a year in which you call your donors, or have one big benefit night per year. Other than that, maybe your nonprofit does not do much to raise money.

It can be overwhelming to think about setting up a fundraising shop. Depending on the scale you're hoping for, the investment on the front end can be *huge*.

There are two pieces of good news: the first is that your fundraising shop should earn you a good return on that initial investment. Frontline fundraisers (i.e., the folks like me who are actually on the road, meeting directly with donors to discuss giving face-to-face) pay for themselves, which is to say that they raise more than they are paid.

The other piece of good news is that a shop can be built piece-meal, which enables you to build over time. While in a perfect world, you'd actually be able to go on a hiring binge and set up a fully staffed shop such as the one I design for you in Chapter 4, it's very unlikely that your executive director or your board will give you the thumbs up to sink tens or hundreds of thousands of dollars in salaries (and benefits—nudge nudge).

In short, your odyssey to establish a fully staffed, well-oiled, aggressive fundraising machine will likely have humble beginnings—and this is okay. You'll have war stories to tell your employees down the road of when your development shop was little more than one fundraiser with a telephone, a laptop, and a desk made out of two sawhorses and a piece of plywood.

Glorified histories aside, you will undergo several iterations, and there will be bumps along the road. The biggest caution, especially in the early stages, is to watch for burnout. Your first few hires will have to be Jacks- or Jacquelines-of-all-trades, so be sure that their workloads are designed in such a way that they have a sustainable, happy work-life balance. The fact of the matter is you will have the work of 20 people with a staff of one or two at the very beginning.

Once you have your fundraisers on the ground and raising money, both through mass outreach (phone, e-mail, and mailed solicitations), as well as through individually based conversations with major donors, you'll then begin to think about support and logistics staff to help with the administrative and clerical work so that the fundraisers can fan out more aggressively. Once the support staff is in place, you can then think about making your fundraisers into specialists, placing them into either annual giving, major gift, or other categories. Then, you can turn your sights toward a stewardship department, and then toward researchers.

Again, we'll discuss staffing at far greater length in Chapter 4, but I want to drive this point home early: your shop will likely build slowly over time. While the ideal would be to hire your entire staff of 10 or 15 right out of the gate, I wouldn't bank on that being a possibility. The likelihood is that you will have to fight tooth and nail, especially at the beginning, to get permission to hire and expand operations. The board members for your non-profit, understandably, will want both forecasted results and proof that you're delivering on those forecasts. They'll want to know that their decision to hire a fundraiser actually resulted in increased funds.

Having taken a broad look at how nonprofits rely on philanthropic support, having explored briefly how wealth is ubiquitous, and having reflected briefly on the evolution of a development shop, let us now turn our attention to the role of the fundraiser and discuss in more depth what exactly what a fundraiser does (and does not do).

The Role of a Fundraiser

In Chapter 4, I'll get into the nuts and bolts of recruiting your stellar fundraising team. But first, I need to discuss the role of the fundraiser, and the development shop in general, within the context of the organization. I want to give you an idea of where exactly fundraising fits into the nonprofit.

Your Context Within the Organization

When I first tell people what I do, I say that I'm a spy. While this is an outright lie, it is not an accidental choice of words. A fundraising shop, while not a top-secret organization, nonetheless tends to operate behind the scenes. We let the advocates, the lobbyists, the professors, or anyone else in the organization who most directly carries out the organization's mission take the glory while we do our job in the background.

In the grand scheme of things, this is a good system. While we might personally prefer to be more in the limelight, it is, in my opinion, wiser to feature your fundraising shop a little less prominently than you might wish. (Note: This is subtly but *very* distinctly different from making the fundraising shop hard for the public to find, whether your website, in person, or by phone). Why do I say this? Because at the end of the day, fundraising isn't exactly sexy. It is necessary, beyond any doubt. But that does not make it glamorous. People who have philanthropic relationships with nonprofits know that a fundraising shop exists, but they don't necessarily want to think about the development team more than is absolutely necessary. Nor do we want them to. We want them to focus instead on the latest and greatest thing that the nonprofit is currently doing, thanks to their last gift. Featuring the development team too prominently can be a turn-off in an already delicate situation.

Note that when I say fundraiser, I mean *anyone* on the development staff within your organization. Whether you are in gift administration, the annual fund, corporate and foundation relations, stewardship, events, or any other area, *you are still a fundraiser.* It's a simple enough dictum on paper, but it can be difficult to put into practice. Granted, researchers or events coordinators are much less likely to be in a position of soliciting someone, but they should at least be comfortable with the idea of being in a situation where a gift conversation could happen. Imagine, for example, the likely scenario in a young, nascent development shop that only one staff person happens to be in the office, and he or she is a stewardship writer or a recordkeeper. You do not want to miss out on a gift because the staff member is unable to take the gift either over the phone or in person. You want that staff member to be able to engage in conversation with prospects about why they should support the organization. You also want everyone in the shop to be able to talk, at least at a cursory level, about all the exciting things that the organization is doing!

Above all, a fundraiser is a revenue source. Every employee on the development team, whether directly or indirectly, adds or should be adding value to the organization's bottom line. For example, a major gift officer is expected to raise much more money in a given fiscal year than he or she will be paid. With researchers or administrative support, it's a bit more difficult to do the exact math, but their role is to enable the frontline fundraisers, whether annual fund officers or major gift officers, to do their job more effectively.

Deciding Institutional Goals

So, who gives the marching orders? Who decides on your shiny new fundraising shop's goals? Who determines whether you're going to launch a capital campaign to build a new center or instead raise money to start a $500,000 trust for long-term financial security? Or, at an earlier stage, if you're simply going to try to increase annual gifts from $50,000, in the last fiscal year, to $75,000?

While rank-and-file fundraisers could (and maybe even should) be part of those executive meetings, they shouldn't hold the chief decision-making power. In the delegation of work, that isn't necessarily considered our forte. Your board, your organization's executive director, and perhaps the director of development, in short, your pioneers and visionaries, should be the ones deciding what your funding priorities are. They should seek out feedback from the top fundraisers (your director of development, director of major gifts, or equivalents—more on staffing in Chapter 4), since they will have their hands on the pulse of the larger donors to your organization and will be able to give you an idea of the feasibility of the goals and priorities that are being set, as well as provide realistic (which can sometimes mean sobering) estimated timelines.

This said, however, fundraisers should be vocal about their successes or struggles in raising funds for each priority. Certain priorities will be inherently more difficult than others, and that feedback needs to be communicated upward, eventually back to the board. It's no use pushing a certain organizational priority if there's simply *no* donor interest. While this is hardly ever the case, it does happen often enough where the original dollar goal or timeline proves too ambitious, despite the very best efforts of your frontline fundraisers.

While the board and the executive director should originally decide for what your shop will be fundraising, *the planning and implementation of the actual fundraising should be left to the development shop*—that is our niche and our strength. I'll talk about planning and goal setting later on in Chapter 6.

Here's a tip for the director of development, executive directors, and board members reading this book: *take your fundraisers seriously when you receive their feedback* from the road. They're the ones in the trenches, scrapping to bring your vision to life. Good frontline fundraisers are smart and intuitive; they know when fundraising for a certain funding priority is much harder than for another one. How, then, are they likely going to lead when pitching an idea to the donor across the table? Unless the donor has previously expressed interest in a priority that the fundraiser has found more difficult to sell, it's highly likely that the fundraiser will lead with a more palatable priority.

What makes fundraising for one organizational priority more difficult than for another? One easy answer is that some naming opportunities are more expensive than others. If, say, it costs $10,000 to name the foyer of the local theater and only $2,500 to name the summer acting class program, well, you'll probably have an easier time naming the acting class program.

Another possibility Is that the scope of a given priority is too narrow. It can be easier, although not always, to raise money for "big idea" priorities than seemingly mundane ones. If you were asked to give $10,000 to name a room in an office at a given nonprofit or asked to give $10,000 to significantly increase the amount of health services and free counseling offered to battered women, which would you choose?

The long and the short of it is that certain funding priorities will be an easier sell than others. Fundraisers should feel empowered to share that information with the director of development, and the director of development should feed it upward to the executive director and the board. That isn't to say that the board needs to abandon the priority altogether, but that they should reconsider the amount they hoped to raise or the timeline in which they hoped to do it.[1]

Board members and directors, here is another quick aside: err on the side of transparency and giving your fundraisers too much information. Trust that they'll treat it with the proper discretion. If some internal document needs to be "eyes only," that's OK; go ahead and share it. Let the recipients know if something can't be communicated externally, but they need to know what it is. When we fundraisers are having those absolutely essential face-to-face conversations, especially at the major gift level, we need to have a ton of information at our fingertips so that we can speak knowledgeably about any aspect of the organization's programming, whether it's related to the funding priorities or not. I'll talk more about the perils of being caught off guard in Chapters 9 and 10, but for now, trust that from a fundraiser's perspective, we'd like to know more than you think we'd like to know.

Excellent Fundraising Depends on Collaboration

As a fundraiser, rather than think of yourself as a godsend to the organization, you need to realize that you fit into the larger fabric of the institution that you are representing. Sometimes, this can be a good thing, as it allows for cross-departmental collaboration. For example, at the school where I work, at certain junctures in a gift conversation, we might enlist the help of a coach, a dean, or a faculty member (and, of course, at the highest levels of solicitation, the president or vice presidents can and often do get involved).

---

[1] Of course, it could also be a question of making the messaging around a certain priority more interesting and compelling. Invite your communications team to help you if a certain funding priority is a flop.

Sometimes, this can be a hindrance, especially if another department within your organization is loath to cooperate on some aspect of your operation. Examples abound: You can't get information that you're hoping to put into an appeal. A department affected by a gift stewards the donor poorly, resulting in a miffed donor.

How do these negative interactions happen? The answer is not that the department whose cooperation you were hoping to get wants you to fail. They just aren't thinking about fundraising the same way you are. That's OK. That's why your job exists in the first place, so that you dedicate your workday to thinking through the gift cycle, from start to finish. It isn't the primary job of other departments to provide John Donor with information on the latest efforts that your nonprofit is undertaking to improve the local public school system. That's your job. Sometimes it requires persistence; it usually requires some patience. But know that the casework that you do on behalf of your prospects is worth it.

So, how do you fit into the organization as a whole? Your role exists because the nonprofit you are representing would be leaving money on the table by not bringing you on board. You help the organization to dream bigger than it would otherwise. You take the pressure of asking for money off them (which they're probably not good at anyway . . . or they don't see it as a priority), thereby allowing them to focus more exclusively on their mission. As noted above, this can *sometimes* be to your detriment. Yours is a specialized role; you are but a piece of the organization, although an essential one.

Getting buy-in from other departments can sometimes prove to be a challenge. If you're reading this book, then it's likely you're the one who will be starting up the shop or developing it further, so it will rest on your shoulders to get that buy-in from the necessary departments, and notably the top brass. Again, while it is logical on paper, institutional inertia, especially in the nonprofit world, can be a plague to any kind of forward movement. I'm not saying that you *will* face a fight with the executive director (or, if you're the executive director, with the trustees or steering committee). Just be ready to make the case. Again, topics such as the bottom line and cash flow aren't necessarily the most fascinating things to talk about when you could be talking about deforestation or rural poverty or toxic materials in your drinking water. Moreover, talking about money makes some people uncomfortable. Even worse, the idea of *spending* money to raise money can sour things further still, especially in a young organization without any pre-established track record in fundraising.

Mastering the Coordination Game

OK, so all fundraisers are revenue sources and help to feed the bottom line. Does this mean that your sole purpose is to craft written, telephone, and electronic appeals and get in front of high net-worth donors? While that is certainly a good part of what a development shop does, *the fundraiser is not always the one making the solicitation*. In fundraising-speak, a fundraiser is often referred to as a prospect's *coordinator*. This term is not accidental. As a major gift officer, I was the coordinator of about 250 prospects scattered throughout the region that I used to cover (the Midwest and Texas). Many of these folks I solicited myself. However, for a good number of those prospects, other key players have entered the gift conversation at certain points along the way, up to and including the solicitation itself.

This is where the term coordinator becomes more pertinent. A proper gift conversation is much more than asking someone for money, just like any good visit is assessed not solely by the content of the lunchtime conversation, but also by the quality of the subsequent follow-up. As one of my supervisors likes to say, a single gift has many moving parts. It is your job, as a fundraiser, to coordinate all those moving parts in a harmonious manner.

Sometimes, as a coordinator, you operate proactively. Other times, it is necessary for you to step in to put out a fire (that you might have set, or that someone else might have made for you).

Proactively, you will be reaching across your institution to bring in those colleagues who can help move a conversation forward, either with an individual donor or as part of a broader solicitation. Having a coach pen a letter to alumni athletes is one example. Simply getting the executive director to sign off on an appeal going out to all current and past supporters is another.

There may be some ego-checking involved in certain situations where you, as a frontline fundraiser, are not the best person to make the ask (development-speak for a request for a donation). As gift officers, we have a tendency to get territorial and possessive about our prospects. It isn't entirely our fault. After all, we are each assigned a region of the country or a set of class years or a certain aspect of the organization's programming. And we are ultimately the ones getting evaluated on whether a prospect has moved along in the gift cycle.

However, sometimes it's wrong to assume a fundraiser is the right person for the ask. Not all constituents are comfortable meeting with a development officer directly. If that's the case, you need to think creatively about how to engage those prospects in meaningful ways without traveling to their hometown to take them out to lunch.

I've come to be thankful when I can enlist the help of others. For purely selfish reasons, it saves me time if I can delegate a certain aspect of the gift conversation to someone else. For more altruistic reasons, it is sometimes more effective when the solicitation comes from someone who has a more direct connection with the prospective donor (again, the example of a coach personally asking former players to step up comes to mind).

I am extremely fortunate to have established a cooperative relationship with a great high-level volunteer on the ground in one of the cities I frequent for my work. She is well connected in this particular city, and happens to be a very good fundraiser. I cannot quantify just how much her support has benefited my work in this particular area, but I can tell you that he has opened doors that I could not, and that she has moved certain conversations along much more quickly than if it had been me taking that donor out to lunch.

"You're a talented young individual," she said the last time we worked together. "But you know, sometimes these guys want the 'elder statesperson.' "

And the thing is, she's absolutely right. Sometimes, she's in a much better position to cultivate or solicit a prospect. At other times, I'm the best person for the job. Each prospect is different, and each constituency is different, so be sure to take the time to strategize and consider who is actually the best person to make the ask. Even if you're technically the frontline fundraiser.

On Being Cool (or Not Being Cool)

I already noted that fundraising isn't exactly glorious work, or sexy. Let's draw parallels with spies once more. If a spy movie were based on your non-profit, your executive director would be the head of the CIA, your lobbyist, policy advocate, and volunteer managers would be the devastatingly good-looking spies who get all the cool gadgets and have wild nights with double agents. The fundraisers would be the computer nerds wearing coke-bottle glasses and Aloha shirts in the background and providing all of the logistical support. In the movie, our scenes would be short, and they would feature us displaying technical wizardry or handing off a sealed envelope to our more attractive costars.

Don't despair, though. Your job is essential.

I will talk about this in Chapter 4 when I discuss recruiting and what to look for in a frontline fundraiser, but I think it is worth driving the point home early: fundraising is not about being cool. It is by nature a somewhat awkward art. You are asking people to do what they wouldn't necessarily do by themselves: give away money that they have earned (or inherited).

Yes, it helps to have social graces, and to be able to adapt to a donor's given vernacular. If you didn't like being called a nerd in an Aloha shirt, allow me another simile: you are like a cheerleader for the organization. You have to be enthusiastic, sometimes uncomfortably so, so that the donors can rise to your level of excitement. People are not usually chomping at the bit to give their money away. For this reason, you have to bring copious amount of enthusiasm, so that they can feed off of your energy. You need to belt out the call to action, and explain why your nonprofit not only needs their money, but is more deserving of it than the other nonprofit next door.

The instant you falter in your step because you're about to do something uncool or unsmooth, you're in big trouble. Fundraisers often have to operate in hyperbolic fashion: you have to lead the call to arms, and you can't always do so by sitting back and trying to be suave.

Part of the reason we try to be cool in fundraising is because we want our donors to like us. That will make them more likely to give us money. We don't want to get rejected. Sadly, getting rejected is part of the trade. Not everyone you ask is going to say yes. In fact, the majority of people you ask will say no, or give at a level lower than you had asked. In Chapters 7 and 10, when we get into planning and discuss the actual ask, respectively, I'll reflect at length on just how often you're going to hear "no," just how much of your work will be steeped in rejection, and how you have to remain optimistic and retain a positive mindset anyway. For now, trust that you'll hear "no" a lot, and that that's OK—think of it as sifting through a desert of "no," which is dotted with some very beautiful oases of "yes."

But remember—and this should help tie things back to why I insisted that being cool is not the objective—when the donor says yes or no, they are not saying yes or no to *you*. They are saying yes or no to their belief in the organization as a worthy recipient of their philanthropic support. So, it's a better use of your time to make the case enthusiastically than to worry about whether or not the donor across the table thinks you're smooth.

The truth is, and I mean this as a high compliment, that the best fundraisers I know tend to be a little strange, which in part enables them to make the case for giving in very imaginative ways.

In this chapter, we've taken a look at just where exactly your fundraising operations, and, more importantly, your fundraisers themselves fit into the broader context of your organization. While not operating behind closed doors accessible only by secret punch codes, the development operation does tend to do most of its work behind the scenes, leaving the more public successes of the nonprofit for the executive directors, program officers, etc.

We also saw that the frontline fundraisers will sometimes have to enlist the help of other members of your organization to close a solicitation. I ended with a brief meditation on why you shouldn't trouble ourselves too much with being cool and should instead work on being the ever-enthusiastic cheerleader of the organization, in the hopes that your prospects will rise to your level of excitement.

In Chapter 4, I'll discuss how to build a top-notch team, but first, let's take a look at the gift cycle. That will help contextualize the role of each staff member on the team.

The Gift Cycle

Setting the Foundation

A fundraising shop does not just ceaselessly ask people for money. There is a lot of strategy behind crafting a message, coming up with an annual plan, and so on. It isn't rocket science, but it's important to know that a lot of thought has gone into those appeals you get in the mail, or those phone calls you get between 5 p.m. and 9 p.m. local time.[1] They were timed that way on purpose. Your efforts must be just as well planned. While annual planning and strategizing are not the primary focus of this chapter (we'll cover these topics at great length in Chapter 6), they'll give you a backdrop for thinking about its contents: an overview of the gift cycle, and the steps you will take to engage donors and maximize their contributions to your organization.

The gift cycle is less about mass appeals and more about cultivating the donors who will be receiving individual attention from your staff in person. Understanding the gift cycle is key to understanding the information I present in the chapters on stewardship and major gifts. It will also provide you with a framework for the contents of the next chapter, on assembling your team.

I am including this information early in the book because all too often, we charge forth, frantically raising money to keep the lights on, without any long-term view. This serves to hurt your organization down the road. You need to set up your fundraising shop with a solid understanding of annual gifts, major gifts, and the steps involved in raising both. The first step is understanding that the actual act of asking for money is only one element in a much larger cycle.

---

[1] Yes, even the really bad pieces of direct mail.

The Gift Cycle

There are five steps in the gift cycle: assessment, cultivation, presolicitation, solicitation, and stewardship, which starts the cycle all over again (after all, it's called the gift cycle, not the gift line). These five steps can be automated, or they can be individually tailored depending on the available staffing resources at your organization as well as the size of the gift.

In fundraising lingo, we often talk about "moves management." Moves management refers to the system of moving your donors along to the next step in the gift cycle. Ideally, each new contact with a donor should move that donor to the next level (although plenty of times they get caught in cultivation limbo, as we'll see later in this chapter).

Let's now dissect each of the steps in the cycle. The majority of what you are about to read is tailored for conversations revolving around larger gifts and donors who merit individual attention from a frontline fundraiser. As I discuss this information early in the book, so should you consider it early in what I'm assuming to be the development of your shop. This is because, again, I want you thinking about the entire gift cycle from *day one*. It's easier to do it now than to have to backtrack when your team is already operating at 90 miles an hour. I want you to appreciate the many steps involved in a professional solicitation.

Assessment

Think of it as your first date, a meeting to get to know one another. Assessment is best executed in person, but can be done via phone or e-mail if your organization does not have the staffing resources (consider that a suggestion to push for such resources if you don't have them yet!). The goal of assessment visits or calls is to get an idea of each prospect's capacity to make a gift (in other words, how high you can shoot), inclination (feeling of warmth toward giving to your particular institution), and the timing (of when it is likely that a gift will occur). You also want to begin to discern where individual donors' interests might lie with respect to your organization, and where they might be looking to make an impact.

Major gift officers, principal gift officers, and senior staff will often have researched a prospect beforehand to discern the prospect's capacity to give, or had research done for them (we'll discuss research in the next chapter). If this is the case, then focus your attention on trying to figure out inclination and timing.

If you're strapped for resources and therefore don't have research staff, then you'll have to start making assessment calls with your already-generous donors.

For nonmajor gift work, assessment takes on a different tone. From raising money chiefly through mass appeals, assessment turns to analyzing the efficacy of each solicitation, and each mode of solicitation, within your shop. What modes (written, e-mail, or telephone appeals) worked best? Which individual appeals or telephone segments got the best response?

However, with individuals at the larger gift levels, the assessment meeting, more than any other, necessitates that you listen actively and with intent. Have your ears open for any cues that will help you perceive the donor's position.

If you're meeting at the prospect's home, drive around the neighborhood to get a sense of the community. You can't judge a book by its cover, but it will give you at least an introductory idea of your prospect's wealth.

Don't fret if you don't get a view of the house. You can drive by it later. And if you can't do that, then you can do homework on the value of the house. The point is that the conversation itself should yield enough clues for you to begin to home in on capacity, inclination, and timing.

Here are some questions for which you want the answers, if you don't already have the information on hand:

- How old is this prospect?
- In what industry does this prospect work? What is his/her job title? Is it possible to know this prospect's annual salary, or at least estimate it?
- How is the economy treating the industry in which this prospect works?
- Does the prospect own property? Multiple properties?
- Does this prospect come from family money? Is there a family foundation?
- Does this prospect have children? How many? How old? Are they going to private or public school?
- What other organizations does this prospect support philanthropically? Where does your organization stand in this prospect's esteem relative to these other organizations?
- What is the prospect's level of awareness of what your organization is doing today?

- Is there a history (positive or negative) with this prospect and your organization?
- Is there anything happening right now in the personal life of the prospect that could affect the tempo of a gift conversation (for example, divorce, lawsuit, bankruptcy, scandal, family illness)?

During this first conversation with prospects, be very up-front with them about your role and your ultimate intention. Never skirt around the fact that you are a fundraiser. In my major gift work, I often say something along the lines of, "Now, I am a major gift officer, so it is my job, at some point down the road in our conversation, to ask you to make a significant philanthropic commitment to us at the six-figure level. Today is not the day that I'm asking you for that commitment, and I want the conversation to advance at a pace that is comfortable for you. But I wouldn't be doing my job if I didn't let you know that up front."

Terrifying, right? On some level, sure, but think of it this way: by frontloading the idea, you are offering them an opportunity to reveal the answers to your questions about inclination and timing.

It is a huge time saver to have prepared some phrases such as the ones I have just used. If they let you know that now is not the right time, or that six figures is totally beyond their current price range (or that your organization is not high on their list for philanthropic relationships), this is very useful information to you. It helps you prioritize your prospect pool. You can put that particular prospect a little lower (or a lot lower) on your call list.

Again, in the words of Stan, from Grassroots Campaigns, "Just move on to the next door."

If they don't jump out of their skin—and you'll be surprised: they rarely do—then you know that this is a good prospect and that you can continue the conversation with confidence. And if they do fall out of their chairs, well, that's OK, too.

Of course, if you're not raising major gifts yet, there's no need for that sort of end-of-meeting language, but it is always useful to let donors know that your ultimate intention in continuing to meet with them is to get them to open their checkbook.

Cultivation

Assuming your first date went well, it's time to start cultivating your prospect. In the dating parallel, this is where you buy flowers, write poetry, and make a mix tape (or an iTunes playlist for the younger readers out there). In the actual world of fundraising, this is where you engage the prospect on the goings on of your organization in a way that is tailored and meaningful to that person.

Cultivation is usually the longest stage of the gift cycle in that it can take a while to move a prospect from cultivation to presolicitation. Gift officers will often refer to their prospect pool, or portfolio, as "cultivation heavy," meaning that an overwhelming number of their prospects are stuck in the cultivation stage.

Depending on how you view it, it can be the most challenging, tedious, or fun part of the gift cycle. It's often all three at any given point within the cultivation process. It is also the most exciting part because it allows you to think creatively about how best to engage your prospects. You are getting them to trust you, or as we say in fundraising lingo, *building (or cementing) the relationship*.

Put yourself in their shoes: What do they want to know about the organization? What gets them excited about the work that your organization is doing? When meeting with them, take note of how they react to what you're pitching to them, of when their posture and body language changes, of when they really perk up or get enthusiastic.

Cultivation can take on innumerable forms. It can be as simple as forwarding a press release they might find interesting. It can be as formal as getting the executive director to meet them for lunch. It can be making a personal phone call to make sure that they plan to be at an event that you want them to attend.

It could even be asking them to host or underwrite an important event that your organization is putting on. Yes, hosting or underwriting costs money in itself, but it engages donors by allowing them to feel, correctly, that they are promoting your organization in a manner *beyond* simply writing checks. Putting on an event, whether it's an "all-come" event or a smaller, invitation-only dinner with a targeted invitation list, donors often feel good when asked to help put something like this together, and it gets them involved in a way that isn't *strictly* monetary (although there is still a check being written).

Here's a trick that I've never worked up the courage to use, but I think it is brilliant. It's not necessarily restricted to a cultivational strategy, but could certainly be a good gimmick to employ. A colleague of mine used to work with someone who once a year would mail thirteen or so of his top prospects a hand-written card that merely said, "Congratulations!" above the officer's signature.

He reported that over half the people who received that card would call him, reference some event (pregnancy, marriage, graduate degree, house purchase, or retirement) and thank the gift officer, asking how he knew about the event! You'd have to be quick on your toes to come up with a reply, or have them canned in advance, which is why I don't do it, but I think the idea is fascinating, and could be useful in cultivation if you can pull it off.

The length of cultivation will depend both on the prospect's inclination and timing, and the scale of the gift that you are hoping to secure. It can take as little as 90 seconds or as long as a year (or more!). As you visit with more and more prospects, and ask for a variety of gifts ranging from $100 to $100,000, you will gain instincts that allow you to gauge how long the cultivation stage needs to take. A general rule of thumb is that the larger the gift, the longer the cultivation. While there are certainly exceptions, it's a safe bet.

There are two things that can elongate the cultivation stage (well, there are many, including any number of untimely changes in personal circumstances). The first is that a donor's interests can change over time. I have a number of prospects in my pool that were once very interested in supporting financial aid. However, when their children began applying for college, the prospects changed their tune for fear that their support of needier students would be crowding out their own children's potential for getting into our institution.

Another example is a prospect of mine whom we had been targeting, with some progress, for financial aid with an eye toward soliciting him upon his son's graduation. Then, he learned about another effort to build an endowed scholarship fund to honor a professor of his, who had recently passed away. He very quickly changed where he steered his support for the college, and to a level lower than we were hoping for.

It isn't always a bad thing when your prospects' interests change. I was meeting with a prospect recently to discuss building his already-endowed fund to $750,000 over five years, when in passing, I mentioned the college's efforts to endow its cross country program. He wasn't a runner in college, but has since become one. His son is now quite an accomplished cross country runner, so he made a gift over and on top of his current pledge schedule. Sometimes a change in interest can be a pleasant surprise. It can just change the time horizon, or alter the direction of the conversation. Or, in the case of this alumnus, supplement an already-robust conversation.

The second reason that cultivation might take longer than you like is that the donor's interests in your organization don't match up with current funding priorities.

A quick detour: Funding priorities are usually set (or should be) by your board of directors and your executive director. Those priorities should be communicated clearly with the advancement shop. It is your job, as director of development, to ensure that this happens. Don't assume that your board or executive director will think to tell you immediately. You need to be proactive, especially early on in your shop's development. There's no buy-in yet, nor is there a standard operating procedure to communicate these priorities.

I want to stress just how important it is for your fundraisers to be receiving top-level communication from your board and your executive director. You do *not* want a situation where your donor knows more about your organization than you do. Having a fundraiser get caught off guard undermines the donor's confidence in your institution. If a development officer asking for money cannot successfully articulate the nonprofit's mission, that officer and therefore the institution are in trouble.

Again, be proactive and interact with your executive director and your board. You need them to understand the importance of keeping the development office in the know. When there's a new project, you need to know. When there is a change in funding priorities, you *really* need to know. Don't leave it to chance—or worse, to your donors—to become informed about the latest and greatest things that your nonprofit is doing.

When a donor's interests don't align with your institution's funding priorities, you need to be delicate, as you want to honor their desire to give and the spirit of how they want to steer their philanthropic support, even if it is in a way that does not perfectly correspond with their explicitly stated intention.

Sometimes, incompatibility with a donor's interests occurs because institutional priorities change. For example, one time I had a prospect whom I was planning to solicit for $100,000. When we got down to discussing where he might like to make an impact, he expressed interest in funding winter internships that would send students abroad to lesser-developed countries. At the time, this was not a funding priority at the school. I had to explain that while I was ecstatic for his support, internships were not a top need at the moment. Would he consider instead a gift that would support bringing students from lesser-developed countries to our college in the form of an expendable financial aid commitment? He ended up making a gift to financial aid; it was at a much lower level than I was hoping for, but he was on board, which was the important part.

Imagine my surprise (and rage) when not six months later I learned that the college had a new goal of pumping up its experiential learning programming. This meant both that there was a push to provide internships to students, but also to raise money so that students who had unpaid internships could have a stipend to live on during their experience.

The good news is that once the aforementioned prospect's current pledge is paid off, we can go back to him and get him excited about a new undertaking that aligns more directly with his original interests. The not-as-good news is that the timing was misaligned and it might undermine his confidence in our ability to communicate clearly and accurately with donors. That, and the fact that we might have been able to get him on board at a higher level of commitment earlier on. I could have had a $100,000 commitment on the books, but now we'll have to wait five years to resolicit him. If your organization runs on a shoestring budget, that five-year waiting period can be extremely costly. If this is the case, it might make sense to communicate the change in priorities sooner, in the hopes that the donor might convert his pledge to cover his original area of interest, at the amount for which you originally asked. Beware, though: asking for another gift while a pledge is being paid off can upset donors. Be diplomatic if you're forced into this situation. And do everything that you can to avoid being caught there in the first place.

Sometimes, things don't fall into place and you are forced to make things work imperfectly, like a Gemini and a Capricorn trying to date. Don't despair—it can be done—it just requires finesse, patience, and an openness to a longer, more drawn-out conversation.

If your organization has a very narrow mission, the chance that your prospects' interests might not line up with your institutional priorities decreases. Of course, each organization has a wide range of *needs*, some as mundane (but essential) as keeping the lights on and having a budget for office supplies, but the narrower your mission, the more focused your donor base will be in the first place.

Sometimes donors aren't particularly excited about your current undertaking. This can be especially relevant for nonprofits that focus on influencing policy, either locally, at the state level, or nationally. That isn't to say that they won't be excited about your next battle. It's just that this project might not be the right one for them to fund.

If, after much effort, you find yourself still finagling an angle that is pleasing to the donor and in line with your organizational priorities, you have to make a decision: do you side with the donor or the institution? Sometimes, it can turn into a bit of a skirmish, and you'll have to be the mediator.

One example is a prospect of mine from the Midwest who had set up an expendable lectureship fund that would bring a speaker to campus once a year to lecture in Japanese on the state of, and trends in, that language. This was done through a gift of $200,000. After a few years, she was satisfied with how the lectureship was being managed and wanted to endow the fund, so that the lectureship would live on in perpetuity.

When I broached the subject with the budget office on campus, I met some resistance. Lectureships were not a funding priority on campus. Would the donor consider repurposing the fund?

After reviewing this donor's history, having spent time with her smoothing over some rough patches that she had already had with the college, and having several conversations with her face-to-face, it became clear to me that it was going to be lectureship or bust on this particular prospect.

For one, she had already reconverted the fund a few years ago from a research fund to a lectureship fund, when she quadrupled the level of the fund with a significant gift. Secondly, her philanthropy to her other alma mater supported the library and its acquisitions. Finally, in conversation, she revealed that her other alma mater had pushed her about financial aid and that she just flat out wasn't interested in supporting that aspect of the university's programming. I floated the idea of faculty support at our college, since she had been a professor, but at the end of the day, she wanted her fund to remain a lectureship fund.

I did my homework and put in the effort, but with all other options exhausted, I had to go back to the budget office and explain that this donor simply wouldn't budge and that we had to go ahead and endow this fund, despite the fact that it did not align with our institutional priorities.

Of course, you can't always take the side of the donors. Sometimes you have to draw a hard and fast line and insist that in order for them to support your organization, they have to change their tune. Ethical questions can arise, and when they do, red flags should go up. Philanthropy is not a quid pro quo arrangement (we'll visit this theme in depth in the chapter on political fundraising). You have to make it very clear to donors what their support does and does not entail. Supporting an athletic club does not give them a say in who coaches. Supporting a college does not get their children into that institution.

In short, cultivation is a critical step in the gift cycle. The majority of prospects that receive individual attention (i.e., your major gift prospect pool) will likely be in cultivation at any given moment. As noted, it requires imagination, creativity, and persistence to move them from cultivation to the next step.

Presolicitation

In the interest of propriety, it's time to stop drawing the parallels between fundraising and dating. I'm confident that by now, you get the idea. Presolicitation is pretty much exactly what it sounds like: you either ask donors if they'll consider a proposal in writing or you simply let them know that you plan to solicit them soon, whether as a part of your follow-up to this visit, or the next time you see them.

Be prepared, in this scenario, to be asked how much you were planning to solicit them for. Some donors don't really want to draw things out and want to cut right to the chase. When a donor is asking for "the bottom line," or asks you outright, "So, what is it you want from me?" you had better be prepared to turn the presolicitation visit into a solicitation visit (find out how in the following section, and in Chapter 10 on "the ask"). You need to have a figure in mind in case this does happen. And it happens often enough.

As noted before, the gift cycle can be as short as a single visit, or as long as years. By the time you are at the presolicitation stage, you have gained a good understanding of where the prospect is interested in making an impact on your organization via their philanthropy. You've done your homework, figuring out which programs would be involved, and you've gotten buy-in from the parties to be affected. More importantly, the prospect continues to be warm to your advances. Even more importantly, you have been able to calculate just how much you think this person might be willing to give you.

Solicitation

The big moment is upon you. You are either going to solicit your prospect for a gift during this visit, you're compiling your talking points for the phone call, or you're preparing a proposal for them in writing.

If you've done your job up to this point, your ask should not catch the prospect off guard. The *amount might*, and that's OK. Believe it or not, at some level, the prospect has been waiting for this moment much like you have (and probably looking forward to getting it over with, much like you have!). Their time is limited as well, and the *last* thing you want to do is leave a meeting with the prospect wondering, "Where was the ask?" It's a delicate balance, as you don't want to be hasty, but again, if you have been up-front with them, prospects will know that there is a solicitation coming. Linger too long, and you'll actually undermine your chances of success.

Chapter 10 will focus on the solicitation itself in much more detail.

Stewardship

The prospect says yes. Tell your boss, tell the executive director, pop the champagne, leave work at four. It's time to celebrate. After all, the development shop has done its job, right? Well, mostly.

Stewardship is the art of thanking your donors for their gifts. It is you reporting back to them on the impact of their generous support. You have to demonstrate to your donors how their philanthropic relationship with your organization has enlivened your programming, helped you to succeed when you otherwise would not have been able to, and how grateful you are for them.

As a gift officer myself, I cannot stress enough how much I value having a strong stewardship team where I work. Solid stewardship renews the gift cycle all over again, and when properly done, makes resolicitation a whole lot easier . . . or inspires a new commitment all by itself. I've devoted a whole chapter to the subject (Chapter 8). It's that important.

So, there is the gift cycle in a nutshell. I spent a good deal of time on assessment and cultivation, and I went a little lighter on the nuts and bolts of presolicitation, solicitation, and stewardship. Again, examples and more in-depth explanation will appear later on in the book. For now, I want you just to have a basic idea of the life cycle of a gift, so that it makes more sense as we move on to talking about staffing your office, which we are about to discuss in the next chapter.

Assembling Your Team

Having taken a look at philanthropy and its relationship to the nonprofit world, the development shop in the context of the nonprofit as a whole, and having discussed the gift cycle at an introductory level, let us now turn toward recruiting an institutional advancement team.

In order to give you a better snapshot of an ideally staffed team, I am going to assume that you have unlimited resources to hire as many people as you want (knowing that this is likely an erroneous assumption). At the end of the chapter, I will talk about how to prioritize when you are cash-strapped and can't recruit everyone you want.

Frontline Fundraisers: A Strangely Effective Team of Black Sheep

It should be no surprise that I start with the frontline fundraisers. We're called many things: gift officers, philanthropic advisors, road warriors, professional beggars. Whatever you want to call us, we're the folks who are going to be asking prospects big and small for money in person, over the phone, and via e-mail; who are going to be writing your individual proposals and general appeals; and who are going to be adding most directly to your bottom line.

Pretty important stuff, right? So, what should you be looking for in a gift officer?

It's a tougher question to answer than you might think, for a few different reasons. One is that there is no universally accepted way to ask for money. This is because every donor is different; every constituency is different—and never mind the fact that there are myriad things that philanthropists could support. Your organization will undertake short-term funding projects and longer-term investments, and your approach to fundraising for each of these types of efforts will likely (and should) differ.

There is another reason that the question of what to look for in frontline fundraisers is difficult: successful fundraising, especially successful face-to-face solicitation, is owed in large part to the personal style of the officer in question, and their ability to relate well with the prospect on the other side of the table.

That said, there are certain traits that tend to make for a solid frontliner. An ideal fundraiser:

- Has a passion for the cause one is representing
- Has an *intellectual* understanding of the cause one is representing
- Does not upspeak (meaning you want people who do not end all of their sentences as though they were questions)
- Is a self-starter that can also play well with others
- Is an engaging and captivating speaker
- Is extroverted
- Can build and manage relationships with prospects
- Can connect to a variety of different audiences
- Has hobbies or interests outside of work (since this enhances the likelihood that the fundraiser will be able to connect with a prospect on a personal level)
- Is comfortable asking for money (I know this sounds really, really obvious, but I've worked with a few fundraisers who actually didn't enjoy asking for money)
- Can write well

I'd advise against dismissing any CV or résumé on the sole ground that it does not have previous fundraising experience on it. The qualities that I listed above are not exclusive to the development field. What's more, a lot of people tend to get into the development field by mistake. This is changing, as the field becomes increasingly professionalized (and as institutions find themselves short on cash), but whenever I am at professional fundraising conferences, I am always struck by the variegated backgrounds people bring to the trade.

There is a burgeoning field of professional study in institutional advancement. A number of universities that have programs in higher education administration now offer masters programs in development or advancement. Not having attended one of these programs, I cannot speak to their value; it's a relatively new field of study, and I am confident that as the fundraising industry continues to professionalize, you will see more and more candidates applying for jobs who have this kind of degree. There is certainly value in studying the industry, its practices, and its historical context. However, it is hard to replace the practical training of getting out in front of donors, making actual "asks," getting actual rejections, and closing actual gifts.

Previous experience in sales is common, and, for all intents and purposes, sales brings to the table a transferable skill set. I have gotten feedback from fundraisers with a sales background that the pace is a bit slower in fundraising than in product or service sales, particularly in the major gift field.

Your next fundraiser could come from anywhere, and as time goes by and the field of development/institutional advancement continues to grow, so will the candidate pool of people with fundraising experience.

If you're fortunate enough to have the resources to hire a number of fundraisers, go for variety. You don't want a team of carbon copies. It's likely that your donor pool is too diverse for a single "type" to cover all of your bases, *even if the nonprofit that you represent is focused on a singular issue.* Some gift officers are formal and buttoned up; others are a little more laid back and casual. Some are better writers; some are better speakers. You'll need all types, so mix it up if you have the resources to make multiple hires. If you're really lucky, you'll be able to construct different divisions of frontline fundraisers. If this is the case, you'll want to focus on establishing two teams: the annual fund team and the major gifts team.

The Annual Fund

The Annual Fund raises expendable gifts, usually revolving around your fiscal calendar and special projects. The annual fund team is the group that will be writing the appeals for your direct mail campaigns, your e-mail solicitations, and your phonathon program if you have one. The job of the annual fund team is to get *as many gifts as possible*, from a $5 contribution all the way up into the thousands. They will be soliciting gifts large and small, and they should certainly push their individually assigned prospects to give as generously as possible. But at the end of the day, their chief focus is on obtaining a high volume of gifts, as opposed to generating large gifts; in other words, quantity over quality.

An annual fund officer will be making face-to-face solicitations, recruiting or managing volunteers (see the section in this chapter on volunteers), and strategizing on how to maximize your organization's exposure to create as large an audience (and donor base) as possible.

You might be asking: Why not just focus on big gifts? Why not just hunt for the biggest buck and be done for the season?

The answer is threefold: First, sometimes you don't have time to wait around while the major gift prospect upon whom you were resting your hopes decides how to steer his or her support. You simply don't know in advance when a major gift will close, and if you're relying on that pledge payment and it doesn't come, you're in *big* budgetary trouble. Major gift prospects come and go: they make their big gift and often move on to the next nonprofit (unless you steward them well and keep them on your roster!). Some stick around, but others don't. And if you don't have an endowment, where that gift is going to live on in perpetuity, the gift's value will eventually dry up and you'll need to go in search of the next big donor. Conversely, you will always have a base of donors who can make smaller contributions.

Secondly, it helps to think of the annual fund donors as major gift prospects in the making. People don't just start giving away thousands of dollars willy-nilly. They do so because they have been gifting for years and it just so happens that now they are able to do so at a higher level, for whatever reason. If you look at *most* major donors at any institution, it is very likely that before they were making six-figure commitments, they were giving small contributions each year to that institution. Sure, there are exceptions (notably with prospects that are preliquid), but for the most part, you'll see this trend.

Thirdly, participation matters. You want a variety of gift levels from a variety of donors. You want mass appeal. If you are applying for grants, for example, foundations will often want to see evidence of other bases of philanthropic support upon which your organization relies. A strong level of annual participation will often be one of the things that these foundations and charitable trusts look at when considering your application.

What's more, if your organization only focuses on raising money from sources that can give you six figures at a time, you're eroding your support base. You're sending a message to prospective smaller donors that their $25 doesn't matter. Not only that, but small gifts add up. At one institution I know of, gifts of $50 or less usually end up totaling around $150,000 each year. If you don't empower the donors that are giving you $10, $25, or $50 a year, you are cutting yourself off at the knees.

Major Gifts

A major gift officer is charged with managing a prospect pool of a set number of individuals and moving them through the gift cycle with high levels of personal attention. The size of the pool will vary depending on how many major gift prospects you have, if you're geographically diverse or regionally focused, and how a major gift is defined at your institution.

In educational philanthropy, major gifts are usually those in the six-figure range, and occasionally into the seven-figure range. For small nonprofits, it is likely that the major gift threshold will be significantly smaller, and that's okay. The same principles and strategies will apply.

We'll focus more on major gifts in Chapter 11. Meanwhile, I'd like to talk about the distinction between the annual fund and major gifts in the context of recruitment. Major gift officers tend to be recruited up through the ranks of the annual fund, but not always. Some candidates have no previous fundraising experience. However, with major gift work, you do want to scrutinize your candidates carefully. The stakes are a little bit higher. While the annual fund team can be depicted as a scrappy but plucky, frenetically paced office, major gift work can require a slightly more refined approach. Again, more on the distinctions later, but know that it's fair to expect experience with direct solicitations when interviewing for major gift officers.

As noted, there is no ideal type of fundraiser. There are ideal traits, but they can be embodied in very different ways among individual candidates. During interviews, ask yourself if you would give them a donation right then if you were asked. It's fair game to ask them to pitch you for a hypothetical major gift at the interview. Also ask yourself: could they have a meaningful conversation with someone half their age? Twice their age? More generally, could they connect with a wide variety of audiences?

Let's now move off the frontline and peek behind the curtain at all the folks who help fundraisers do their job.

Administrative Staff: A Gift Officer's Life Line

Again, I'm boldly going to assume that you're able to hire an entire shop. In reality, it is more likely that a small number of you will have to be jacks-of-all-trades. However, by giving you an idea of what a fully staffed shop might look like, you'll be able to get a broad idea of the tasks necessary for a well-run shop, and plan (and delegate) accordingly. It will also give you a hiring roadmap, so that as your operations expand, you can turn back to this to know what your next recruitment step should be.

Recordkeeping and Reporting

The staff member responsible for recordkeeping and reporting is your reference librarian, who is responsible for making sure that you have the most accurate, up-to-date information on your donor base as possible.

You should capture as much information as you can on every single donor. How you design your gift forms, both on paper and online, will help you in this endeavor. Every time you have an event, you should provide a sign-in sheet that asks for each guest's e-mail address, mailing address, and phone number.

You should make sure that your gift officers are feeding your recordkeeper all of the information that they learn, whether it's new work e-mail addresses, new cell phone numbers, etc.

Ideally, you should have the following information about each of your donors:

- Full name and spouse's name
- Maiden names (for possibly family wealth connections)
- Employment information (and spouse's)
- Personal e-mail, work e-mail
- Personal phone number, work phone number, mobile phone number, fax number
- Primary mailing address
- Alternative mailing address (read: other properties)
- Birthday
- Other family information (such as children, parents, family foundations)

Recordkeepers will need database software in order to do their job well. This type of software can be expensive, but if resources are an issue, there are free, reliable options available, such as OpenOffice. You could even get away with using Google Docs if you have to.

The Raiser's Edge, by Blackbaud, is software geared specifically toward fundraising operations; it is quite fancy, and thus coveted by a lot of fundraising shops. It does come at a cost, though, and if resources are tight, you can make do without it.

Other institutions have database software that isn't geared specifically toward fundraising, but does include fields where development officers can enter and retrieve critical information (solicitation plans, visit notes, and so on). How you keep your data and records will depend on your resources, but at the end of the day, you need to make sure that you are keeping your records accurate and up to date.

Besides budgetary constraints, another question in terms of what type of database software you will be using is what the rest of your organization uses, which inevitably raises the question of compatibility.

Records isn't just a dump site for the data listed earlier. You want a history of how you're communicating with donors. The point of having a designated recordkeeper is to use that person as the conduit for getting information captured into the database. Granted, this person shouldn't act as a gatekeeper, restricting other support staff from accessing or contributing to the database, but the recordkeeper's utility is in making sure there are standards on how to capture, enter, and report on information about individuals, about the efficacy of certain appeals, and other data.

In the next chapter, I explore the role and importance of records at greater length. For now, trust that it is impossible to have too much data on prospects. In addition to their personal information, you will want information that clarifies and explains their relationship with your organization to date. This type of information should include answers to the following questions:

- How much has this person given to your organization in the past?
- Has this person made good on their pledges historically?
- Has this person requested not to be contacted by any particular means?
- Who from your organization has contacted this person? For what purpose? What was the outcome of that contact? Was it an in-person visit, a phone call, or an e-mail? Was it possible to catch the donor's mood or personality on that visit?
- When has this prospect visited your organization?
- Which events has this prospect attended in the past?
- Does this person volunteer for you?

The more data you have on someone, the more prepared you can be, and the less likely you are to get caught off guard (see the section on disaster stories in the next chapter), when you do contact a given donor.

Logistics: Mailing, Technology, Printing

This staff member (or members) will be responsible for getting the great ideas that your annual fund team comes up with onto paper, into HTML format, and out the door. They are your operations managers, in a way.

A logistics staff member implements your great ideas and takes point on getting the message of your organization out there, whether it's a direct appeal, a thank you, or an invitation. This person must be extremely detail oriented, with a good understanding of all the tiny steps that are involved in mailing or e-mailing your donor base, as well as an appreciation of the repercussions if there are errors.

I received an e-mail once from a small business in my area, with a subject line reading "Template for my b*tches." I responded to the e-mail, inquiring if perhaps there had been an error in sending this to their e-mail distribution list. I got a quick reply, apologizing for the error and explaining that the template subject line was intended only for e-mail test runs. It was an honest mistake. But it did beg the question: why was there a cuss word in the template subject line, even if it was meant for internal use only?

Details like this are things that your logistics personnel should be considering. In fact, they should spend a good amount of time thinking about how things can go wrong: it is so much easier to spend five extra minutes on the front end, doing one last proofread or sending out one last test e-mail, than to have to respond to innumerable inquiries about why a link did not work, where one clicks to make a gift, or why the recipient received this appeal (in the case of e-mailing to an incorrect segment or constituency).

You want a logistics person to be inquisitive, with a mind that likes to get under the hood. This staff member should be comfortable with technology, including mail merging software and HTML formatting. Also an asset is the inquisitiveness to ask the questions that will bring an appeal from the planning session to the mail drop in the shortest timeline possible. It is this person's job to think about the minutiae, the details that the big-idea people often don't have a feel for. Granted, you need the big-idea people, but you also need a counterbalance, someone who has a realistic idea of what it takes to implement the big ideas. Without this person, you have a plethora of big ideas and no clue as to how to bring these great visions to life. The result is burnout and embitterment toward whoever dreamt up the visions in the first place.

This person isn't necessarily a pessimist or a Negative Nancy, but will be able to ask the right questions, or to give honest answers when asked about implementation. You want someone who has a can-do attitude, while at the same time recognizing your organization's limits in terms of timing, costs, and so on.

If your logistics person raises an objection to a certain idea in a meeting, it is in your best interest to hear out the argument. While you don't want your operation to slow down, you need someone in shop who is thinking things through. Take the logistics staff seriously, and listen to their concerns; they appreciate how long things take and the cost of correcting errors once something has gone out. If it takes an extra day or two to get an appeal out because you need to test the data one more time, do it. It is worth the trouble, and is much easier than having to craft an apology to a certain segment of your donor base who received a message in error.

The Donor Relations Team: Thanking Donors, Throwing Parties

The donor relations team has two overarching tasks that dictate their workflow, stewardship and events. Donor Relations is the new *en vogue* term for these two jobs; sometimes, they are each separate departments. At the college where I work, we recently combined them, and there is logic in doing so. Both tasks involve contact with your donor base where solicitation is implicit, but not explicit. (Remember my earlier comment about how *everyone* on the institutional advancement team is a fundraiser, whether directly or indirectly?)

The donor relations team engages donors in meaningful ways that aren't directly tied to a solicitation. On the events side, you will want someone similar to your logistics person. This staff member is, in essence, a party planner, and party planners need to have an eye for the finer details: which vendor will provide the catering (whether a donor is underwriting the event affects the answer to this question), whether there will be flowers at the event, what expectations the host has, the capacity of the room/home in question, when to hold the event, who will staff the event, the follow-up plan on how to communicate with event attendees, and so on.

You want someone who, while not a frontline fundraiser, is at the very least comfortable talking to affluent donors. This is because it is often these affluent donors that will be hosting the event, either at their home, or at a club or venue through their connections. If you are lucky, the donor will be underwriting the event, so your events coordinator should be comfortable talking a donor through that process as well (since you can count the underwriting that event as an "in-kind" gift if the donor wants). In the average office, the pace is such that the director of the shop won't have time to be checking in with the host every step of the way, so you need to be able to trust and defer to the events coordinator to handle things independently.

It's important to explore the crucial stewardship role to enable you to make a good hire.

Stewardship brings a donor's gift to life by demonstrating, in as much detail as appropriate, the impact of his or her charitable giving at your organization. Donors must be thanked individually for their gifts. Granted, this can be automated, but donors should all still receive a thank-you note with their name on it as opposed to a general salutation of "Dear Donor" or "Dear Supporter."

Personalized thank-you notes should be mailed or e-mailed as soon as possible after the gift is made. Nonprofits that have phonathons should dedicate additional time to thank-you calls.

Still, you need more than a good thank-you note template to steward donors properly. One of the most common ways to steward your donor base is to provide an annual or quarterly report to all donors that provides substantive updates on what your organization has accomplished in the last period, and how philanthropic support made that possible.

As someone whose chief role is to ask for money, I rely *heavily* on quality stewardship, at *both the front end and the back end of my solicitations.* My duty at the back end is obvious: after people make a gift, we need to thank them. I cannot, in good conscience, go back to a donor and resolicit for a major contribution until my office has taken steps to demonstrate just how meaningful that donor's gift was and the impact that it has made. As we'll see later, stewardship resets the gift cycle that we discussed in the previous chapter.

A good stewardship report can also play directly into a solicitation effort. Often, when I am submitting proposals to prospects of mine, I will pull up a stewardship report that we have given to another donor in the past, take out identifying information, and then include the report in my proposal, citing it as an example of the kind of impact that this prospect could have if they give at the level I am requesting. Good stewardship is therefore a very powerful tool in making the actual ask: I am, in essence, showing donors their future relationship with our organization (provided that they say yes to my solicitation). Your stewardship writer needs to have strong, clear writing skills, and a creative mind for how to make giving sexy. You need someone with an imagination that can bring the gifts which your organization has received to life, and construct an inspirational narrative around those gifts.

This employee also needs to be able to forge positive relationships through-out your organization, since ostensibly, the money that you're raising affects other departments more directly than it benefits yours. Your stewardship writer will have to collect stories from these departments, interview the appropriate parties, work with them to construct a rich thank you note, and also collect numerical data on the program on which a certain gift had an impact.

When hiring a stewardship writer, you will want someone who understands that stewardship is primarily the business of saying thank you, but also sees clearly its role in resolicitation, or even presolicitation.

We will explore stewardship in even more detail in Chapter 8, but what you have just read begins to put forth the justification for recruiting donor rela-tions staff members.

Researchers: Your Wealth Detectives

I saved researchers for last because, of all the jobs within a fundraising shop, this line of work is the most likely to make people uncomfortable. We don't really like to think about a team of people snooping around, digging up our financial history. However, if you want to discover your potential big do-nors, you will want to have a researcher on staff to help you figure out when someone can be approached, in good faith, for a significant gift to your organization.

An ideal researcher must have an inherent sense of curiosity. After all, he or she will be spending a good amount of time on the computer, searching tire-lessly for information about individuals. A former colleague of mine admits that if you aren't naturally curious, and you don't enjoy digging deep and turning over every stone, you will get bored doing this kind of work.

Researchers are not only responsible for figuring out how much people are worth and how much they can give. This is certainly a big part of the job, but researchers should also be involved in the strategy process with pros-pects. After all, they are the ones figuring out where prospects are steering their other support and at what level. They can help gift officers with the initial approach, as well as suggest ways to direct the topic during the be-ginning stages of a gift conversation.

A researcher will be looking for the following data:

- What a prospect *paid* for their house (or houses). This is different than the current assessed value of a property. How much they actually spent on the house is a better gauge of wealth
- All of the donor's employment information, including employment history
- Indications of connections to family wealth
- Other philanthropy
- Stock
- Boards upon which the donor sits

A good amount of this information is publicly available and can be found for free. Google, Bing, and Yahoo will be able to provide you with some of this. You want someone who is proficient with search engines and has a knack for crafting queries that will provide a more exact match. For example, if you have a donor named John Smith, you had better include some other terms in your search if you hope for any accuracy.

There are also paid services that will help you with your prospecting. The two programs that come most highly recommended are WealthEngine (www.wealthengine.com) and Noza (www.nozasearch.com). These two services complement one another and will assure you that the John Smith that you are looking at is the John Smith you had in mind. WealthEngine, for example, gives you access to household, individual, private business, and public company information.

There are limits to research, of course. The researcher is, after all, only making calculated, educated inferences based on publically accessible information. This can mean that an assigned rating (an indication of giving potential) could be off, or that the rating is accurate, but there is a very low inclination to give to your particular organization.

Here's an example. A prospect of mine was initially given a rating of $100,000–$249,999. Our research staff, based on data they had collected, figured that this individual was able to donate between $20,000 and $50,000 a year to the organization, or $100,000–$250,000 over a five-year giving period. However, it eventually became clear that we could confidently approach a million-dollar conversation with this person, based on her own admittance.

What happened here? Why were we so far off? The research team came up with the calculation based on the normal criteria: profession, real estate, and other philanthropy. She was the chief information officer of what we thought to be a somewhat small (although self-funded) company, and her husband was a self-employed artist, but we weren't able to gauge his financial success.

They owned their house, but it was pretty modest. So, the rating was accurate based on the information that was available to the research staff.

The error arose because her employer was a private company doing far more business than we had been able to gauge. Because it was private, we were not able to gain an accurate understanding of how much volume the company was seeing.

The point is that research is essential, but it has its limits in terms of what it can provide you. It is up to the fundraisers to get out there and figure out someone's inclination. Research provides you with clues, cues, and talking points before you pick up the phone for your assessment calls.

Tips on Recruitment

So, you have permission to hire a fundraising team, and you're ready to go. You've written your job descriptions and posted them on your organization's website. Good enough, right?

Sadly, it's not. You need to advertise. With the field of institutional advancement growing the way that it is, and with more and more nonprofits in need of money, there is increased competition among them to attract talent.

There are a number of ways to get the word out. You can post for free on your local craigslist classifieds. You can also advertise in the local papers. The Chronicle of Philanthropy is a website that fundraisers tend to visit often as part of the trade, so posting there is also a good idea. You'll also want to advertise in industry-specific publications. Get resourceful and get aggressive with respect to your recruitment process. You can't expect to post something on your website and magically have your phone ringing later that afternoon.

You might even consider hiring a headhunter if you have the resources to spend on one. The point is that you can't expect a lineup outside the door trying to fill your open positions. Even where I work, a college with a reputation of having a pretty solid fundraising shop, is still waiting to fill some critical advancement positions at the time of this writing. Why? Because we have been sitting back waiting for positions to fill instead of actively hunting for the talent we need. Don't let this happen to you. Every day that goes by in which you don't have a fully staffed advancement shop is one in which you are leaving money on the table.

Volunteers: A Blessing and a Curse

Volunteers are a wonderful asset to add to your operations. They can also be a royal pain and, in the worst case scenario, a management nightmare. The scope of your volunteer program will vary, but here are some thoughts.

Someone I met at a fundraising conference, who worked for a college with an incredibly well-run fundraising shop and an especially well-regarded volunteer program, said that there were three categories of volunteers: 1) the superstar volunteer who goes above and beyond the call of duty, who is proactive and can be relied upon to get the job done; 2) the volunteer who does just the work assigned, and usually only when asked; and 3) the volunteer who does nearly nothing, and requires a significant amount of prodding.

The advantages of having a core of volunteer fundraisers are:

- You don't have to pay them.
- They can often open doors that you cannot.
- Sometimes prospects respond to volunteers more positively than professional fundraisers.
- They can keep you fresh when you're tired of dealing exclusively with donors.
- They are a solid base for funds, and they can serve as a good sounding board for new ideas.

The *potential* downsides to volunteers:

- You can't control the messages that they disseminate in the same way that you can with a paid employee. In the worst of situations, they have a negative interaction with your organization and then spread toxic invective about you to everyone they know.
- They can be unreliable/inconsistent.

Despite these potential downsides, it makes sense to think about a volunteer program, especially if your development shop is nascent and understaffed. Volunteers bring great energy to the organization, and you'll find that oftentimes, folks who can't give you a ton of money will be willing to volunteer for you as a way to make up for it. If, for example, a volunteer can contact ten friends and get each of them to give $100, that's $1,000 that would have been harder for you to access without that volunteer's personal touch. Aggregate that model up to 100 volunteers, and you can see the potential impact that a strong volunteer program can have.

If you do go down the road of recruiting volunteers, it will make sense to have a volunteer coordinator/manager in your office. What you don't want to do is recruit a large number of volunteers and then have them sitting idle. They want to know that you have your act together, and providing them with clear tasks, deadlines, and expectations is the first step.

How can you find volunteers to help with fundraising? The first step is offering the opportunity to sign up on your organization's website. You can also include a section on any giving form (whether online, on paper, or in the script for a telephone solicitation), asking if volunteering time might be of interest to the donor.

Another strategy is sending out a designated recruitment message to everyone who has donated to your organization in the past. The language of the appeal can begin by thanking them for their support, followed by outlining your need for volunteers and asking them to respond (either by joining as a volunteer, or by renewing their financial support).

Should you decide to pursue a volunteer program, treat it with the same eye as you would any other aspect of your fundraising program. You should set goals around the number of volunteers that you want to recruit, and write up "job descriptions" for the roles for which you're recruiting. You want to do good work at the front end of recruitment by establishing clear guidelines. You don't want a bunch of rag-tag loose cannons that are just in it for the free lunch they get when you thank them in person for volunteering. You can professionalize your volunteer corps, and when you do so, they can become a potent weapon, since it happens often enough that a donor actually responds more warmly to a peer than to a paid fundraising staff member.

How can volunteers help your fundraising operation? With proper training and management, volunteers can be entrusted with tasks at all levels of the giving pyramid. Where I work, we have some volunteers asking for grassroots-level commitments of $25 to $100, and others making major, $1-million solicitations. You will have to vet your volunteers to assess their willingness to ask for certain levels of gifts (not everyone wants to ask for six- to seven-figure gifts) and their ability to do so effectively (you don't want certain volunteers asking for six- to seven-figure gifts... or certain prospects being asked by certain volunteers).

At least some of your board members who are volunteering for the organization should be helping with the fundraising. Chances are that they are already giving money to the organization, so they should be able to help stir up philanthropic activity at some level. Granted, not every board member will be willing to do this, nor will every board member be good at it, but you should have your eyes open for which members you want to enlist.

I have had the good fortune of forging a very positive relationship with a trustee, which has turned out to benefit my work as a fundraiser immensely. I cannot tell you how many conversations in one region that I cover have been aided, if not simply executed, by this trustee's participation.

Of course, it helps that this trustee has lived in the city that I have frequented for decades, that she is extremely well connected, and that she is semi-retired. Therefore, she has free time, knows people, and is unafraid to pick up the phone and call someone to make an appointment. She has also made a few key solicitations in my place, which, given the donors' personal connections with this trustee, simply made more sense.

I am extremely lucky in this case, as fundraisers and trustees don't often work together in such a systematic manner. However, it would behoove you to take a critical look at your board and discern whom you might consider either taking on the road with you, or whom you might want to contact in advance when you're making a trip to New York, Boston, or Dallas. You could also benefit by pushing for access to board members/trustees, if you don't already have it.

Not to pile another staffing need onto your plate, but you really should consider having a volunteer coordinator within your shop to get the maximum output from your volunteers. This coordinator is oftentimes one of your frontline fundraisers, who, in addition to making direct solicitations, is charged with recruiting, training, and managing a volunteer corps. A well-managed volunteer force can do wonders for your bottom line, both in dollars and in the number of gifts acquired.

The volunteer coordinator should check in monthly with the volunteer base and provide them with updates on the organization. This should include where you stand relative to the relevant fundraising goals, a reminder of their tasks, and a call to make their gifts to the organization if they have not done so already (after all, they should be leading by example), as well as non-fundraising-specific updates that the volunteers can share when making their solicitations.

Another way to engage volunteers is by doing conference calls. Conference calls can be a hassle, but they are worth the preparation. The difference between sending monthly e-mails and holding a monthly conference call is that you have your volunteers' uninterrupted attention for 20–30 minutes. Granted, you can't make people join the call, and sometimes attendance can be thin, but I argue that occasional conference calls are worth the preparation.

The formula that I have found works best is as follows:

- Notify your volunteers a month in advance. Include the date and time of the call. When choosing the time of day, consider time zone differences if you are working with volunteers across different regions.
- The week before the call, send a reminder.
- Two days before the call, send another reminder. Notify them that you will send call information and the agenda tomorrow.
- The day before the call, send a final reminder, complete with agenda and call-in information.
- You should be on the line five minutes before the appointed time. Wait until five to seven minutes after the appointed start time to begin going through the content.
- Take attendance.
- The call itself should last no more than 30 minutes. Ideally, the call will be five minutes of waiting for people to join, ten to fifteen minutes of updates, five minutes of questions and answers, and then a wrap-up.
- After the call, send your volunteers a detailed summary of what was covered on the call.

One other note: While I will visit the subject of travel later on, one thing I do want to point out is that your frontline fundraisers should be putting volunteers on their call list when they are planning a trip. It is always a nice gesture to take them out for a coffee or a meal to say thank you for volunteering their time for the organization. Another reason that it is worth the time: Your volunteers are more likely to be responsive and engaged if you take the time to get in front of them. It is harder to ignore your organization once they have a direct, personal point of contact within your ranks. When I was working intensely with volunteers while managing the Young Alumni program, the volunteers whom I visited were, almost without exception, those that were quickest to respond when there was a call to action.

The main thing to remember about volunteers is that they have their utility, but be aware, in advance, of the potential limitations of that utility.

The Minimalist Shop: What to Do When Resources Are Tight

So, you can't afford to hire *everyone* I just mentioned? Who is indispensable and who isn't?

It goes without saying that you can't have a fundraising shop without a fundraiser, so you'll need at least one gift officer. If you can have an annual fund officer and a major gift officer, so much the better. If you can't immediately hire both, I would err on the side of hiring an annual fund officer initially, and delegating the major gift work to the organization's executive director. Some may disagree, but I think it wise to increase the breadth of your donor base first, creating a potential pipeline for major gifts down the line. It might be tempting to chase after the bigger fish right out of the gate, but I think good strategy dictates that, if you need to choose between major gifts and annual gifts, you should start with annual gifts.

If you're in this situation, and you don't have enough resources to pursue a major gift program immediately, then you can, *for the time being*, forgo a researcher. Researchers are going to offer the most help at the top of the gift pyramid, so if you are concentrating on simply building a base, the researcher isn't critical.

Note: If your organization is about to launch a large, systemic fundraising campaign, then you will definitely want a major gift officer on hand. As we will discuss later, campaigns, and their accompanying gift pyramids, are top-heavy, meaning that the majority of the dollars raised in a major campaign come from a small number of large gifts at the top. It's the Pareto principle in action: 80 percent of your donations will come from 20 percent of your donors.[1]

Administrative support—recordkeeping and logistics—could be rolled into one position if need be. Know up front that you run the risk of burnout, as administrative staff can often get saddled with an inordinate amount of work in a small, growing shop. If you do need to limit your administrative staff to one person, please be sure to compensate that person well. It is hard to exaggerate just how essential administrators are to keeping the whole operation in clean, working order. All too often, they are paid too little for the impact they have on keeping the office on task and organized.

You can get away without a donor relations team initially. A single event can be delegated to a frontline fundraiser with the help of the administrative support. Thank-you notes can be quickly personalized from a template, and sent by automated software or by a gift officer. Once your shop grows, however, you'll want to provide more personalized, in-depth stewardship,

[1] The qualifier here is that in recent history, with large, multimillion-dollar campaigns, we've actually seen the ratio take on dimensions more along the lines of 5% of the gifts from 95% of the donors.

and as you turn your sights to leveraging events more systematically, you will want to bring someone on board to focus solely on these tasks.

While not all the staff members I have listed are critical for starting a fundraising shop, I do want you to take home the knowledge that each added member is added value, ensuring that the minimum amount of money is left on the table.

Having discussed in detail the composition of your team, let's focus in the next chapter on the importance of gathering good data and keeping good records.

The Basic Tools

Collecting Good Data, Keeping Good Records

Gift officers all too often take data for granted. In well-established development shops, there is sophisticated databasing software that allows you to look up a donor's name, address, employer, spouse's information, phone numbers, e-mail addresses, the boards upon which the donor sits, press releases on their company, their stock options, their previous philanthropy to your organization and others, as well as a detailed history of the direct contact that your organization has had with this donor through significant phone calls, e-mails, personal visits, etc.

It's all essential information. And the biggest problem is the very fact that we take it for granted. A very complete donor profile is a rare and wonderful thing, and it is made possible only through diligence, attention to detail, and sometimes painstakingly tedious data entry.

The aims of this chapter are to make the case for collecting good data and to walk you through how (and why) to build a good database. We'll also take a look at some examples of what happens to fundraisers when data is wanting.

The Mack Truck Philosophy

I've gone on in previous chapters about the importance of good data. Why am I working so hard to drive home the point?

Effective fundraising at all levels, whether a small participation gift of $25 or a transformational gift of $5 million, is derived from the establishment and continuity of solid relationships with your donors. Fundraisers are the thread that allows for that continuity, but data needs to be maintained and updated vigilantly if the relationship is to be sustained.

Fundraisers come and go; turnover within the profession can be high. Good records on prospects allow for a new fundraiser to come in and be able to hit the ground running, without having to rebuild the relationship from scratch.

A colleague of mine called this mindset the "Mack Truck Philosophy." The Mack Truck Philosophy is really more a practice than a philosophy and is aimed at having a large amount of useful information on a donor entered into a database and easily accessible. That way, if the current fundraiser is hit by a Mack Truck and killed, a new employee should be able to step in and continue the conversation from right where it last left off without much hassle.

Another reason that the importance of information capture has been so driven into my head is my own upbringing. My father worked for several banks on the operations side and, in the second half of his career, was in charge of what was originally called "disaster recovery and emergency management" before it got the euphemism "continuity management." In other words, I was raised by a man whose job it was to think about how to keep a bank going under extreme circumstances—from bank robberies to hurricanes to deer jumping through a branch window (true story).

The problem, of course, is knowing how much information to include. Whereas it is easy to know when there is too little, knowing the threshold of what is too much information is a bit tougher.

The other problem is the fact that this data collection, this reconnaissance, can be time consuming, especially if you are relying on free software or search engines. I know that it's tempting, especially if you're scrambling and under pressure to bring in money to keep the lights on. It's tough to balance: do I spend time trying to capture all the relevant information about a donor or do I make another phone call to ask for money? I argue that, even though it is time consuming on the front end, you make up for it later and also prevent your frontline staff from getting caught off guard by bringing outdated information into a conversation. We've all heard the saying: information is power. With fundraising, this is certainly the case.

We probably don't need to know about *every* phone call or *every* e-mail that's passed between a fundraiser and a donor. Here is what should be recorded for each donor:

- Full name, aliases, maiden names
- Mailing address (or addresses), e-mail, and all phone numbers

- Religion (this matters so that you know when *not* to call folks)
- All business information (as well as previous employment information if possible)
- Special appeals that a donor has received
- Which appeals a donor has responded to positively (i.e., he/she made a gift)
- Events that a donor has attended
- Every visit to the donor from a staff member (whether it's a fundraiser, executive director, or otherwise)
- Any phone call / e-mail with the donor *that moves the gift conversation forward*
- Any phone call / e-mail with the donor that suggests an increase or decrease in either giving capacity or inclination.
- Any information that your organization has gleaned from the donor or from other sources that might have implications for a donor's giving capacity or inclination. This could include any number of things, including the following:
  - A change in job (promotion, layoff, new company, etc.)
  - A liquidity event involving a donor's company
  - An IPO involving a donor's company
  - A bankruptcy filing involving a donor's company
  - The selling or buying of a new home
  - Any information on a donor's children, in terms of schooling

How do you get this information?

The easiest, but least common way, is when donors send you their updated contact information. It's nice when they do this, but don't count on it. Donors rarely think about telling you when they move or that their company has just been sold.

Make sure your gift forms, both online and print, allow for maximum information capture. You'll want the full name, including middle name (for research purposes), address, primary and secondary e-mails and phone numbers, employment information, etc.

Once you have a donor's name and business information, you can plug them into Google Alerts, which will deliver news to your inbox based on queries or topics that you are interested in. It's a good way to stay on top of donors, especially the ones at the top of your pyramid (we'll get to gift pyramids in the next chapter).

Another good way to gather information: read. If your organization is based locally, make sure you're reading the paper, scanning it for information on your donors. If you've gone to a performance lately, study the donor roll: who are the platinum, gold, or silver donors? Are any of those names in your donor pool? Local news will oftentimes include examples of significant philanthropy that can open the doors of a certain organization. Keep your eyes open.

Oftentimes, donors tend to know one another, especially if you're a locally based organization. You should never be afraid of asking donors, whether in person, via e-mail, or over the phone, who else you should be talking to. You can run by them a list of donors in the area, both to see who you should be tapping for larger gifts, and also for informational updates on other donors. This does two things: it gets you information you wouldn't otherwise have and gets the donor even more invested in your cause. Any kind of non-monetary form of engagement is a good one!

I can't tell you how many times I've gotten good information on donors from other donors not only with respect to new addresses, but also with information on their jobs, their children, and their wealth. You would be amazed how connected some folks are and just how much they know about one another.

Another reason why it's good to ask your donors who else you should be contacting is that it gets them involved in a non-monetary way. They get to feel (correctly) as though they are helping your organization beyond the act of writing a check. They can also help open doors that you might not be able to open. When asking your prospects who else you should be seeing, ask if they might be willing to introduce you.

Sometimes, because of privacy concerns, a donor might not be able to di-vulge specifics (because they are clients, for example), but will be able to say, "It'll be worth your time to call this person." So never be afraid to ask your donors who else you should be contacting. More often than not, you'll be pleasantly surprised.

Let's now turn to an essential part of the fundraising process: taking notes when we meet with donors.

Taking Good Notes

Fundraisers should, ideally, submit contact notes for each donor they've met or spoken to within 12 to 24 hours. This is not just in the interest of timeliness—this is also in the interest of *remembering* the content of the conversation.

When spending a day outside the office, conducting face-to-face visits, you can (and should) have many visits a day. Three to five prospect visits is a good target for a per diem visit count. It is hard enough keeping those visits straight in your head at the end of the day in your hotel room. The longer you wait to type up your contact notes, the poorer the quality and the less relevant the details will be.

All fundraisers have their own strategy for capturing notes. Here is what I and other successful fundraisers do. These practices should result in sufficient data capture.

- Bring a small notepad with you to each visit. It will ideally fit in a jacket pocket, so as to be discreet. If you're traveling, hotel notepads often do the trick.
- Immediately after the meeting, jot down the most important things that came up in the meeting.
  - Themes in the conversation
  - Mood of donor towards your organization, or, more pointedly, to the efforts of the fundraising shop
  - Any of the aforementioned data points
- Do this for each visit you have that day.
- At the end of the work day, in your hotel room (or back at your office), type up all of your notes in a narrative format. Err on the side of including more details than you think you need. You don't need to include how they took their coffee, but with respect to information that could be pertinent to development work, include it, even if its usefulness might be a little remote. Again, if you have a researcher, they'll be able to sniff out subtle details that might be more significant than you think. Examples could include mentioning a certain investment, in, say, a copper mining company. While it could seem like a random, passing reference, if there's a huge spike in the construction of wind farms, which require a significant amount of copper, you'd be wise to check in with that prospect to see how his or her investment is doing. Another example could be a child changing schools (to public or private, to a less or more expensive school). That will affect a donor's immediate capacity to make a gift.
- E-mail those notes to yourself, your supervisor, and your support staff. Make sure that the notes get entered into your organization's database.

I'll admit it: it's hard at the end of the day to sit down and spend an hour typing up notes, especially if you've had a glass or two of wine with dinner. But if you don't get those notes typed up within 12 hours of that visit, then the quality and detail level of those notes will suffer. It is worth it for you to hunker down and hammer out those notes that same night.

Capture the Moment

One of the main purposes of taking these notes is to capture a donor's inclination, capacity, and timing *at a specific moment in time*. You can and should make projections based on your visit. However, keep in mind that things can (and do) change. While good contact notes are indispensable for coming up with a good strategy, it should be acknowledged that a donor's inclination and capacity can (and all too often do) shift between contacts with your organization.

For example, say you visited a donor who managed private wealth on Wall Street in March 2008 before the Bear Stearns collapse (and before the even bigger meltdown in the fall). The donor hinted that a significant gift to your organization was quite possible. She said, "Let's get back together in the fall and we'll have that conversation."

Well, when you called to set up a meeting in October 2008, you got the cold shoulder. In the immediate aftermath of the financial sector's collapse, you should not have been expecting to continue the conversation *at the same pace* at which it was being conducted in March. You were right to still call this donor, of course. But you might have expected a very different conversation than the one you anticipated after the March visit.

Good notes, therefore, capture three things that we've already discussed:

- Capacity
- Inclination
- Timing

Stories from the Road: Why Notes Are Important, and Their Limits

To illustrate the point, I'll give you three examples from my own experience.

In the fall of 2008, I was in the Midwest visiting with a young alumnus who graduated from the institution that I represent. I was a little over a year into the job, with a full fiscal year under my belt.

My colleague, who preceded me, and I had cited this particular alumnus as a potential lead donor for his upcoming 10th Reunion (and, to her credit, she turned out to be absolutely spot on). The plan in the spring of 2008 was to visit him in the fall of 2008 and solicit him for $60,000, to be made over five years. $50,000 ($10,000 a year for five years) would be used to set up an endowed fund, and $10,000 ($2,000 a year for five years) would be used as an expendable fund.

Once I got to him in October 2008, the conversation did not go as planned, as you can imagine. He worked for a small investment bank, and he said that there was way too much uncertainty for him to commit either to a gift of that size or a five-year time horizon. What is more, his interests were, at the time, in setting up an internship fund to send students to Africa. At the time, internships were not a funding priority.

So, all in all, the visit was not a success. I came away empty handed and couldn't satisfy his primary philanthropic interest. But I did my best to capture all this information when I wrote up my notes.

The diligence in writing up a thorough summary of the visit paid off. A year later, my colleague on the major gifts team was looking for filler visits for her Midwest trip, and I recommended this particular prospect. Between my unsuccessful visit and her trip, a lot of things had happened that would change the color of the conversation.

For example, internships were now a funding priority at my workplace. One of this alumnus's former professors took a job at our graduate school, thereby increasing the level and frequency of institutional contact this alumnus had. Furthermore, his cousin was graduating from the school and had had a wonderful time.

Even if work at the investment bank still engendered a good deal of uncertainty, enough had changed since the last visit that my colleague had a wonderful meeting with this alumnus, and they remained in contact.

Granted, my colleague might have eventually tripped upon this alumnus, but having the notes to reflect back upon certainly made her initial visit a lot more substantive, both because she had a clear idea of how my visit went, and what had changed since then.

The second example of a contact note that was accurate at the time but didn't stand when I was ready to visit someone occurred when I took on my role as a major gift officer. In the transition that took place, one of the prospects whom I inherited was mid-conversation with my predecessor about an impending liquidity event involving his company. He had been looking to sell the company for the past year and half. Around the time of my transition to my role as a major gift officer, we were expecting the event to occur, meaning that he was going to be looking to give away a good amount of money to avoid paying capital gains taxes.

This alumnus hadn't been visited in about a year by the time I got around to putting a call out to him. The first time that I tried contacting him, he wasn't available, but I had other prospects to fill my trip to the city anyway. So I made the trip.

While on the road, I mentioned to another alumnus that I had tried to see this particular prospect but couldn't make an appointment. This alumnus then mentioned, "You know his company went bankrupt, right?"

I didn't. But I sure as heck did my homework when I got back to the office. Based on that comment, I entered that information into the particular prospect's record. And that information certainly did change my approach for my next outreach. As it turned out, he moved out West and was reassigned to my colleague who covers that territory.

We'll round out this section with a happier example. I had a mid-range prospect on my list for one of my trips to a city in Western New York. I had avoided seeing him for a while, since all of the previous visits from two other gift officers painted him as a very lukewarm prospect with low inclination. Their notes had indicated he was more interested in giving to his graduate school than to my employer. This prospect was definitely on my B-list and not at the top of it either. Compound this with the fact that it took at least three attempts to get him to agree to see me.

I wasn't terribly excited to meet with him and wasn't particularly optimistic about the visit.

As it turns out, I was more than a little surprised at the outcome of the meeting. He revealed a lot of information that belied the pessimistic notes of the past. He said that while he wasn't terribly liquid at the moment, and that he had young children and was on the board of a local museum that was currently receiving the bulk of his philanthropic dollars, he was beginning to "get over" his previous hang-ups with his alma mater, my employer.

He made it clear that, while he was not in a position to give a lot right now, he was thawing out as a donor and would someday be interested in supporting financial aid. And, in the short term, he received an appeal from us that was aimed at establishing an endowed scholarship fund named after a former coach of his, to which he planned to contribute $20,000. That was five times what he normally gave to the school in any year since graduating.

So this visit revealed that his capacity had changed slightly (although his giving didn't increase enough for us to reevaluate his rating). His timing was still remote, but most significantly, his inclination had changed in our favor. Finally, and of equal importance, we were able to glean his philanthropic interests.

The point is that contact notes are extremely important to providing gift officers and supervisors with a summary of a prospect's capacity, inclination, and timing *at a given moment in time*. These three factors can change, for the better or worse, depending on the circumstances. But it is a gift officer's responsibility to capture them as accurately and as in-depth as possible with each new point of contact.

If, for example, you are reporting to your board (or even your boss) on planned solicitations for the previous fiscal year, you want to be able to account for why a solicitation did not happen. You'd be surprised how often you refer back to notes to provide color on a stalled or delayed solicitation.

In short, I hope you have gained an appreciation for the importance of taking good notes, as well as their limitations (which by no means detracts from how important they are!).

Notes, Continued: Examples and Analyses of Notes from the Donor Visits

It's worth spending more time analyzing contact notes. I'll provide you with some examples, ranging from terrible to good, and take some time to explain.

Here is an example of a bad contact note:

> JDS plans to visit with Joe. Notes to go here.

How often does this note exist as the only capture of the visit? More often than you'd think. Sometimes there isn't even a record of the visit. That lack of information can haunt a new fundraiser if a donor has just been visited, or the last visit went poorly. It's even worse if the fundraiser who originally met with that donor no longer works for your organization. The new fundraiser going into that situation must, essentially, start cold.

In such a meeting, the new fundraiser might frontload this potential information gap by asking the donor to narrate to him/her where the conversation had last left off. Of course, the potential problem here is that you have to take the donor at his or her word, which isn't always correct. I have had times where the donor did downplay where the conversation had stood at last visit with a prior gift officer. I have even had conversations where the donor downplayed where the conversation stood the last time *that I personally met with them*. Needless to say, it has helped to have the backup of a good contact note.

Here is an example of a good contact note of a visit from an annual fund prospect:

> *22 September 2010: JDS met with Josephine over coffee. He thanked her for her consistent support of the annual fund. He provided her with an update from campus, with a focus on social life, financial aid, and the political science department. Josephine asked about Professor Smith, and JDS explained that he was still teaching, and was coming out with a book in the fall about campaign finance reforms. Talk turned to Reunion. Josephine is planning on being back at Reunion. Regarding her gift, JDS asked Josephine if she would consider making a stretch gift of $1,800 this year in honor of her 20th Reunion. Josephine said that she'd consider that level, and had to check with her husband. JDS asked if it would be okay if they touched base around Thanksgiving to follow up on the gift conversation if they hadn't spoken by then. Josephine said that this would be a fine arrangement. JDS to send a follow up thank you note, which includes Professor Smith's book title, as well as information about financial aid.*

This note provides the reader with Josephine's capacity, inclination, and timing. We can see that her capacity is that of a mid-range (by my school's standards) annual fund donor. Her inclination is high, since she gives every year. And the timing is soon: we'll know about her giving within two months. What is also good about this note is that it includes the content of the conversation, as well as follow up items.

If the fundraiser were to quit between now and November, their replacement should be able to pick up the conversation where it left off, with the $1,800 solicitation, potentially designated to Financial Aid or the political science department if Josephine so desired.

Here is an example of a good contact note for an initial visit for a major gift prospect that did not go as well as planned—at least for now:

> *JDS met Robert for lunch. Robert played in CA at the US Whiffleball Championships this past summer with his team: Smiths (classes of 88, 83), Stevie Jackson, Mark Fish, and others. Robert was excited to see the pre-tournament dinner grow to include more [school] constituents. Rob-*

ert in general seems to be hungry to stay connected to the school; was somewhat jealous that a lot of his friends are closer to campus. His oldest son is @ Dartmouth. Has 2 younger kids, a daughter, junior in HS and a son, 9th grade, both @ Academy, a top private school in his city. Hopes one of them will attend [school]. Lots of talk revolved around sports. JDS gave update on men's soccer and asked Robert if he was in a position to be a big donor to the effort. Sadly, now is not the time for a big gift; Robert made very heavy allusions to some transactions that could be very lucrative; in the interim, b/f that all shakes out, he's holding on tight to any expendable money that he has. JDS to keep on Robert for how the transaction goes, as from the sounds of it, it could mean Robert's net worth could increase significantly. Robert is very, very much on board for hosting an event in the area. JDS to send a listing of regional alumni and parents to give Robert a sense of who's in the area. Robert said the next few months are too hectic, given this transaction, but that May/June or September/October would be ideal. A time of year where the event can be half indoor/outdoor would be ideal. Rest of conversation is around languages/revenue. Language instruction links in follow up. Other flu: when [school] played again US junior nationals, what percentage of soccer players take a gap year to play intensively, info on schools abroad. Also, a reminder to call JDS when Robert brings daughter to campus. Might make sense to arrange meeting w/head coach of soccer team.

Here is an example of a good contact note for an initial visit for a major gift prospect that went well:

JDS had a lengthy and interesting meeting with Robin at his office. Robin walked JDS through the hardware system that Robin invented, and explained the history of it, which can be found in previous notes. Robin owns 4 properties in the area. He has a $2.5MM planned gift to his undergraduate alma mater and a $1MM planned gift to the City Foundation, both bequests. He is also paying a $210K pledge to his undergraduate alma mater for a professorship there in the Russian department. He says that currently, his major giving is going to his alma mater, but that he is open to a conversation about giving to [my institution]. He is very, very grateful for his experience, and joked that the $5K gift he made in '05 was a late payment on an outstanding bill that he never paid back in the 1980s. He said the $5K was that payment with interest. He did say that he will consider a project that excites him, *and is open to continuing the conversation with JDS. He is also open to coming back to alumni career talk. He mentioned two different figures with regards to revenue; the lower figure would be $75MM / year in sales. Higher would be 75MM units sold per year @, on average, $15K per unit. Sells in 3 continents. Currently developing Thai. Robin is also hoofing the bill for a family friend's nephew at his undergraduate institution in Seattle. Robin is single with no children. A very good prospect with lots of cultivation and follow up required. JDS to send TY note to Robin and Alexander for meeting and for treating JDS to dinner. His special collections of rare books and other antiques must also be worth a fortune. The collection at his office is easily worth many, many thousands and he said his home collection is even larger.*

This was a first visit. This particular donor had never been visited before; we only knew to research him in the first place because he sent in a $5,000 check one year, unsolicited. After some preliminary research, we slapped a $100,000 rating on him. When I made it to the city where he lived, my visit was an assessment call. It quickly became apparent that the $100K rating was too low, based both on his outright and planned gifts. The contact note includes information about his company, as well as other indications of wealth (his private collections), his family life (never married, no kids), and his other philanthropy. We can glean from this note that this prospect has very high capacity (we bumped him to a rating of $1 million after further research), moderate to high inclination (he is subsidizing someone's tuition at our school already, and said he is open to the right project), with a medium time-horizon (he is currently paying off another six-figure pledge).

I realize that dissecting a meeting at this level of detail might come off as quite mercenary, ruthless, and cold. But there is a positive intention to all this. A gift of a million dollars *anywhere* can have a *huge* impact. Here, again, I want to reiterate that the role of a fundraiser is to act as an intermediary between the donor and the organization. You are facilitating a donation that will feel good for all parties. It is thus your responsibility to have as keen an eye for detail as I'm suggesting. Your detective work will have a lasting impact both the donor and your organization.

Here is an example of a good contact note for a cultivational visit for a major gift prospect:

JDS met w/Patrick & Richard for dinner (3.5 hour) in downtown Austin. Patrick entertaining JDS's proposal. Admired bold tone. Conflicted with philanthropic relationship towards [school]. View 200k fund they are setting up as drop in the bucket. Building to 2MM isn't even the end of the road for their giving, either. Patrick said at some point they should be considered 5-10MM candidates. Patrick has reservations about school's endowment and spending policies with need blind admissions. Patrick not convinced need blind is a good financial decision, wants data that can convince him need blind policy graduating grateful students who are giving back. JDS to form a narrative that will hopefully build the case for this. Patrick said if he wasn't serious about his philanthropic investment in [school], he wouldn't be having the conversation; Patrick and Richard want to support scholarships to create opportunities to allow deserving, passionate kids to attend. What they do not want is to create a culture of students who feel entitled to their experience based on high school qualifications. He wants to know that students graduating feel grateful and continue to provide the fuel to allow the need blinds mission to continue, as opposed to just riding on the sponsorship of alumni. Want to support short-term projects as JDS, Patrick and Richard figure out the long term horizon for philanthropy. Baseball might be an area of support, because Patrick, interestingly enough, believes student athletes get a perspective on life. They hope to visit campus 1x yr, since sister's children are there. Patrick is a big fan of the VP, would love to meet him. They remain skeptical of endowment as "black box," they are ready to increase their annual fund support to 100-200k / yr over the next few years. Should be considered for alumni advisory committee.

This is a couple that I have visited more than once, and corresponded with via phone and e-mail numerous times. They are fantastic prospects and I know them quite well at this point. They've essentially pledged to half a million dollars over the next few years. But what if I leave? What then?

There are a number of things to notice on this note, some obvious, some less so. The obvious things: Pat is very opinionated and very savvy about his philanthropy. He is also very interested in the happenings of the college. He notes out loud that the reason that he's so inquisitive (in the meeting he was downright belligerent) is that I'm challenging him to explore a new level of philanthropic commitment (which, he noted, was a positive thing). To give $50,000 a year was one thing; to Patrick and Richard, that was a drop in the bucket. But I had already asked them to consider more than tripling that to the tune of $150,000–200,000 a year. This note reveals that their capacity is extremely high, that their inclination is also very high (if not hard-earned!), and that the timing is imminent. Of course, it also notes where the fundraiser (in this case, me) has a lot of work to do. I did spend the next week back in the office working meticulously to craft a narrative that would appeal to Patrick and Richard in a meaningful way, concentrating my efforts on demonstrating the gratitude of students.

The less obvious thing to note: we went to dinner. This is different from going out for coffee or even going to lunch. Dinner can last longer. This dinner lasted 3.5 hours. The first dinner with this couple also lasted four hours.[1] This should tell the fundraiser who inherits these two prospects to allot sufficient time to meet with them. That they want to make it back to campus once a year is also worth noting, as it allows the fundraiser to think of ways to engage this couple while on campus. For future trip planning, the fundraiser should budget one evening for this couple alone.

Another small, but important, thing to note is that Patrick liked the bold tone of my proposal. It was a passing comment, but has informed our subsequent conversations; I have been given Patrick's permission to push the envelope with him. If the reaction to my admittedly bold proposal hadn't been as well received, I would have reacted accordingly. This brings up another point when dealing with donors: what degree of formality they expect. It can, and does, vary quite drastically. I am not just talking about dress code, but also the degree of familiarity that one can use with the donor. It varies, and I'll talk more about this when we discuss face-to-face visits in depth, but given that this appeared in the note, I wanted to call attention to it. It is a good idea, when possible, to try to capture *how* a donor speaks to you.

These were all notes from visits I had while on the road. Know that you can, almost as effectively, conduct similar, substance-rich conversations over the phone, via Skype, or e-mail if your company does not have the budget to send your fundraisers on the road. While nothing can replace a face-to-face conversation, you do have to work within your means.

Databasing: Information, Organized

So you have all this great data. Now arises the Herculean task of how to organize it all. Ideally, you will have a database into which to dump all the information. If your organization does not have databasing software already, it does make sense to invest.

What you want to avoid is every gift officer keeping their records in "stand-alone" mode, which is to say on the privacy of their own computer. This

---

[1] This isn't to say, of course, that you can't accomplish what you need to over a 20-30 minute coffee. Not all meetings need to last 4 hours. In fact, my colleagues who have Metro NY as a territory rarely have prospects who will take that amount of time to meet.

violates the Mack Truck philosophy. If the gift officer gets hit by that Mack Truck and leaves this earth, along with all their passwords, then all records of his or her prospect pool are effectively erased. This is a very bad situation.

There are several companies that offer specific fundraising databasing software. As mentioned previously, one very popular product is Raiser's Edge by BlackBaud (www.blackbaud.com/products/fundraising/raisersedge.aspx).

There are other possibilities other than simply purchasing new software. If your organization already has databasing software that does not have fundraising information built in, it makes sense first to see if development fields can be added (they often can be).

And there are free products out there as well. OpenOffice (you can find it at www.openoffice.org) offers database software at no cost.

If you're looking to be truly minimalist, you could get away with creating a file folder for each and every donor that contains your contact notes, giving history, contact information, and research dossier. This can become a maintenance nightmare, although it is doable.

Whichever level of sophistication you choose, you must have as much information about every donor centrally located and universally accessible for your development team. Information in silos is worthless.

Having discussed in depth how to collect data, why it's important, and explored the universe of note-taking, let's step back in the next chapter, take a look at the fiscal calendar, and describe how to create an annual fundraising plan.

The Annual Plan

Setting Goals, Charting the Course

One of the smarter fundraising colleagues I worked with lived by the six P's: Proper Planning Prevents Piss-Poor Performance. She was right (if a little crude).

Then why does planning get overlooked so often? The answer is because it's easy to overlook Indeed, it is so incredibly tempting to make that one additional phone call, to send one more e-mail, or schedule one more meeting on the road. Because every moment a fundraiser spends in a meeting or planning is a moment that he or she is not raising funds, which is his or her purpose.

Planning often gets overlooked, but an organization does so at its own peril. Planning is important for a few simple reasons.

- It provides you with a framework for your year (or quarter).
- It gives you goals against which you can measure success.
- It enhances workflow and helps you prioritize the innumerable tasks that you have.
- It gives you a chance to strategize out loud, as a team, about micro-goals (i.e., certain prospects) and macro-goals (dollars to be brought in).

Why Set Goals?

Why bother with setting goals? Why not just get out there and ask for as many gifts as possible? Setting goals achieves the following things:

- It challenges and empowers your fundraisers.
- It provides you with material to bring to your supervisor/board.
- It informs your strategies and planning, both at the individual, targeted level and at the more general, participatory level in a way that cannot be achieved without goals.

In other words, goal-setting and planning are inextricably tied together. Let's explore both of them.

Goal Setting: Dreaming Big, Realistically

Goal setting is always a fun exercise—it allows you to dream big, to think broadly about your organization's fundraising capabilities, and to think creatively about how to improve upon last year. It also empowers you to think about the impact that your operation can have upon the institution as a whole.

Where do you start? Well, it's best to begin by asking the central questions: What can our organization currently NOT do due to lack of funding? What incremental increase in funding would we need in order to carry out those wishes?

It's a better place to start than by looking at last year's data, especially if your shop is still in its nascent stages. The expectation should be that you'll raise more money than last year, especially if you've been able to expand your fundraising staff.

My own bias is to start as big as possible and then pare back once you get into planning the implementation. This is an evolved opinion—I have often been accused, somewhat accurately, of being the one to shoot down big ideas, big goals. While the accusation has merit, it is motivated by the fact that I'm very much implementation- and process-oriented; so, while I sometimes come off as someone who enjoys shooting down big ideas, I like to think of it more in terms of me serving as a counterbalance to the dreamers. The "idea people" have their place in the organization, without a doubt, but so do the folks who devote their time to thinking about pitfalls, capabilities with limited resources, and getting from A to B without losing their sanity. In other words, you need both types of folks (remember the operations and logistics staff member from Chapter 4?), and both of them should be given equal voice when setting goals and coming up with your annual plan.

Goals should be ambitious, yet achievable. On the one hand, you want to challenge your staff to think creatively about how to improve both themselves and the organization, while on the other hand, not sending them over the edge with completely unrealistic figures.

Gift Pyramids: Your Dollar Goals, Visualized

When it comes to setting your dollar goals, the classic way to visualize them is with a gift pyramid. At the top of your pyramid sit the largest gifts in the smallest numbers. From there, you make your way down the pyramid, with a larger number of anticipated gifts at each subsequent level.

There are two general guiding principles to keep in mind when setting your dollar goals:

1. Eighty percent of the money you raise will come from 20 percent of your solicited base.[1]

2. On average, you will receive $0.20–$0.25 for every $1 you ask for.

Regarding the second point, this can mean that for every person that you solicit for $1, each one gives you $0.25, or for every four solicitations you make for $1, one solicitation is successful. This pattern tends to play itself out at all levels, whether you are asking for $100 or $1,000,000.

In other words, if you are hoping to raise $500,000 this coming year, you need $2 million in solicitations.

If we continue with this hypothetical example, and bring in the first principle, then you will need to raise $400,000 from your top 20 percent, meaning that you'll need $1.6 million in solicitations among that echelon, with the remaining $100,000 coming from the remaining 80 percent of your solicitable base (and yes, with $400,000 in solicitations).

Even within that top 20 percent, there will be a range of gifts. Every organization has its top donor. How that top 20 percent is divided will depend on the composition of your donor base, but it is good to recognize that even that top 20 percent is not distributed evenly. It might not be an exact microcosm of the 80/20 split that we tend to see in the overall pyramid, but you will certainly still see a range.

---

[1] With certain large-scale campaigns, this ratio actually becomes more skewed. You will see certain gift pyramids in which 95 percent of the money raised comes from 5 percent of the donor base. As you professionalize and your goals and ambitions get bigger, and as you continue to build a solid donor base and steward your major donors, you might find yourself tending toward a 95:5 ratio—but when you're first starting out, go for 80:20.

On the 4:1 ratio of dollars solicited to dollars raised, why build that level of rejection into your goals? It's a sobering but good idea to frontload that truism that 75 percent of the money you ask for will not come in.

Fundraisers need to get used to hearing *no*; it is part of the trade. Rejection is unavoidable. It doesn't matter how valid your mission, how talented your staff, and how urgent your need. There is such an intense competition for a limited supply of philanthropic dollars out there, that the demand far outpaces what is actually available.

Of course, that isn't to say that you still shouldn't give each personal solicitation your best effort, or that you should slack off in your follow-up. The point is, get used to rejection; get used to that 20 to 25 percent rule.

Going too far over that 4:1 ratio can get an organization into trouble. In good times, you can see that ratio inch towards 3:1, but it isn't wise to rely on that for very long. Where I work, we got ourselves into trouble pre-fall 2008, when the economy was strong (or appeared to be strong), and people were being quite philanthropic. We did see a solicitation to gifts-in ratio that was pushing 3:1. That's a good thing, right? Yes, so long as you don't get too used to that notion.

My organization (and others) began forecasting 3:1 ratios three to five years out. Not only were they reporting out to the board such optimism, but there were also budgetary assumptions based on the 3:1 ratio that would, in a very short time, come back to haunt the entire organization. The overarching message: a few years of good times do not preclude a spate of bad times. It is better to err on the conservative side of a 4:1 ratio, and be able to report a surplus, than overstretch yourselves going for 3:1.

The interesting thing about this rule is that you can't necessarily predict who will offer a yes or a no; some years, your designated "go-to" donors might come up short, and other years, donors who have been reticent to give at the level you were hoping for might have had a fortuitous change in circumstances, allowing them to step up their giving. In other words, ask everyone, don't be surprised by the no's, and be grateful for every single yes, even if it's a quarter or a fifth of what you had originally asked for.

When I first began fundraising, standing on the streets of Boston with a clipboard and a DNC t-shirt, our average yes-rate was closer to 20 percent, with the average contribution of around $20. During each shift, which ran from 11 a.m. to 4 p.m. with a quick lunch break; we would have, on average, thirty conversations. It was gritty work—and at times, downright miserable—but it did train me very quickly in taking no for an answer, while also instilling in me the need to ask absolutely everyone, even if I thought there was no chance that someone would make a gift.[2] Some of the more pleasant surprises in that summer of 2006, came from conversations that I was pretty convinced were a waste of time. The converse is also true: some of the biggest disappointments were folks I thought I had pegged for a good gift (a good gift was $50 or more at the time).

Again, pursue each conversation until it has unequivocally expired, in your favor or otherwise.

Let's return to the goal of $500,000 and break it down into a hypothetical gift pyramid.

Here is a look at the top of the pyramid:

Gift Pyramid: The Top 20 Percent			
No. of Gifts	Ask Amount	Total Solicited	Anticipated Cash-In
1	$250,000	$250,000	$62,500
5	$100,000	$500,000	$125,000
8	$50,000	$400,000	$100,000
10	$25,000	$250,000	$62,500
20	$10,000	$200,000	$50,000
Total: 44		$1,600,000	$400,000

In this particular instance, I set up the pyramid and took into account the 4:1 rule in such a way that I assume that each solicitation will result in a yes, but those yes-results will come in only at 25 percent of my original ask.

I could have just as easily altered the pyramid in a way that assumed a 25 percent yes rate, but at 100 percent of the original ask. That is to say, I could have made the first column "Number of Asks" instead.

---

[2] The amount of *daily* rejection also taught me to sniff out the differences between a hard no and a soft no. A hard no, in the street canvassing scene, is one in which the person says "no" and walks away. A soft no is someone who hesitates, stays put, but says the amount you're asking for is a bit much. We'll cover more on how to deal with soft no's later in Chapter 10.

Such a pyramid would look something like this:

Gift Pyramid: The Top 20 Percent			
No. of Asks	**Ask Amount**	**Total Solicited**	**Anticipated Cash-In**
4	$100,000	$400,000	$100,000
8	$50,000	$400,000	$100,000
16	$25,000	$400,000	$100,000
40	$10,000	$400,000	$100,000
Total: 68		**$1,600,000**	**$400,000**

One way is not necessarily superior to the other, so long as you build in, somehow, the two basic assumptions of the 80/20 ratio for gift size and a 4:1 ratio for dollars solicited to dollars received.

Returning to the first mode of assumptions, in which we have a 100 percent yes rate, but at a quarter of the original ask, a hypothetical remainder of the pyramid would look like this:

Gift Pyramid: The Remaining 80 Percent			
No. of Gifts	**Ask Amount**	**Total Solicited**	**Anticipated Cash-In**
20	$7,500	$150,000	$37,500
20	$5,000	$100,000	$25,000
30	$2,500	$75,000	$18,750
35	$1,000	$35,000	$8,750
50	$ 500	$25,000	$6,250
60	$250	$15,000	$3,750
(Plus Smaller Participation Gifts)			
Total: 215	**$16,750**	**$400,000**	**$100,000**

Granted, this is a hypothetical pyramid, and the math is such that the top 20 percent in dollars is slightly less than 20 percent of all the gifts in; in addition, I didn't provide a breakdown of smaller participation gifts of $1 to $249. Granted, each pyramid, from year to year, from project to project, will vary. It will be largely dependent on your solicitable base; you can't raise more than your base's capacity. If you have a small donor pool, you will have to start with modest goals.

Each year, you should set overall goals, such as the ones above. Also, each project should have its own, specific pyramid to make it more manageable. When I say "project," I could mean anything from constructing a new building for your organization or renovating a current one (a "capital campaign," in the industry's parlance). It could mean launching a short-term, concerted effort to lobby for or against certain legislation at the state level. Any undertaking that merits special attention beyond the ordinary level of engagement merits its own goal-setting session, the outcome of which should be a gift pyramid.

Of course, each of those gifts (or solicitations, depending on how you structure your pyramid) should correspond to individuals. It's no good dreaming up figures if you don't have donors to back them up. It might be a good exercise, as you read this, to think about who your top 20 percent is, and what the individual and combined philanthropic capacity of that top of the pyramid is.

So, when drawing up goals annually, be sure to consult with your frontline fundraisers, your executive director, and anyone who has donor contact to ask them about anticipated solicitations in the coming year.

Participation Goals: Building the Movement, Investing in the Big Donors of the Future

Dollar goals are the first ones you'll want to set—they have the biggest implications for your programming, your budget, and, as you expand your fundraising operations, your staffing requests.

Dollar goals are not the only goals that your organization should focus on, however. You also need to take some time to set participation goals. Participation can be measured in different, non-exclusive ways. You can either measure participation as a percentage increase (or decrease) over last year's participation (as measured in the total number of gifts in), or you can measure it as a percentage of your entire solicitable base. If you are a small non-profit looking to expand your visibility, but you have a distinctly limited number of people to solicit, it might make more sense to take the first approach of percentage increase in gifts, as your potential solicitable base is much less defined than that of a college or university.

I made the case for annual fund gifts when we talked about staffing, but let's revisit why we need to focus on participation at all. Participation is important for many reasons. Here is a short list of them:

- It empowers smaller donors to feel like they are part of something bigger.
- It helps you to "build your movement."
- Foundations that might be considering giving to you will want to see how broad a base of support you have, as measured both in dollars raised, as well as absolute number of gifts.
- It does, at the end of the day, help your organization (consider that all gifts to my organization that were $50 or less last year added up to $250,000).
- It gets people on your radar for informational updates and stewardship opportunities (including newsletters, thank you phone calls or face-to-face visits).
- You are creating your pipeline: most major donors today were small, annual donors in the years leading up to their big gifts.

Let's focus for a minute on the notion of the pipeline, as it validates the importance of celebrating participation gifts. In fundraising lingo, the *pipeline* refers to the donors who are currently giving participation gifts, but who will later be major donors to your organization (with proper cultivation and stewardship, of course).

If you look at the majority of major donors to a given organization, you will notice that before they were supporting the institution at the major gift level, they were making participation gifts in the years previous to their becoming major prospects.

Granted, there are exceptions to the rule. You will get the rare unsolicited gift of $10,000, which will cue you to do some homework on that donor.[3]

---

[3] Remember: If you *do* get a large unsolicited gift, follow up immediately with a personal phone call to that donor, or visit to say thanks. Turn the thank you into a conversation as to why and how they decided to amp up their giving unannounced, with an ear toward developing the philanthropic relationship further.

For the most part, though, your major donors will be discovered through sifting through the $25–$100 donors and finding the diamonds in the rough.

This philosophy holds true at institutions where the fundraising operations are quite developed. Participation gifts are an investment for major gift operations down the road; or at least, re-solicitation.

I'll let you in on a little secret to prove my point. When you see a canvasser, like me in 2006, standing on the street corner with a clipboard, a smile, and a tragic amount of enthusiasm, or when you get that knock on your door on a weeknight around dinnertime, and you make a gift to that canvasser, it might pain you to know that the canvassing operation, on the whole, loses money.

Unless a canvassing operation is extremely well run, it loses money. It simply costs more to pay those canvassers to stand on the streets with their clipboards, or send them into the suburbs to knock on doors until 9 in the evening than the average amount that the operation brings in.

So why do so many non-profits invest in it? Because by canvassing, by getting those $5–$50 gifts every day, they are building their base. It is a glorified data mining expedition. Canvassers are encouraged to get a donor's contact information, including mailing address, phone number, and e-mail. Why? So that they can be re-solicited by the far more efficient means of phone, snail mail, and e-mail. Canvassers are building the lists from which organizations can then most efficiently micro-target. Those lists are then converted into e-mail lists and phone rosters for follow up solicitations, which do make money—and lots of it.

Canvassers who hustle day in and day out to meet their daily quotas might not appreciate this bitter truth, but they can go home happy knowing that their toils have helped set up a number of donors to get re-solicited. It's a little less glorious than the picture we have of canvassing operations: the noble young people spending their summers raising support for some worthy causes, but it is important to recognize their indisputable utility. The fact that canvassing operations are standard practice for large, nationally recognized non-profits is a testament to the importance of encouraging participation gifts, regardless of the amount.

Not all participation gift efforts lose money, of course. The canvassing example is simply one way of illustrating how important participation is; how much well-established non-profits invest in it because of its value in building the movement, if not immediately helping the bottom line.

Setting participation goals, as with most things in fundraising, is a combination of science and art. Take a look at last year's level of participation—how many gifts did your organization bring in? As you professionalize your fund-raising operations, you should see distinct increases in participation levels, as measured by the percentage increase over the number of gifts from last year. How much your participation increases will depend on a variety of factors, including the following:

- The reach of your organization: Are you locally or regionally based, or state or nationwide?
- The specificity of your mission: Does your institution focus on a single issue (reproductive rights, environmental justice, filling judgeships with conservatives, etc.), or are there multiple items on your agenda that your organization is seeking to advance?
- The target audience: Does your institution have universal appeal to a wide demographic of potential donors, or are you more likely to garner support from very specific segments of the population?

At some point, you will see the participation curve line flatten out, or at least see a decrease in the level of the slope. This just means that you are maxing out your donor base (which is good), and there are fewer and fewer stones left unturned (which is also good). You should still strive to bring in more gifts each year than the previous year. Just be aware that you will hit saturation points along the way. If you find that your curve is flattening out, it will become a matter of maintaining that level of support. Pushing that curve back up will probably require a combination of expanding your staff, automating or systematizing certain operations within your shop, and altering your message to attract a larger, broader audience.

One very important thing to keep in mind as you set goals and come up with annual plans is that you cannot—cannot—take any donor for granted. At the beginning of each fiscal year, you are back at zero, and you have to get out there and raise those participation gifts all over again. Just because a donor has given for five years in a row does not mean that he or she will give six years in a row. Or that he or she will always give at the level he or she historically has. Granted, with each year that a donor gives, he or she is increasingly likely to give again, but you cannot afford to make the assumption that a 10-year donor is automatically an 11-year donor.

I don't mean to make participation sound like a Sisyphean task, but you do need to appreciate this hard truth. Just because you received 5,000 gifts last year does not mean that you can rely on those 5,000 gifts this year. To put it another way: if last year you brought in 5,000 gifts, and this year, your goal is to bring in 5 percent more, as measured by the crude number of gifts, you are not just bringing in 250 new gifts. You have to bring in all 5,250, starting from zero.

Another cautionary word: If you have had a professional shop for a few years, if you see a year in which you don't meet your participation goal, and participation actually decreases from the year before, don't be discouraged. If there has been a ton of bad news on the economy, unemployment skyrockets, or if any number of factors beyond your control have had unfavorable effects on the philanthropic climate, know that, try as you might, participation rates will sometimes flag.

The flipside, of course, is that sometimes participation increases can be achieved even amid bad news. In fact, during economic crises, the message of participating, of throwing whatever you can into the bucket, will resonate across gift levels—from the major donors all the way down to your $5 donors. Furthermore, during economic crises, the urgency of your message is already implicit. In other words, don't throw your hands up when the *Wall Street Journal* is predicting Armageddon. Forge onward.

Planning, Planning, Planning: Charting Your Course to Goal Achievement

So you've done some data analysis on last year's participation. You've taken a look at your institution's goals, and spoken with the appropriate fundraisers and other staff to calculate your dollar goals, and figured out whom you will target as your top- and middle-range donors. Now comes the fun part—planning it all out.

As noted in the above section, I do think it is good, when coming up with goals, to think big. However, be flexible with those goals as you enter the planning process; a rigid dedication to goals when certain aspects are unattainable does you no good. It is a good idea to defend the goals you have come up with, but remember that this planning stage is about considering your organization's capacity and your solicitable base's capacity, and the goals must be in alignment with these factors.

Retreat for a Day or Two

When planning your year, it makes sense to set aside a day (or two) away from the office, away from the internet and phone, so that you can discuss your coming year without interruption.

I'm not a huge fan of team-building exercises, as we seem to do them at every planning retreat where I currently work. I'm simply not convinced that they do much to add to a productive conversation. This could be narrow-minded of me, but I don't think you need to spend half the day doing the Myers-Briggs test, DiSC training, trust falls, or similar exercises. The point of these exercises, in my understanding, is to give everyone a better understanding of one another, but I'm not sure that these time-consuming exercises cannot produce similar results as honest, one- to three-minute narratives from people at the planning session that include the following information:

- What they hope to accomplish in this session
- Their style of interacting with others
- What they're afraid of
- What they bring to the table

During your planning retreat, assign the following tasks:

- The mediator/facilitator keeps conversation on track, mitigates disagreements and defuses tension (by acknowledging that there is tension!).
- The scribe, logs the plan, either on paper (think: butcher block!) or on a computer.

The planning session is an exercise in dividing up the many chunks of work that go into fundraising. Each staff member and each division within your department should come to the table with tasks that they are happy to take on, tasks that they are willing to take on, and tasks that they would prefer to delegate (knowing that they might get stuck with it anyway). The goal of planning is to have a solid idea of the division of labor and the pace at which it happens.

Let's take a look at some of the areas you will likely be discussing.

Retreat Topic #1: Direct Mail

Let's start with the most basic form of soliciting: direct mail. As electronic as communication is becoming, direct mail is not dead. There are trade-offs, yes, but they exist with any form of solicitation.

The advantages are as follows:

- Letter appeals won't get caught in spam filters, like e-mail.
- It's easy to code your return vehicle—envelope, form, etc.—to gauge the efficacy of each appeal (that is, if you include a return vehicle).

- Longer form narratives do resonate with some people.
- It's the only way to reach certain audiences (i.e., our silver-haired constituents).

The disadvantages:

- People move, and don't always update their information, whereas e-mails remain pretty constant.
- There are the associated costs of printing and mailing.

  - A note on this: if you include a return vehicle, do not pay for postage. It often backfires on you when you do so, as donors will raise the complaint that their gift is going towards paying for the postage.

When thinking about your direct mail campaign, and really, all aspects of your direct solicitation methods, you need to give some thought to *segmenting* your appeals. What I mean by this is that it behooves you to have more than a "one size fits all" mentality when crafting your written appeals. This allows you to think creatively about your donor base, and give serious thought to its composition.

You will need, of course, to find a balance between segmenting and standardization. It is easy to go overboard when dividing up your donor pool into smaller pieces.

Here are some examples of how to segment your population:

- Age groups
- Giving levels
- Giving consistency
- Affinity within your organization, if appropriate (that is to say, if people give to a specific aspect of your programming)

Here are other questions that you will want to have in mind when planning your mail campaign:

- How many general appeals will we be mailing this year?
- How many segmented appeals will we be mailing this year?
- Will they all be letters, or will some be postcards?
- What other, non-solicitation mailings will our donors be receiving from our organization (newsletters, event invitations, etc.)?
- When will these appeals be mailed?
- Who will write the appeals? (Executive Director, Director of Development, Staff Members)?

- Who will edit the appeals once drafts are written?
- Who will the appeals be signed by (Executive Director, Director of Development, Staff Members, Volunteers)?
- What is the turnaround time needed to go from finalized draft copy to ready to mail?
- Who is responsible for doing the mail merge, for pulling the mailing data?
- Who's folding the paper and stuffing the envelopes? In other words, are you handling these appeals in-house or outsourcing the mailing operations?
- What type of paper are you printing on?
- What type of postage will you use? First class? Third class? First class is faster and will forward to a new address.
- Are you including any information other than the appeal and a return vehicle (e.g., giving history, information about the organization, etc.)?

You should also, as noted, be sure to track the success of each appeal by coding the return vehicle with an appeal code, so you know which appeals did better than others. You don't have to get fancy. It can be as simple as W11 for Winter 2011, S12 for Spring 2012, etc. Either way, you want to be able to collect data to help design your future solicitations.

In the next chapter, we'll focus on how to write a good appeal; the focus here is more on the logistics of things.

Retreat Topic #2: The Phonathon

The telephone is a great, often underestimated way to engage people as a substitute for in-person visits. It is also a great fundraising tool. Telephone fundraisers get a bad rap for interrupting dinner, but when on the phone, you often have someone's undivided attention, a luxury you do not have with mail.

Again, we'll get to how to craft a telephone message in the next chapter, but for now, you should focus on asking questions similar to those in the preceding list for your mail campaign.

A phonathon is any concerted, direct effort in which a number of volunteers or employees of your organization call donors with the express purpose of asking them for money. A phonathon can be a once-a-year or a year-round operation.

- How many times a year will you conduct phone solicitations? Will the phonathon be a year round operation or seasonal?
- Will you segment your phone list into multiple segments and scripts, based on past giving, giving levels, or affinity giving? Or will there be a simple, general call script?
- Who will be making the calls? Staff, volunteers, hired callers?
- Who is writing the script?
- If you hire telephone fundraisers, what is your budget for paying them?
- If you use volunteers, how many will you need per shift?
- How many hours are required to make it through all the segments that you are looking to call three to five times each?[4]
- Who is pulling the data? Who is reviewing the data to make sure that it is sound (see the following section on recommendations)?
- Will you be calling during the day or during the evening?
- Will you be calling work numbers and cell phone numbers or just home phone numbers?
- Will you be leaving messages?

Some general recommendations on phonathons:

- If you have to choose between day time and night time calling due to staffing concerns, it's advisable that you call in the evening. You have a better chance of reaching people and of having their attention for longer periods of time. It's okay to interrupt dinner. You might irritate folks, yes, but at least you're getting them on the line.[5]
- If appropriate, remember to account for time zone differences.
- Call from your work line. Yes, if you call from your cell phone, it's more likely you'll get someone to pick up, as they don't recognize your number, but it's a little deceiving.
- Don't call a single prospect multiple times in one evening, unless you are really short on numbers to call and/or really close to the end of a campaign/fiscal calendar.

---

[4] Calling through a single list three to five times is usually how long it takes for the list to be "exhausted," which is to say that it is no longer worth calling through it again. You should move on to another segment or list after that point.

[5] If you DO interrupt dinner, apologize sincerely ONCE, and only ONCE; then, move on to your script. You're interrupting dinner because you want to talk to them about some serious stuff!

- Collaborate with your fundraisers to see if there are individual prospects they want to contact personally; make sure that these prospects are removed from the calling data.
- Utilize your phonathon to complement your other contacts with donors. For example, you can use it to secure RSVPs to an event if your numbers are lagging, or to follow up on a written appeal that was recently mailed out.
- Some organizations will send out a pre-call postcard or e-mail to donors, letting them know that the phonathon team is going to call them. This often spurs people to make gifts to avoid the phone call.

One final note on telephone fundraising: make sure that whoever is calling, whether volunteer or staff member, has very thick skin. Telephone fundraising can be downright brutal work, perhaps more so than canvassing. At least with canvassing, you have the face-to-face aspect, which usually prevents most people (although by no means all) from getting too out of line. Telephone fundraising can really bring out the worst in donors. Getting hung up on is often an act of mercy compared to the verbal lambasting that can happen. You really do need the folks calling out on behalf of your organization to be able to take heat.

Considering the potential brutality endemic associated with telephone fundraising, *why bother with the phonathon program, then?*

The answer is simple: it gets results. Phonathon programs do bring in good money. Nonprofits wouldn't be investing in the technology and expenses (and staffing challenges) inherent in phonathon programs if the operation wasn't cash positive. While you probably won't be able to afford an autodialer, server, and programming to automate your phonathon operations at the outset, you should still find that your phonathon program brings in money.

Retreat Topic #3: E-mail

Of course, to remain relevant in today's world, you need to be able to communicate with your constituency electronically. E-mail is cost-effective and fast, and the returns are more immediate than snail mail. You can, with the proper software,[6] track what percentage of e-mails were opened; how many bounced back; how many got swept into spam filters; what percentage of opened e-mails were read (as tracked by scrolling to the bottom); and

---

[6] Lyris, Inc. (www.lyris.com) has a software suite that offers such services.

what percent of opened e-mail resulted in a "click-through" (that is to say, the reader clicked on a link leading them to a web-page—hopefully your giving page!).

You need to be cautious though, as mistakes can still happen. Data can get messed up and you can end up erroneously e-mailing a segment of your donor pool that you did not intend to, sometimes with very messy consequences and no small amount of clean up (both in terms of donor relations and in terms of time spent mopping up the damage). Before sending the e-mail to your donors, send a test round of e-mails to staff members. Get their feedback: make sure that there are no typos or grammatical errors and that all the links work (especially the link that takes you to your giving page).

For example, sending a thank you e-mail to non-donors, which has happened where I work, is never a good thing. Especially when it gets sent on the last day of our fiscal year and we are scrambling as it is to hit our targets. That added another layer of work onto an already stressful week, and it could have been avoided with a little more vigilance and coordination between divisions.

Don't trust your data. Even though data and reports should come out clean, you need a set of human eyes to do a thorough scan of each list to make sure that you are not crossing your wires. This is true of snail mail, the telephone, and e-mail. For whatever reason, though, it seems that the errors in external communications happen more often with e-mail than other forms of communication.

With e-mail, there is always the challenge of trying to stay on peoples' radars. Striking a balance between establishing a connection and over-communicating can prove difficult, since, in today's world, inboxes are bombarded incessantly on a daily basis. So, how much e-mail is too much? Do you alter the frequency of your communications when you get one irate response asking not to receive e-mails from you? Probably not; but at what point do you acknowledge that you are becoming a nuisance?

It's a difficult question to answer, and I'm not certain there is a golden rule on this one. For each person who responds saying that we are sending too many solicitation e-mails, there is another thanking us for the constant reminders. It is often the case that on the *last day* of the fiscal year, after constant reminders to give, with that final e-mail saying that there are less than 24 hours to make a gift, you will get tons of responses saying that they'll make their gifts, and *then say how glad they are that you sent the final reminder.*

Again, it's tough to come up with a magic number in terms of how often to send an electronic solicitation. People do respond differently to e-mail.

On the whole, I tend to err on the side of assuming that people are more patient than we give them credit for. I hear people complain that they receive "so many" e-mails from this non-profit or the other, but rarely do I hear them saying that they've responded to the sender asking to be removed from their mailing list. With e-mail, our attention spans are short. It's usually easier to click delete than to write an e-mail asking to be removed, or to go through the steps associated with unsubscribing.

Having your message deleted is acceptable; having someone request to be removed from your mailing list because of the high frequency of receiving e-mails is a bit more problematic.

Here's what you should be considering when devising your e-mail strategy. You'll see that there is some overlap in the types of questions.

- Will you be dividing this appeal into multiple segments?
- Who is pulling the data?
- Who is reviewing the data?
- Who is in charge of loading the data?
- What program will you be using to send the e-mail: Outlook, another program/software?
- Will you be sending in html or plain text?
- Who is writing the appeals?
- Who is editing/reviewing the appeals?
- Who is signing the appeals? From which account will each of these e-mails be sent?
- What is the turnaround time from the approved final drafts to the e-mails being sent?
- What will your subject line be for each appeal?
- And, of course, how frequently will you be e-mailing your donor base?

It makes a lot of sense to do as much planning around e-mail as you possibly can at the beginning of the year. When things get crazy mid-year and in the third and fourth quarters, and you're just beginning to come up with e-mail strategies for later that month, the solicitation will be a little lackluster, a little rushed; the data pull will be hasty; the data review will be cursory; the likelihood that mistakes will arise increases.

It is natural for the frequency of your e-mail solicitations to increase as you approach deadlines, whether fiscal year ending, campaign deadlines, etc.

Retreat Topic #4: Events

Let's not forget about events, which are a great way to engage donors. It is a good setting to keep folks connected without making them feel singled out for contributions. It is also beneficial to your organization because you can get your message across to a large number of people in a short amount of time with their (mostly) undivided attention if you have a content-rich message to share with them. This should include updates on your organization, your latest issues, etc. It is also a strategic way to engage individual prospects who might not currently be worth your time to visit individually, but who you would nonetheless like to meet/keep engaged. Also, on the subject of those prospects not currently worth your time: events can serve as a good low-pressure cultivation opportunity for them, a way to have them stay connected to the work of your organization.

Here is a list of important questions you need to answer when planning your events:

- How long is the event?
- What is the budget? Is there a donor (or donors) who might be willing to underwrite the costs of putting on the event?
- Who is the point person for organizing the event?
- Who is designing the invitations?
- Will invitations be mailed or e-mailed?
- Who is collecting the RSVPs?
- Are you charging or not? If so, is that going to be considered a gift to your organization?
- Is there a pitch at the event, or is it merely a meet-and-mingle type of affair?
- Is this event content-rich (i.e., with a speaker, lecturer, etc.)?
- Is this event an "all-come," or a smaller, exclusive event?
- Who will be in charge of setting up/breaking down?
- If appropriate, who is catering?

You will want a mix of all-come and targeted events, and a mix of social events and ones with pitches at the end.

You have to find a balance in terms of how often to have events. Your donors will tend to like them and will often push you to have more of them. You have to acknowledge your own limited bandwidth, though, and realize that event planning is very time-consuming. If you have a designated events person, please listen to them in terms of what they can deliver and how often. You want events to flow perfectly, and if the events manager has too much to do such that quality decreases, it is time to slow down the pace at which you put on events.

You also have to realize that events are an investment where the return is not always immediate and is usually indirect. Events do provide good opportunities for follow up and individual attention. Here are some pieces of advice:

- Make the RSVP list accessible to all of your advancement staff (not necessarily such that they can edit responses, but such that they can see who was invited and who has responded).
- If you are a fundraiser and you see prospects who have not RSVP'd, contact them and encourage their attendance. If they have RSVP'd and indicated that they can attend, let them know in advance that you'll be delighted to see them.
- Events also provide ample opportunity for engagement with your donors post-facto. E-mail them or call to say it was good to see them there (if you attended), and that you'd welcome their feedback on the event. Don't just pay lip service. Take note of what they have to say, both good and bad. Reaching out to them is always good—they feel empowered when they are solicited for their opinions—not just their money.
- You can also use events to initiate a targeted e-mail, phone, or mail solicitation. You can use language like, "We hope you enjoyed the event!"

Retreat Topic #5: Face-to-Face Visits

We've arrived at face-to-face visits at last: the most costly, least efficient, but best, most compelling method of solicitation. I will cover trip planning and how to maximize your time meeting with donors in Chapter 9, as well as how to conduct the visit. The focus here is to talk about planning your year in travel/visits.

The number of visits that you have with your donors each year will vary greatly, depending on the size of your donor pool, your geographic reach, and, most importantly, the budget that you have to spend on travel. It will also depend on the size of your staff. If you are fortunate enough to have fundraisers who are designated road warriors, this is a wonderful thing to be exploited. If not, you will have to find a balance between being away from your desk and getting in front of donors and prospects. You will need to analyze how much time you can afford to spend away from the office.

Bear in mind that face-to-face visits are labor intensive. First, you have to secure the visit, either via phone or e-mail. Then, you have to work the donor's schedule to have the face-to-face visit; and then, you have the even more important task of providing meaningful follow up to the donor with whom you visited, which often can (and does) take more time than the planning and actual visit itself.

Here are the questions you should be asking:

- How many working days out of the month, quarter and year, can you designate as travel days for your traveling fundraisers?
- Who is on your A-list, your B-list, and your filler list?
- Will any of these visits require other key players to be involved (prior to the visit, on the visit, after the visit)?
- When do you need all hands on deck *in the office*, thereby precluding staff to be on the road?

We will talk at much greater length on travel and face-to-face visits soon enough. This little section is kept short because it is solely to help you think about how travel will fit into your overall fiscal calendar.

Let's turn our attention now to crafting your message, which is where the process of direct solicitation begins.

Crafting Your Message
Standing Out Among the Crowd

This chapter will focus on the development of a consistent, compelling message of need for your organization. While the content of your message will inevitably vary based on your institution's goals and mission, there are still some basic guiding principles for how to construct an effective message.

Foremost, you need to capture the attention of the audience you are soliciting. This can be more difficult than you might imagine. Numerous organizations need money just as badly as you do. Always, be aware that there is significant competition even for the thirty seconds of undivided attention you need to deliver your message. Assuming that you get your message delivered, expect even more competition for those precious philanthropic dollars for which you are asking.

I will begin by providing some general principles for creating the message, for your written, e-mailed, and telephone solicitations. You'll find tips on face-to-face solicitations in Chapter 9. To illustrate the principles, in this chapter, I'll provide a telephone script that you will be able to adapt for the use of your own organization. You'll also find useful examples of e-mail and written solicitations in the appendix.

Composing a Message that Moves People

Your message not only needs to inform people of your mission, but it must also *inspire* them to take out their wallet and give away their hard-earned money. The former is significantly easier than the latter and this is to the point where I often see appeals where the letter is information-heavy and inspiration-light. You need a balance.

A former colleague from Boston captured this sentiment in a moderately unsophisticated way:

> *Think about it. Can you name one thing that Greenpeace has actually done in terms of helping to pass legislation for conservation or environmental justice? No, but they throw themselves in front of harpoons, so people give them money.*

Also, consider the words of another colleague as they discussed the seemingly incongruent difficulties in raising money for different clients:

> *Save the Children has been such a great client to canvass for. You're essentially saying to the people you talk to, "You don't hate children, do you?" And it's like magic. They give.*

The point here is that these non-profits have inspiration in abundance, which makes for a powerful message. My colleague, in speaking about Greenpeace, probably exaggerated a bit, but she was revealing a very important truth about philanthropy: it is an affair of the heart just as much as, if not more so, an affair of the head. We want an inspirational story just as much as we want to know the nitty-gritty details of how our money is going to be spent.

In a time where everyone is so busy, we often deal in images: the pelican covered in oil, the starving child in Somalia, a deforested region in the Amazon, a bald young boy in a hospital gown with tubes running in every direction. We try to summarize both our ethos and our mission in a picture.

This is okay—there is a place for those images: on your company's website, in newsletters, on supporting material that you leave behind with donors on personal visits, and in selective mailings.

However, that is not to imply you should not spend some amount of time writing appeals. You need to paint that picture. You need to do it in as few words as possible and then you need to make the case for giving.

Elements of a Fundraising Message

So, where do you start? What should you include in your fundraising message? Let's discuss the key elements that you should include in every appeal.

- *Identification:* Who is your organization? On written appeals, include your logo, website, mailing address, and a phone number. Also, don't assume that people will remember your organization. It's best to state your mission again, just for the record.
- *The problem:* What is the problem you are currently addressing? This does not necessarily have to be your core mission, but rather the problem at hand that you want to discuss right now.
- *The solution:* How is your organization addressing the problem? What steps are you taking to improve the situation, or hoping to take, with proper funding?
- *The urgency:* Why do you need the support right now? What are the consequences of a donor sitting idle? Why can't the donor afford to wait?
- *The ask:* Don't forget to ask for money! Yes, it's implicit; the reader has already guessed that this is coming. But deliver on that expectation and ask. Be sure to include all the ways in which people can give, whether by mail, phone, online, PayPal, etc.

Of course, the challenge is to include these elements as *clearly and concisely* as possible. It is incredibly easy to overdo it; in an attempt to include every single bit of information to make the case for giving, you soon find that you do tend to write too much. It is very difficult, a true challenge, not to indulge this temptation and keep your message to a single typed page: single-spaced (with regular margins and a normal-sized font), or to a sixty-second telephone call.

On Consistency

Your messages need to be *consistent* across the different media, especially if you are launching a coordinated campaign of written, phone, and e-mail solicitations. It does you little good to pepper your audience with multiple messages; they will get confused over your actual needs and likely end up throwing their hands up in frustration at the lack of clarity and consistency in what you're asking for. Granted, it is likely that your organization has multiple funding needs. If that is the case, and each one carries equal importance, make sure that each one appears in every single medium in which you solicit money.

This said, you must be wary of overwhelming your audience with too much information.

It takes an audience longer than we care to admit to absorb a message. It takes them even longer to absorb multiple messages.

A former colleague, who had worked in advertising, mentioned to me once that it takes the average consumer *twelve times* of seeing a commercial to realize they had ever even seen it.

Look at the presidential campaigns of 2004 and 2008. Whichever side you were on, I want to call attention to the consistency of the campaign messaging that the winning side displayed. George W. Bush campaigned on the message of "America is safer," and the very vague, but admittedly effective idea of "moral values."

In 2008, throughout the primaries and the general election, Barack Obama based his message on two words: "change" and "hope."

Both messages were little more than empty platitudes, but in terms of communication, both presidents got the point across. The point is that you have to choose your message carefully and then you have to blast it forth mercilessly.

You need this kind of consistency to get the message across to your constituency. But your frontline fundraisers need consistent, constant, and similar messaging as well. If you change the message too often or provide them with too many talking points, you run the risk of confusion, mixed messages, and out-of-date communications.

We tend to dread the thought of our message getting stale so we continuously search for the new, sexy thing to communicate. However, I would make the argument for staying on a given message a bit longer than you think you need to. It might make you feel a bit uncomfortable that you're repeatedly parroting the same words; but you would be surprised at just how long it takes your audience to get the point you were trying to communicate in the first place. You need to keep in mind that whereas you, as a fundraiser, spend your whole day thinking about your organization and its messaging, your audience spends next to no time at all thinking about the work that you do... or the work that any other nonprofit does for that matter. What we see on the inside as repetitive on the outside seems little more than consistency, which is generally a good thing in this field.

In drama, one of the first things you are taught (other than face the audience at all times) is that your motions need to be exaggerated, that each dramatic pause needs to be just a moment longer than what you think is necessary. When you're first starting to act: that exaggeration, that lingering pause, can feel extremely uncomfortable. But, to the audience, it appears normal and that is exactly what you want in order to get your point across. I am making the argument for lingering on a given message in the same way, even if it begins to feel a little stale.

When you launch a big campaign, it takes a while for people to realize it. Remember: Whereas you and your team think about your fundraising efforts, methods of communication, etc., every day: your constituency does not. You're lucky if they think about it more than once a week. Or once a month, for that matter.

Here's an illustration to clarify the point:

We had a five-year challenge gift to increase participation each year for five years straight. If we succeeded, each year we received a very generous sum of money from an anonymous donor. That five-year challenge ended, and I still have people asking if the now well-known "participation challenge," was still going on.

Moreover, during the lifetime of this challenge gift, we launched a multi-million dollar comprehensive campaign. It took no small amount of work to distinguish between the participation challenge and the comprehensive campaign among our donors. Most people, in their daily lives, see the form letter or the e-mail and decide yes or no without reading the majority of the content. It takes a while, so continue with consistent messaging beyond what you think necessary.

Of course, at some point, you do need to change your message; just use restraint in the frequency with which you do so. Yes, there is a place for nuance; however, that is in the face-to-face visit or the lengthier, personal phone call to prospects or volunteers, when you have time to paint a bigger picture. Remember, when it comes to letters, e-mail appeals and telephone solicitations, you have to deal in sound bites. It is all that the audience can realistically digest in a single sitting.

On Stealing

Picasso said, *Good artists copy. Great artists steal.* Recently, at an art showing, graffiti and street artist Banksy had a plaque with that quote on it—with a slight modification:

Good artists copy. Great artists steal.

~~Pablo Picasso.~~ Banksy.

Banksy understands the importance of this statement and you need to as well. You must receive mail or e-mail soliciting you for money. What messages resonate with you? Which ones don't? What style of writing do you find yourself more likely to read? Encourage your other staff to bring in examples of pieces that they find inspiring.

Oftentimes, at fundraising seminars, there are "appeal tables" to which attending organizations bring examples of appeals they have been using over the last year or so. Help yourself; be greedy. Take copies of the appeals home and do you own analysis:

- Does it read well?
- Is it too long?
- Is there a very clear call to action?
- Does it contain the elements mentioned above (identification, problem, solution, urgency, ask)?
- Does the giving form capture sufficient amounts of personal information?
- Is it inspiring? What do you feel after reading the appeal?
- Would you give to this organization?
- What changes would you make to the letter?

I'd encourage you to take those printed appeals and use a pen to mark them up. Circle or highlight phrases that you particularly like and then edit them to the point where you find them satisfactory.

Now, to be clear, you can't copy an appeal verbatim and *just* change the name of the organization to your own. You can imitate the ideas, the style, the tone, and maybe even the gist of the message itself (for example, citing similar problem, how greater cooperation with the government is needed, or how federal programs are being slashed, meaning that the need for private support is even greater)—those things are not copyrightable. Specifically, you can't copyright an idea, but you can copyright the execution of it. Seriously, don't just Photoshop your logo onto the letter, change the name of the nonprofit, and slap your signature on it. Show some originality—you will need to bend the idea or style to your goals. You need to make any piece you use your own. After all, was Picasso *really* copying from others? Or, was he learning from them and using their ideas?

To call it stealing is a bit gauche, but seriously, it is a time saver to borrow a good idea. While you want to tailor the message you're communicating to your audience to represent your own organization, you can still mimic the tone and style of a message honed through years of practicing the craft of written solicitations, and no small amount of market research.

One great place to begin your research into other institutions' solicitations is the SOFII website, "The Showcase of Fundraising Innovation and Inspiration," at www.sofii.org. The SOFII collection's goal is "to be the most comprehensive, best organized, and most inspiring collection of fundraising related content from around the world." They're not too far from achieving that goal.

In Hall 4 of their site, you will find samples of mail, e-mail, telephone, and face-to-face solicitations. It's a great place to begin your search for inspiration.

Composition 101

Creative writing instructors often implore students to read for inspiration. It is no different for the writing of good appeals. Scan every appeal that comes to your mailbox. Listen to every phone call you get asking you for money. Force yourself to read each e-mail solicitation from start to finish. Then, ask yourself if you would give based solely on the virtue of the strength of the appeal. Now, let's examine each form of solicitation.

The Telephone

When you get a call from a telephone fundraiser, don't interrupt them. Listen attentively, and let them get all the way through the script to "the ask." Yes, they're following a script; or at least they should be. Time the call. How long does it take them to get from the introduction of who they are to the ask? Did you get bored during the call? Did your mind wander or were you listening with rapt attention the whole time?

Here's a quick advisory on creating telephone appeals: I would advise against the common strategy of beginning the call by confirming a prospect's contact information. Many organizations use this approach to keep the caller on the line, and to use the well-worn sales technique of getting the prospect to say "yes," early in the conversation. The more a prospect says yes during the dialogue, the more likely the conversation will end in a yes, or so the wisdom goes.

I get a lot of phone calls where they ask if I still live at my current address, is this still the best number at which to reach me, etc. Because I already know what's coming, I always get a little cranky when the call begins like that. Get to the bottom line. Keep it short; you're probably interrupting dinner.

I argue against initiating a phone call with a request to confirm contact information for two main reasons: 1) it's somewhat disingenuous to disguise your call as anything less than what it actually is (a solicitation), and 2) from an efficiency standpoint, it takes longer to get to a "no" if you frontload the call with data collection. You should save the data collection for the end of the call, once you've confirmed that you're going to get a gift.

If the ultimate purpose of the phone call is to ask for money: *front load that information*. Don't cover it up by asking for information, or disguise it as a survey. You *really* undermine the donor's confidence in you and the organization when you do that. If a donor interrupts you during your pitch to say, "Are you asking me for money," *do not back down;* if asked, be transparent about your motives. Your response should be honest and enthusiastic. Yes. You are. Because your organization is in dire need and this donor has been helpful in the past, you need them to be helpful again now.

The Telephone Script

Here is an operating template for you to use when creating your telephone appeals. Make the following assumptions:

- The segment of the population that you are calling has given in the past.
- The organization is a state-based environmental advocacy group.

GREETING: Hello, may I please speak to Mr./Mrs. [Donor last name]?

INTRODUCTION: Good evening, Mr./Mrs. [Donor last name]. My name is [Your name] and I am calling from Green Means Go.[1]

THANK: First, I would like to thank you for your past support. It means a lot to our organization. Over the last year, it has allowed us to make huge strides in accomplishing our goal of making clean energy accessible to Connecticut residents.

PURPOSE: I am calling today to expand support for Green Means Go.

---

[1] Certain states have different disclosure requirements as to what information is required at the beginning of a telephone solicitation. Sometimes, callers are required to indicate if they are paid fundraisers. Be sure to check the laws in your area.

PROBLEM: While we have been making progress at the local levels, we still face numerous obstacles. Despite gains in certain parts of the state, Connecticut is still largely dependent on nuclear power and coal. As I'm sure you've been reading, the Bridgewater Power Plant has failed safety inspection after safety inspection and the state legislature is likely to permit it to continue operating. The consequences of doing so are dire. Because of the faulty cooling system, the water temperature of the nearby Gerety River is rising, causing the number of fish species to plummet. This could have disastrous consequences for our ecosystem.

SOLUTION: We here at Green Means Go are taking this one straight to the legislature and demanding that they recognize the dangers in allowing the Bridgewater plant to continue its operations. We are reaching out to citizens and asking them to phone their representatives and we are sending our activists directly to the capitol to put pressure on the government.

This kind of direct action relies upon the financial support of our donors. Without the continued generosity of our members, we cannot take this fight to the house floor nor to the courts if it comes to that.

URGENCY: The house is going to be voting on the fate of the Bridgewater Power Plant at the end of the month; so, we really need to build as much support as we can now in order to win this battle.

ASK #1: With this in mind, Mr./Mrs. [Donor last name], we are asking all of our members to renew their support tonight. I am hoping that you will support Green Means Go with a gift of $[twice their largest gift].

IF NO, ASK #2: I understand. Are you still in support of the work of Green Means Go? That's great, and I'm grateful that you still believe in what we do. It's just that, in addition to fighting the nuclear power advocates in Hartford, we're also working hard at raising awareness statewide about alternative fuel sources such as biomass and biomethane. With this in mind, can I ask you to consider a gift of $[one and a half times largest gift]?

IF NO, ASK #3: That's fine, Mr./Mrs. [Donor last name]. Our aim tonight is really about building up as much support as possible from as many of our most consistent donors as possible. Your last gift to Green Means Go was $[last gift]. Would you consider renewing your support of our work tonight at that level?

IF NO, END CALL: Not a problem, Mr./Mrs. [Donor last name]. Thanks so much for your past support and for taking the time to speak with me tonight. Have a wonderful evening!

IF YES: Wonderful! Thank you so much. I am delighted to count on you for such a generous amount.

DATA CONFIRMATION: May I confirm that you still live at [address], and that your email address is still [email address].

CREDIT CARD ASK #1: Will that gift be made via Visa, Master Card, American Express, or Discover?

IF NO, CREDIT CARD ASK #2: I understand. It's just that making a gift by credit card does save us the cost of mailing you a pledge packet and allows us to put your gift to work right away. With this in mind, may I ask you to reconsider?

IF NO, PLEDGE: That's fine. I'm happy to mail you a pledge packet. Just to confirm, you have pledged [gift amount], correct? And we're mailing that to [address]?

Wonderful. We're asking everyone tonight if they would please mail their pledges back by [date]. Is that something that you can do?

CONFIRMATION: Great! I have you down for a gift of [gift amount], to be mailed to us by [date]. Mr./Mrs. [Donor last name], thank you so much for renewing your support, and for taking the time to speak with me about the work we are doing here at Green Means Go. Have a terrific evening!

Points to Remember

The following points are important to remember.

- In ASK #2, there is the question: *Are you still in support of the work of Green Means Go?* The idea behind the "focusing question" technique, lifted from the sales world, gets the prospective donor to go from saying "no" to saying "yes" again. Founded upon the assumption that the more a donor says yes during the conversation, the more likely the conversation is to end in a "yes," you are refocusing the conversation away from the fact that the donor has already said no, and working, once again, to find common ground.

- The confirmation at the end of the call seems repetitive, but it is important. Again, chances are that your prospect might be somewhat distracted while being solicited over the phone. You want to say the amount and return date repeatedly, especially with pledges (as distinct from credit card gifts, where you already have the

money-in-hand). This is so that when donors receive the pledge packet in the mail, they are more likely to remember having made the pledge.
- When making the call, it's a good idea to have the donor's complete giving history in front of you.

The Written Appeal

When writing the drafts of your appeals, shuttle them around to a few employees. If you have willing volunteers, have them review it, too. Take their responses seriously; they represent your audience. Of course, if a volunteer is "signing" the appeal, you need his approval before putting his name on it.

Once you think you are finished writing an appeal, read it aloud. Do any of the sentences sound clunky or awkward?

Here are some general pieces of advice on writing effective direct mail appeals:

- Keep the solicitation to one page. It's okay to have a second sheet to include information, but your appeal, the actual letter in which you ask for money, should be limited to one 8.5 by 11-inch sheet of paper in a readable font, with regular margins, and with your organization's logo and general contact information at the top.
- Write based on the same formulaic elements you would in a telephone script: introduction, purpose, problem, solution, urgency, and ask.
- When in doubt, err on the side of formal language. If appropriate, you can change your vernacular and tone in face-to-face meetings; but when writing a generalized appeal, it is best to assume that the reader is more conservative than you are. This is *especially* true if a trustee or your executive director is signing the letter. The written appeal is not a place for clever word play. It is all about simple, direct, and frank language that is unashamed to ask for what your organization needs.

The Electronic Appeal

The e-mailed appeal is last. It's fast, it's efficient, and it provides you with very quick feedback on its effectiveness.

Here are some tips on e-mail appeals:

- Spend some time thinking about your subject lines. You'll need a subject line that:

    - Is inspiring enough to get people to open it.
    - Is not misleading or disingenuous.
    - Will not get picked up by spam filters: avoid all capital letters, or numbers.
    - Satisfying these three conditions is harder than you think—it is worth your time to work with your team to shoot some ideas back and forth. If you have a dry erase board or butcher block paper, toss up a bunch of subject lines and see which ones satisfy these three parameters; it can be tougher than you think.

- Keep it short. Shorter than you think. People's attention spans are limited when it comes to reading e-mail. You have no guarantee that that your appeal is the only thing they are looking at. With face-to-face conversations and phone calls, it is a safer assumption their focus is on you; but by no means guaranteed.

- Keep the length within a single window. If your audience has to scroll past one single screen, it is too long.

- To help keep it short, you can include links to other pages on your organization's website. This should obviously include a link to the giving page.

- Of course, the challenge is to communicate your goals and aspirations convincingly—yet briefly. Here again, we return to the utility of the subject line. The subject line can introduce any of the necessary aspects of a good written appeal. Most often, the purpose or the problem can be summed up in a compelling subject line, such as *Calling all loyal supporters* (purpose) or *Help us stop deforestation in the Amazon* (problem and purpose).

- Again, be sure to vet your data and perform at least one test send before sending it to your entire donor base.

- If you have software that allows for a mail-merge, such that you can have the donor's name associated with an e-mail address so that the e-mail reads "Dear Jeff," instead of "Dear Supporter," so much the better. Including names in the subject line is hit or miss though, since sometimes spam filters pick that up as spam.

This chapter has provided you with useful tips on how to write effective solicitations for telephone, direct mail, and e-mail solicitations. In the appendix, I have also included examples of effective appeals that both work and meet the necessary criteria. Each one contains the elements of a good message, but, like any real-world example, isn't perfect. I do a brief analysis of each, to call attention to what works and what doesn't work for each.

Let's now turn our attention to stewardship, where the gift cycle ends ... and begins.

Stewardship
The End and Beginning of Every Gift

I know what you're thinking: why are you talking about the stewardship of giving before you talk about the "ask," the solicitation? You haven't even gotten into the nitty-gritty of the face-to-face gift conversation, so why are you skipping ahead to saying thanks? Isn't it a bit presumptuous to be doing the victory dance before the victory?

I put this section ahead on purpose, because it's easier for an organization with a million things to do to overlook the importance of thoughtful stewardship than it is to overlook the importance of asking for money.

I also want to talk about stewardship first because stewardship is the last step in the gift cycle, but it also *reinitiates* the cycle anew. The more compelling the stewardship, the more effectively you narrate your case for follow-up giving. Good stewardship is indispensable not just for resolicitation, but also for asking donors to *increase* their giving to your organization. If you haven't thanked them well enough for their current level of giving, don't expect them to step up their level of support.

By giving donations "flesh and blood" through stories of how the gift has helped, you are restarting the dialogue and rebuilding the case for giving again. In the chapter on major gifts, I will focus a lot on storytelling, and you'll be able to use parts of what you read here to come up with your narratives for major gift solicitations.

The new frontier is actually to create synergy between stewardship and events, combining them into a department known as "donor relations." It's a logical combination, truth be told. You're assembling a team of folks whose job it is to engage donors and to keep them connected to the work of your organization beyond the explicit gift conversation. Events are an important way to do this, so I'll cover that at the end of the chapter.

Big advancement shops have entire teams devoted to the art of "stewarding" donors, which boils down to communicating gratitude as well as bringing life to the gift. It isn't enough to issue a sincere thank you to donors, especially your bigger ones. You really do need to provide them with content-rich examples of how their philanthropic commitment is positively altering the landscape of your organization.

The Art of Proper Thank You(s)

Let me begin at the basic level. Every donation needs to generate a gift receipt, which can either be mailed or e-mailed. The receipt needs to include the amount, the designation of the gift, the method, and the date of payment. This receipt should be accompanied by a form letter (or text in the e-mail) with a note of thanks. It can be signed by the executive director (ED), the director of development, or others. It can be a few sentences or a single page.

Here is a sample of a short text:

Dear Randall:

You will find attached a receipt for your generous gift of $25. Per your request, we have designated your gift to support our after-school athletics program.

I would like to thank you for your support of the work of Keep The Kids Safe. The generosity of you and others makes it possible for us to carry out our mission of making the city of Milwaukee and its surrounding towns safer by engaging our underserved youth.

Please know that your support has a direct and positive impact on the work that we do here at KTKS and merits our deepest gratitude.

Sincerely,

Jeff Stauch

Your frontline fundraisers, both in annual giving and in major gifts, should be writing handwritten thank-you notes to their prospects as well as to donors who aren't assigned to them per se, but with whom they have had personalized contact.

If your organization has set up different giving levels for annual gifts (and it should), you need to determine best practices regarding which gift levels receive thank-you notes from whom. The highest-level annual gifts should receive a thank-you note from your ED or president. The next level should receive notes from the director of development. The next level down should receive notes signed by one of your frontline fundraisers (and include his or her contact information). Again, the actual levels that you set will be dependent on the constitution of your donor base; the point is to take time to figure how to divide it up.

Of course, these letters can be templates that are then altered slightly for each individual gift. In fact, one of the tasks of the stewardship department should be ghostwriting these templates for the president, ED, or director of development.

Thank-you notes can be mailed or e-mailed, depending on your gift officers' and donors' preferences, so long as the thank-you notes get out the door in a timely manner. Many of my colleagues prefer to write handwritten thank-you notes. As for me, I have very atrocious handwriting, so in the interest of legibility, I either e-mail my thank-you notes or print off short notes and sign them in pen. My opinion is that it won't do much good to send a thank-you note if the donor can't read a single word of what I wrote. It's also an efficiency question—if I do want to make my handwriting legible, my thank-you notes take a *long* time to write, both because I need to go slowly to make it legible and because I make mistakes and have to start over again. Typing thank-you notes, for me, ends up being quicker, and I don't think there is much decrease in quality—it is clearly my voice that comes across, as opposed to that of the president or vice president. It will be up to you to figure out which you prefer and what your standard operating procedures will be. I wouldn't be nervous about thanking people by e-mail, especially if the majority of your correspondence with that individual has been via e-mail.

At lower gift levels, you will want your stewardship to be standardized, especially if your office has strained resources. Create a small set of interchangeable templates that are easily customizable, with a limited number of fields that can be changed. As unsexy as it is, it makes sense to think of this type of stewardship as an assembly line. You have to standardize in order to keep up with your volume. Again, here I'm assuming that your shop, at least in its nascent stages, will be scrambling to keep up with all the work. As noted earlier, without a system in place, it is easy to gloss over the thank-you process, which you do at your own peril.

All Phases of the Gift Cycle Are Related

As fundraisers, in terms of our decision-making logic, we know we are primarily responsible for *bringing in* money first, with all else being secondary in importance. We know that our work has budgetary implications: certain aspects of our organization's programming depends on us hitting our goals. So, first and foremost, we need to solicit. Everything else is subordinate to that.

The trouble here is that all parts of the gift cycle are interconnected, such that if you cut corners on any of the seemingly secondary items, you sacrifice your ability to resolicit with confidence.

Not long ago, my office had to do some damage control with a top prospect who wasn't happy with the reporting that we had provided on her funds. This delayed our ability to resolicit her until we were able to show her the impact of her giving in a way she found inspiring.

It is for that reason that I am stressing the importance of setting up a cottage industry of stewardship activities as you build your shop. In other words, *you need to professionalize your back-end shop (stewardship, records, and data) at a rate in proportion to the rate at which you professionalize your front-end shop (your direct fundraisers).* If the front line's operations expand too quickly for your back end to keep up, there will be fallout (even when you are fully staffed, there can still be fallout). This will become especially true at the mid- and top-levels. I know it sounds very intuitive, but donors want to be thanked. They want to feel validated by their giving, and, of equal importance, they want to know *how* their giving is impacting your organization. This is one way in which philanthropy has changed over the last decade, and especially so since the 2008 recession. Donors are viewing their philanthropy as *investments*, and they want to make sure that their investments are performing well. The stewardship shop's job is to construct a narrative and provide evidence that this is the case.

The Three Levels of Stewardship

One of my senior colleagues talks about the "three levels of stewardship," which I'll dissect for the bulk of the remainder of the chapter.

The first level of stewardship will apply to the vast majority of your donors. It is the basic level stewardship to all of your annual, participation-level donors.

The second level of stewardship is for your donors who have established legacies, named funds, or have otherwise had a significant, longstanding relationship with your organization.

An example of the latter would be a donor who has given you tens or hundreds of thousands of dollars over the years, but has designated it all towards general usage.[1]

This level of stewardship merits individualized reporting on the impact of the donor's fund or impact on a certain program. You want these reports to appear individualized, although you should create a process of standardization that streamlines the process.

The third level of stewardship is for your megadonors, the very top of your pyramid, or, as we say in the industry, those who have made *transformational gifts*. This level of stewardship might actually not apply to your organization until later on in its life, once you have cultivated those mid-range donors to become huge donors. This level of stewardship is more often than not customized, because these types of gifts, as the name *transformational* implies, are having an impact at the frontier of your organization's programming, making it inherently difficult to have canned templates on hand. Of course, if one of your megagifts goes to a traditional, existent program, you will have a template on hand from level-two stewardship, but take some extra time to think creatively about how you might add on to that report.

At this level, you can actually ask the question outright: how do you want us to thank you? It's a valid question, and while it might sound awkward, it can actually be an empowering question to pose to the donor.

One final thing to note: donors receiving level two and level three stewardship should also be receiving that level one stewardship.

Now, let me spend some time discussing at greater length what you should be offering your donors at each of these levels.

Level-One Stewardship

Let me begin by exploring the basic annual level stewardship. I want to reiterate: level-one stewardship will be the type of stewardship that applies to the *vast majority* of your donors. Remember the 80/20 rule? This is the stewardship for 80 percent of your donors.

At the basic annual level, donors should be receiving, in addition to a gift receipt (which includes a form thank-you note signed by the director of

---

[1] This can actually be a very challenging stewardship situation: how do you thank someone who has only given to general usage and hasn't designated any of it to a specific purpose? I don't want to be prescriptive, but I do want you to think about this.

development or other appropriate personnel), *an annual, bi-annual, or quarterly newsletter (or e-newsletter)*. This should be written by the stewardship office with input from the director of development and other departments within your organization, such as your Communications or Public Relations department, as appropriate.

The newsletter should include informational updates on what the organization has been doing since the last newsletter, with an eye towards highlighting specific examples of philanthropic support that have made certain accomplishments possible.

The newsletter should open with a short thank you from either the executive director, or director of development, which frames the rest of the content of the letter.

If space allows, it makes sense to include a profile of a current donor. The type of donor can vary, whether it's an annual donor, a major gift prospect, or a planned gift prospect.[2] Or, it could be a volunteer. The profile should include what the person is supporting and a paragraph or so on why he or she helps the organization in this way and at that level.

The donor profile serves two purposes. On the one hand—especially if it is a major gift or a planned gift—you are providing donors who are currently just giving at the annual gift level with an example of folks who are giving more than they are. We call that "sight-setting" or "sight-raising." You're presenting annual donors with an example of someone who has increased their giving beyond an annual check; the implication, by featuring the major or planned donor and giving voice to their testimonial, is that you're inviting annual donors to step up their giving, especially given how happy and satisfied the interviewed donor will (hopefully) sound.

Secondly, the act of asking a donor to be featured in this newsletter is a form of stewardship in and of itself. You are asking her to be an example to other donors and prospects out there. You are saying to her: we want to feature you in hope that more will emulate what you have done to help our organization. In fact, in your outreach to such people, when you pitch the idea, use language to that effect: we want you to narrate why you give, so that others will do the same. It should feel empowering to the donor. Of course, some will say no to this offer, as they would prefer to remain anonymous, or at least under the radar publicly. Even if they say no, it is likely that they will be flattered by your asking.

---

[2] Planned giving, which is not covered in this book, refers to gift vehicles such as trusts, annuities, as well as estate gifts and gifts of property.

The newsletter can be mailed or e-mailed. If your postage budget is small, go with e-mail and accept the fact that the "open rate" probably won't be too high. That is not to say it is not worth the trouble. You just need realistic expectations. There will be a sufficient number of donors who do take the time to read the newsletter in depth for you to spend time making it a quality product.

In the newsletter you send at the end of your year, whether it's your fiscal or calendar year, include two key things in the summary of your fundraising efforts. The first is a report about your annual goals versus actual results. Believe it or not, donors *are* interested in knowing if the goals that you reported at the beginning of your fiscal year were met. You will want to include the following data:

- Dollars raised
- If applicable, a breakdown of dollars raised by funding priority/category
- Number of gifts
- Percentage increase (or decrease) in dollars raised and number of gifts
- Total dollars raised from all gifts under $100—or $50. The point is to show that small contributions add up.

The other thing that you will want to include with your annual report is the donor roll. The donor roll, as the name implies, is an alphabetical listing of all your donors. You shouldn't include the amounts that people give. What you can do is star or highlight people who have given above a certain threshold, with a legend at the end of the donor roll. In addition to leadership-level giving, you also want to highlight planned givers, volunteers, and—most importantly—your consistent givers.

Giving Societies

Let me detour for a minute to talk about "giving societies" or "giving levels"—or whatever you end up using for terminology with your organization. Giving societies exist for sight-raising and sight-setting, as well as giving you a good stewardship opportunity. In previous chapters, I've referred to the playbill that you get at a performance, where you have platinum, gold, silver, and bronze patrons. These are giving levels. You can get more creative than this, to make it more directly relevant or specific to your organization. For example, a nonprofit that does work to improve literacy in urban schools could have giving levels such as the following:

- $0–$100: Pupil
- $100–$250: Class Representative
- $250–$500: Valedictorian
- $500–$1,000: Teacher
- $1,000–$2,500: Vice Principal
- $2,500–$5,000: Principal
- $5,000+: Superintendent

Your two main giving societies should be leadership annual givers and your consistent givers. Leadership annual giving levels will depend partly on the composition of your current donor pool. It's not an exact science. You want the level to be a reach for your annual donors, but an attainable one. The other thing to note is that, over time, the leadership annual giving levels *can change*, especially as you gain traction with your existent donor base.

If you really are at a loss as to where to start, an arbitrary but good enough dividing line for leadership giving and simple annual giving is $1,000. A four-figure gift does confer a certain amount of seriousness, especially when a nonprofit is just beginning to systematize its fundraising operations.[3]

Of course, once you establish this line in the sand, it should be a goal of your frontline fundraisers to get out and encourage as many donors to give at the leadership level. This will, in turn, create a need for your stewardship employees to engage this new crop of leadership donors.

There is tension among the fundraising community as to whether the leadership givers or your consistent givers are more important in terms of your investment of time and resources. I think both deserve attention, but if push comes to shove and you have to spend time on one more than the other, the stewardship office should spend time creatively engaging the consistent donors as opposed to the leadership donors. Chances are, in a small- to medium-sized development shop, the leadership donors should be on the radar of your front-line fundraisers. And, if you follow the advice I gave above, front-line fundraisers will be writing personal thank-you notes to that demographic as well.

One reason for this stance is that, oftentimes, your leadership annual givers *are also consistent givers*. To use a very loose analogy (and to dust off your high school geometry), all squares are rectangles, but not all rectangles are

---

[3] One thing to keep in mind: If someone is giving you $500 unsolicited (i.e. without personalized attention from your organization), chances are they can give $750 or $1,000 if asked. If someone is giving you $1,000 unsolicited, they can probably give you twice that if you spend some time with them.

squares. I say loose because sometimes leadership donors are one-offs that give a bunch of money and then never give again. But, I'm guessing that if you take a look at your data, the majority of folks that are giving at whatever you have established as your leadership annual giving level will have already been consistent donors to your organization: hence, my reasoning behind urging you to spend time developing a systematic stewardship program for consistent donors at the expense of leadership donors in the event that you have to choose one.[4]

One final justification for this opinion is that the two societies don't have to be exclusive for a majority of your stewardship activities.

With that in mind, in the following paragraphs on the type of substance you want to provide for each giving society, understand that you often duplicate what you are doing for one of them without having to fear repercussions.

Once you've established a giving society, you need to communicate the heck out of it to get donor buy-in. This can be a Herculean task, but it's worth your time. It isn't enough just to create a society on paper. You have to give it life, celebrate it liberally—within budget, of course.

Upon the creation of the giving society, you need to mail or e-mail everyone in that society. This can be done either as a special appeal or just as a simple congratulatory note, welcoming them to the society. When generating automatic thank-yous for gift receipts, you might consider having a leadership level template and a consistent donor template. Again, it's up to you which trumps which, but for the thank-you note, it would be wiser to celebrate the consistent donors first and the leadership donors second if push comes to shove.

Do you need to provide gifts in return? There is something to be said for kitsch or trinkets that boast your organization's name. Don't go overboard and spend a ton of money on this, but you do want to send something either to your consistent or leadership donors or both. The reason is as much to thank them with a token item as it is to *remain present in their daily life*. You want to remain on their mind, so you need to make it into their home beyond the solicitation letter, the solicitation phone call, or the solicitation e-mail. And you want to do so with greater frequency than a quarterly or annual newsletter.

---

[4] I am making this argument for stewardship *within level one*. I do *not* want to give the impression that you can skimp on your level-two and level-three stewardship for your mid-range and top donors.

Think about what you use in your daily life and figure out how to send such a product to either or both of these societies. Examples are as follows:

- Pens
- Notepads or self-adhesive notes
- Paperweights or magnets
- Return address labels
- Bookmarks
- Key chains or carabiners
- 12-month wall calendars with photos of your organization, the people helped, etc. (one of the best ideas, in my opinion)

You can tailor your mementos to parallel your organization's mission. If you're representing an environmental nonprofit, for example, sending paper notepads might not make too much sense unless you prominently display that it's all-recycled material. If you're representing an organization that focuses on workers' rights and labor union advocacy in the US, you might not want to send something that's manufactured overseas. In other words, make sure that the mementos align with the mission. Believe me, things like this will *not* go unnoticed. And then, instead of increasing the donor's appreciation of the work that you do, you are undermining their trust and confidence in your institution, and they also might begin to wonder if the money they are giving is being wisely spent.

Level-Two Stewardship: Mid-Range Donors

Now, let me focus on the medium-range donors. Note that these mid-range donors *should also be receiving level-one stewardship for their gifts*, since they will be part of your "leadership" annual giving society if you create one (and are likely consistent givers already, too).

These are the folks that aren't the top of the top (your top 20 percent), but are well above the minimum threshold to be considered leadership annual donors. They have an ongoing relationship with your development staff. They have established philanthropic legacies at your institution, and it is possible to construct a narrative around the impact of their giving.

It's worth repeating that this group, through proper cultivation and stewardship, is also your future top of the pyramid.

Treat this strata of donors in a special manner, *but in such a way that you can still standardize the process.* You should create customizable templates of longer, narrative reporting, along with some data on the program or funding area supported (in addition to level-one stewardship, which includes a gift acknowledgement letter, your organization's newsletter, etc.). For example, if you're a civil liberties group, you should have a report prepared on recent cases that you have been able to fight thanks to special funding. If you're an environmental group, report on improvements to your expanded urban outreach program since you've started raising money from targeted individuals.

There should also be a lengthier thank-you note written *by someone directly impacted by the funding* (i.e. not generated by an employee of your department). If you're working for an educational nonprofit, for example, ask a current student who's benefited from a program funded by a donor to write a note of thanks for publication. If you're stewarding a gift for a battered women's shelter, have someone who's had the experience of living there write the note.

While you should ask these folks who are not directly employed by you, but are directly affected from the work of your organization to write the letter, you *need to review the letter for content* before mailing it out. Whereas your stewardship employees are ghost writing for your VP and ED, and your frontline fundraisers are writing their own thank-you notes and therefore will stay on point, asking a beneficiary of your nonprofit's work can present certain challenges. When you ask a beneficiary of your organization's work to pen a thank-you note, you run the risk of their tone being too loose or colloquial, or their writing skills being nothing less than abominable. You want to edit not just for grammar and syntax but also for content. You want to maintain control of the message. This might involve considering more than one thank-you letter candidate or coaching the person writing the note, taking the time to explain why they are being ask to write a note and *who it is that they are thanking*. I have seen examples that are perfect as is, complete disasters, and everything in between. I recently saw an example of a thank-you note written by a scholarship recipient that likened his scholarship to receiving a pet for his birthday. We had to ask him to rewrite the note.

Your office needs to have the final say in how you communicate your gratitude. It's always a bit delicate when you have to edit something like a thank-you note or throw it out all together, but for the purpose of stewarding a medium-level donor, it's worth it.

The thank-you notes themselves can afford to be a bit lengthier than your standard half sheet or notecard.

The thank-you note should be printed on your organization's letterhead and include a photograph of whoever is authoring the note. If it isn't mentioned in the note, include a short profile on the author. This will ensure that the impact of the giving is made apparent.

Any fund that is named after or by a donor should generate a report.[5] If the original donor of a particular fund is deceased, it makes sense to track down the next of kin. You'll be surprised at how much good reporting can do for the families of donors. They'll at the very least appreciate that you took the time to report on the donor's philanthropic legacy at your institution, and— every so often—you'll find the family decides to continue supporting that fund to honor the legacy left behind. It's another one of those moments where you have to embrace the fact that it might feel awkward at first to be sending a stewardship report and thank-you note to someone who hasn't been directly involved with your organization yet.

The standardized report should include both quantitative and qualitative data of the impact that that donor's philanthropy has had on the program that he or she is supporting. If you're strapped for time and resources, you can zoom out and give a broader overview of the impact of *all* philanthropy on that particular funding area. However, I would recommend taking the time to customize reports for each donor.

Again, you do need to take some extra time to steward your medium-range donors. They will, after all, be your future top donors and trustees, so invest in the stewardship.

The reporting that you compile for this level of gift range gives vibrancy and color to the gifts made by these donors; it validates both their generosity *and your organization's need for their support.* Good stewardship is a subtle resolicitation; in each of these reports is the implied request for continued support.

Level-Three Stewardship: Megadonors

Individually tailored stewardship should exist at the highest giving levels. Again, your top 20 percent should get that special treatment. If you have the bandwidth to expand that to your top third, by all means do so.

Before I dive into this section, I have a caveat: this level of stewardship, given your limited resources, especially at the outset of your quest to professionalize your development shop, might not be needed in the beginning stages of your work.

---

[5] I say "after" or "by" a donor because donors often choose to have a fund named after someone other than themselves. Granted, many donors do choose to have funds or programs or buildings named after themselves, but sometimes they want to honor a family member, teacher, coach, or someone else important in their life. Sometimes, they don't want the fund, program, or building named after them so as to avoid other nonprofits sniffing them out!

This isn't meant to discourage you. It is my sincere hope that you will eventually have to steward megadonors. I just want to paint a realistic picture, and I don't want you to invest your limited time and limited resources creating customized stewardship projects when level-two stewardship would suffice.

Of course, there is no hard-and-fast rule for distinguishing a megadonor from a mid-range donor. One organization's mid-range donor is another's chief patron. But the level of stewardship that I am about to describe should apply to a very special class of donors. Don't sell yourself short and strain your finite resources by throwing yourself into this level of stewardship until you have identified, assessed, cultivated, and solicited a new class of gifts for your organization. This level of stewardship should be something that you should *desire needing even if currently you don't need it.*

The approach to this kind of stewardship will require a creative mind. You need a stewardship writer who can give serious thought as to *how* a given donor would most appreciate being thanked. This will require coordination with the gift officer who closed the solicitation.

This is a word of advice to gift officers, the front-line fundraisers, since you are the ones most likely to be dealing with the donors themselves: when having conversations with your prospects, be sure to listen for cues on how they have been thanked by other organizations. What did the donor like or not like? I've received comments from prospects that say that my office does a far better job than the other stewardship reports they've received. Of course, I've received comments going the other way, too. Ask them what about a certain report made them happy, made them feel good. If they have received stewardship communications from your organization before as a medium-range donor (or even basic-level donor), what have they liked? What have they felt lacking? Ask these questions to help your stewardship writers later on.

Tune your ear for what makes them feel warm and fuzzy. Sometimes, it's not a letter or glossy report at all that makes the donor happy. Sometimes, it's viewing firsthand the impact of their work. This could involve a visit to your office to meet a student that your after-school programming has helped or meeting the residents of your homeless shelter. It could involve a coordinated site visit to a particular nature preserve that the donor's gifts have helped to conserve. It could involve an invitation to your winter concert if you're a musical organization.

But a solid report is a good base line, so let's focus on that for a moment. Again, your stewardship writer will need to think beyond the simple 8.5 by 11-inch double-sided report and thank-you note and really imagine a longer narrative. I'm talking either multi-media or booklet form. You'll want to interview multiple parties who have benefited from the gifts of this donor and compile a story of positive change and attitude. Take photos, record the interviews, get written testimonies, and compile it all, either in color print or on a dedicated web page.

It's labor intensive, and yes, only thanks one person or family, but it is well worth the effort. It's an investment in the resolicitation.

At the highest levels of stewardship, you have to bear in mind that it's not enough to produce a very glossy report that you're very proud of if the donor doesn't appreciate it. It is always a good idea to check in with the donor not just to verify receipt of the report (which, if sent by mail, is sometimes a problem), but also to garner their opinion on it. Often enough, the reviews come back positive, but don't just assume that. Reach out to the donor a month after you've sent the report and ask them what they thought about it.

While your shop will have a standard operating procedure for constructing stewardship reports, and it will fit most of your donors, it won't fit all of them. And, it is worth your time to listen and alter your reporting accordingly in those instances. Donors will appreciate the extra effort, and it makes that next gift more likely.

Some donors will want more or less quantitative data, and some will prefer a more narrative form of stewardship communication. Others will want data on the broader program they're supporting. Others still will want very specific data on their fund beyond the standard quantitative information (such as the value of a named fund), including specific breakdowns of how the funds availed from the gift were allocated. While it can be a headache and involve some getting into the weeds with your budget office, give the donor what she wants. She's already given you a substantial amount of money. The least you can do is get on the phone with your budget office to be able to report back to the donor how the money was spent.

The stewardship report should come with a cover letter from your organization's executive director, president, or equivalent, thanking her for her giving, inviting her to call should there be any questions or concerns, and encouraging her to stop by your offices. There should also be a broader statement about the importance of philanthropy and how this particular donor sets the example for others to follow.[6]

---

[6] It might be implicit, but let's make it explicit: you can repurpose this customized stewardship as a way to inspire your donors receiving level-two stewardship when the time is right. It's a way of saying, softly, to the mid-range donor, "See what we'd *really* like you to do"?

Events: Parties with a Purpose

Events are important. Events are, by the nature of the time, money, and labor cost, investments, but I would argue that they are worth it. They build good will and get a lot of people dedicated to a similar goal in the same room. They are a great way to engage your donors, especially those who you can't touch individually with personal visits, but who should nonetheless be made to feel special.

Events should be approached strategically; they shouldn't just be held for the sake of having them. Each event needs to have a purpose and a goal. Events should be held both at your offices (if space allows) and off-site. I'm going to divide this section by the considerations you need to take into account.

Scope

The first question you need to ask yourself when planning an event is, how big you want it to be? Do you want the event to be an all-come event, in which your entire donor base (or entire donor base in a certain region) is invited to come? Or, do you want the event to be limited to a certain number of people? If the latter, do you want the event to be limited to a certain giving strata? Is this a social gathering, or will there be an ask? Is the ask hard or soft? Who is making that ask: the executive director, the director of development, a board member, or any other key volunteer? Who from your organization is staffing the event, or is it completely volunteer driven? Will there be remarks made and by whom? What will be the content of those remarks, and who is in charge of preparing them?

Paying for It

If yours is a locally based organization, with your board and a number of your high-level donors in the area, you should consider asking leading donors to underwrite the cost of the event. This is a good idea for more than one reason. The simplest is that it doesn't have to come out of your budget. Another reason is that it is actually a cultivational opportunity for the prospect underwriting that event. They get to feel good about helping your cause, and you get to highlight them at the event by thanking them for their generosity. You can also highlight them before the event, on the invitation, saying that the event has been made possible thanks to their support.

Of course, this puts pressure on your organization to pull off a really solid, well-attended event. But if you do pull it off, you can consider that a cultivation step, even though it's already technically a gift. The reason you can count it as cultivation is that it makes the donor feel really good about collaborating with your office, and he or she can bask in the general *bonhomie* of the event itself. It also provides you ample opportunity to follow up with the prospect and keep them engaged at the personal level.

You shouldn't be afraid about this kind of solicitation. The first time I asked one of my prospects to underwrite the costs of an event in one of the cities I covered, I had clearly come across as nervous. I gave her the reason for the event, justified it, talked about its importance, and finally, slipped it in under my breath that I was hoping she might consider funding the event. To which she said, "Jeff, I knew you were going to ask me, I was wondering what took you so **** long." Major and megadonors understand that putting on an event is both important and expensive, and that your organization doesn't have a ton of cash lying around.

Planning

Where is the event to take place? Your office? A prospect's office space? A prospect's home? The location will influence the time of day you should have the event. The time of day that you have the event will affect who can and cannot attend. Do you want a morning breakfast downtown at someone's office? A cocktail hour in the city? A dinner in the suburbs? Will invitations go out via hard copy or e-mail? How many follow-up reminders will you be sending? Who in your office is responsible for taking RSVPs? You need to be strategic about these kind of decisions; again, tailor these answers such that they address the purpose and goals of the event.

Follow Up

Follow-up to events is very important and *very easy to forget*. Events are a good way to track a donor's interest in your organization, so be sure to have a record of who attended the event (with a sign in sheet) and have that attendance list entered into your database.

If a gift officer staffed the event, he can use the event as a hook when reaching out to a prospect.

More systematically, if the event is staffed by the executive director or another high-level staff member, a thank-you note should go out (e-mail is okay), thanking all attendees for coming and expressing the hope that they enjoyed the event. If possible, the note should reference specific content that came up either in the prepared remarks or in the Q&A.

If the event was tailored to high-end donors with a relatively small invitation list, it makes sense also to send a note to folks who could not attend with a brief note on what was covered. If appropriate, send materials that were distributed at the event.

If there was an ask at the event, there should certainly be a follow-up solicitation coming from whoever made the ask.

The point is, you've put in the work prepping the event, so you don't want to drop the ball by not continuing to engage the attendees once they've returned home. The importance of follow up is a theme to which we'll return in subsequent chapters: both its importance and the ease with which we do a sub-par job of it.

So that's stewardship: saying thanks and throwing parties! I hope that if nothing else, I have driven home the importance of the work of the stewardship department, and shown just how crucial good stewardship is to maintaining good relationships with your current donors and also to open the door for resolicitation. Whether it's a level-one thank you note that's automatically generated and mailed or a high-touch report customized for a million-dollar gift, you need to give some serious thought and attention to your stewardship program. You need to be able to keep your donors connected to your institution through not-strictly-monetary ways; events and thank-yous are a solid first step. Remember: good stewardship cements the relationship, completes the gift cycle, and begins it anew.

Let's now turn our attention to travel and the face-to-face visit.

Face Time

Visit Planning, Face-to-Face Contact, and the Dreaded (but Essential!) Follow Up

And so we get to the face-to-face conversation and travel. When I say travel, I specifically mean planning a trip of a day or a number of days in which you are out on the road visiting with donors face to face. The scope and range of your travel will be based on the location of your donors. Whether you're traveling across the country or across town, the principles of how to plan a trip, how to set up appointments, what to cover, and so on will remain the same. Face-to-face visits are an essential part of your fundraising operation. While it might initially appear not to make sense to spend a full day (or week) away from the office, and while it might seem to be an inefficient use of your time to spend up to an hour with only one or two individuals, you can rest assured knowing that in-person contact will be one of the keys to your success.

Face-to-face conversations allow for many things that less-direct methods of donor contact do not. It is the best shot you can get at having a donor's undivided attention for a given period of time. It allows you to engage the donor in an in-depth, detailed conversation about the work that your organization is doing, and it allows them to ask questions and/or voice opinions that they might not take the time to do over phone or through e-mail. It also makes them a much more likely future donor, as well as someone who will be more likely to increase their giving in the future, when asked.

This chapter will start by outlining all the various types of visits and then launch into the nuts and bolts of how to plan a trip and how to reach out to your donor base. We'll then dissect a visit before getting into the follow up. Finally, I will regale you with a couple of examples from the road.

The Taxonomy of Travel

There are many different types of visits. Not every visit is a direct solicitation, although many are (and should be). Remember the gift cycle we talked about earlier? Each of those points in the cycle (assessment, cultivation, presolicitation, solicitation, and stewardship) is worth a visit. There are other types of visits, too, depending on the scope of your operations. Let's take a look at all the valid reasons you might want to call upon a donor for a face-to-face visit, beginning with the stewardship call.

Thank-You Visits

We just got done with a chapter on stewardship, so why not begin with the simplest reason to visit someone: to say, "Thanks." Of course, the meeting will consist of a more robust conversation, but reaching out to someone in the hopes of meeting only to thank them is perfectly legitimate, especially if they are among your top donors. If you've learned nothing else from the previous chapter, it's that saying thanks is the first step toward your next ask.

If your outreach to a donor is for a stewardship visit, let them know up front that, first and foremost, you would like to thank them for their generous support of your institution and that you'd like to sit down with them one-on-one to provide an update on the organization, answer questions that they might have, and discuss the specific impact of their philanthropic commitment on your organization. You can even go so far as to mention that you aren't going to be asking for money this time around and that the visit is strictly to say thanks.

At this meeting, be sure to bring along any reports or informational brochures that might be relevant to the donor's interest. If there is a report generated specifically around this donor's contributions, be sure to bring it along and deliver it in person. If appropriate, also bring a handwritten (or hand-signed) note from the executive director or, if appropriate, from someone who has directly benefited from that donor's generosity.

The meeting provides you an opportunity both to thank the donor and also to find out *how that donor wants to be thanked*. There are standard operating procedures, yes, and even best practices, but there is also something to be said for customization if you have the time and resources to do it. You can ask this donor questions designed to prompt useful answers: Does she read the reports that you send them? Does she enjoy them? What else can your institution provide to help give life to the gift?

Don't make false promises, but honor requests when possible. If you have done a good job stewarding the donor with good reporting on her gifts, chances are that the donor will already be happy. The very act of asking can be enough to make folks feel good; much like inviting someone to an event, even if they cannot attend, it is a good cultivational, or stewarding, step.

Remember, the stewardship visit closes out the gift cycle, but it also reinitiates it. So bring some conversation points to the table. What is the next frontier for the programs that the donor is supporting? What is the next frontier for other programs that might be of interest? While you won't want there be an explicit ask during this meeting, you'll at least want to provide the donor with a very clear idea of where the organization is heading and suggest very clear ways in which she can remain involved or increase her involvement.

An e-mail reaching out to a donor for a stewardship visit might look like this:

Dear Joseph:

Greetings from sunny Salisbury! I hope this note finds you well. My name is Jeff Stauch, and I'm the Director of Development at Children First Vermont (CFV). As such, I am responsible for connecting with supporters of CFV, providing them with updates on the work that our organization is doing, answering their questions, and, when appropriate, exploring potential avenues for developing significant philanthropic relationships with CFV.

I am planning on being in Montpelier the second half of next week and would love the chance to meet with you. It would be wonderful to introduce myself to you and thank you in person for your very generous support of CFV. I would be honored to be able to explain to you in person just how much your philanthropic commitment to CFV has impacted the work that we do.

I propose meeting over coffee on either the morning of October 7th or 8th. I am early on in the planning stages of this trip, and I have flexibility in my schedule over those two days. If you let me know what day and time works best for you, I am confident we can find a time to meet.

In advance, Joseph, many thanks for your time and consideration. I look forward to hearing from you and hopefully to meeting you in a few weeks.

Sincerely,

Jeffrey David Stauch

PS – I hope you won't mind if I follow up with a phone call in the event that I do not hear from you by the week's end.

You should adjust this letter to fit your own voice and institution, but it should give you an idea of how to reach out.

Recruitment Visits

This section may vary in relevance depending on the resources that your organization has to devote to a volunteer program. But I want to expound on the topic briefly here just in case you are fortunate enough to be able to develop this type of programming.

When reaching out via e-mail (or phone) to set up this visit, it is good to have a job description at the ready. The job description will include the basic tasks involved with a particular role along with a rough estimate of the time commitment. (The question of time commitment arises in nearly every single recruitment conversation I have ever had.)

Here, I actually differ with some of my colleagues on how best to approach this kind of outreach. When I call or e-mail, I tend to frontload what I am hoping to accomplish in my meeting with them. In other words, I go so far as to outline the exact role I am proposing, and I generally include the job description.

I explain that I want them to consider this volunteer role and explain why I am contacting them. I might say that someone recommended them, that they're a good giver, and that they could help the organization even more through volunteering in a certain capacity. I then explain that I am going to be in their city or town and that I would welcome the opportunity to discuss the role in greater detail. I also make it a priority to tell them I will answer any questions they might have.

I have had colleagues who tend not to include the job description. They allude to the volunteer opportunity without explaining specifically what is at hand, preferring to outline the details in person. This method is valid, and it could be more likely that you'll get a visit out of it, but I would rather get the "no" up front than travel to see someone and get it in person.

If the potential donor declines up front, that allows me to call the next person on my list in the hopes that they might be interested in learning more about a volunteer role. If the response is not negative, it is essentially a guarantee that you have a new volunteer. Your meeting can then be focused less on recruitment and more on the process of getting the prospect set up with any materials that he might need to do his job. It can take on more of a training tone, so that at the conclusion of the meeting, the newly recruited volunteer can hit the ground running.

It is up to you which strategy you choose when making calls or sending e-mails, but if you have limited time and resources with which to travel, I would argue that it makes more sense to frontload your intentions. Get the rejection up front and move on to the next prospect, or get the acceptance up front and use the time during that meeting to answer their questions about the role. Then you can take the next steps to get them trained and providing them with the volunteer guidance they need to succeed.

Again, here's a potential template for your outreach:

Dear Joseph:

Greetings from sunny Salisbury! I hope this note finds you well. My name is Jeff Stauch, and I'm the Director of Development at Children First Vermont (CFV). As such, I am responsible for connecting with supporters of CFV, providing them with updates on the work that our organization is doing, answering their questions, and, when appropriate, exploring avenues of volunteer involvement and potential philanthropic relationships with CFV.

I am planning on being in Burlington the second half of next week and would love to introduce myself in person and thank you for your support of the work that CFV has been doing over the last four years. It will also be a good opportunity to provide you with the latest news from our offices.

I would also like to discuss with you a volunteer role which I am hoping you will consider. CFV is currently in the process of building a volunteer program to increase the impact our organization has locally and across the state.

I hope you will consider becoming involved as a CFV Sentinel. Sentinels are volunteers that help us build our donor base by reaching out to five or ten of their friends or family members and making the case for supporting CFV. It is a great way to support CFV and has a huge effect on how folks respond to appeals to get involved philanthropically. To give you an idea of the difference a Sentinel can make, on average just under a third of the people that we call from our offices here make a gift when we solicit them over the telephone. When those same folks are approached by a Sentinel they know personally, that giving rate jumps to over forty percent.

The time commitment is minimal because we know you're busy. On average, it takes about five to ten hours per calendar year. My office provides you with the information and resources that you need to do an effective job.

I would love the chance to discuss this in further detail next week when I am in Burlington. I propose meeting over coffee on either the morning of October 7th or 8th. I am early on in the planning stages of this trip, and I have flexibility in my schedule over those two days. If you let me know what day and time work best for you, I am confident we can arrive at a mutually agreeable arrangement.

In advance, Joseph, many thanks for your time and consideration. I look forward to hearing from you and hopefully meeting you in a few weeks.

Sincerely,

Jeffrey David Stauch

Recruitment calls are a great way to engage your donors in a way that is not strictly monetary. You're asking them to continue their financial support, yes. But you are also asking them to deepen their relationship with your organization by helping out beyond the act of writing a check—whether it's hosting an event, calling their friends to get them to contribute, or volunteering their time at your organization's office—and you're more likely to get them on board if you ask them to do so in person. Now let's move on to a conversation you're more likely to have at the higher end of the gift pyramid: the assessment call.

Assessment Visits

Assessment calls are one of my favorite types of visits. Again, it's a first date, getting-to-know-you kind of affair. These are folks who have the capacity to give a ton of money to your organization, but they haven't done so yet. Some of them are annual supporters of your organization but at small participation levels. Others have made a gift in the past but not recently. Others have gotten onto your radar screen through the work of your research staff or through the intel of other donors.

I covered the nuts and bolts of an assessment call in the chapter on the gift cycle, but a few things are worth repeating.

Remember: It's reconnaissance disguised as small talk. Your goals in this meeting are to get as much information as you can to determine a prospect's capacity and inclination to give, whether the timing is right, and, hopefully, their areas of interest with respect to your organization. Assessment calls are generally reserved for higher-end donors.

You can be direct: You can ask them where else they're philanthropic and where your organization ranks relative to others. You can ask them pointed questions about their business. Ask about their kids, their spouse, and their hobbies. All of this will help you construct a profile of these donors.

And remember: Always divulge your endgame. Never leave someone in the dark as to your intentions. From your very first point of contact, be transparent about what you do. Again, it is easier and more worth your time to frontload what you do than to have it come out mid-conversation.

Now, in the first meeting, although it is very unlikely you'll be making a major solicitation (although it can happen, as you'll soon see), show your cards. Be honest. You can say something along these lines:

> As my job title suggests, my primary goal is establishing significant philanthropic relationships between our organization and interested donors. Today is not the day to have the conversation about a major gift to [Organization Name], but it is my hope that we can continue a dialogue at a pace that is comfortable for you regarding a philanthropic commitment.

What you will say will obviously depend on your own style, but this is language that is clear and states your intentions. Of course, in the interim, encourage them to continue giving to your organization at the level at which they've historically given. If they haven't yet made a gift to your organization, encourage a small participation gift this year as you continue the dialogue. You can get away with a little bit of self-deprecation at the end of your meeting by saying something like "I wouldn't be doing my job if I didn't encourage you to continue supporting our organization at the generous level you already do."

You will ideally have some sort of information on the donor prior to the visit. This would include their giving trends and hopefully some research about their capacity to give. Even without pre-existing research, you can learn a good deal in that initial assessment call, so don't waste the opportunity.

This holds true for all types of visits, but I'll raise the point here: You should have a clear idea of what you want to get out of the meeting. It's best to go into a meeting with more to talk about than you think possible (in case the prospect has very little to say and you're having the conversation for both of you).

I have had colleagues who carry a small, pocket-sized notebook with them with the topics they hope to cover written down in point form. It is important to always have more than one topic prepared, even though sometimes you only end up talking about one of them. The point is, have clear goals. Don't waste your time and don't waste your donor's time.

Here's a sample paragraph in which you explain your motivation for meeting with them. Adapt as necessary.

> I am writing to you today as I am going to be in Springfield in two weeks, from the 3rd to the 6th, and I would love to meet with you. I would welcome the chance to thank you in person for your ongoing support of our organization, to give you an update from headquarters, and to answer any questions that you might have about StayOnTrack. In particular, I'd like to tell you about our latest efforts at closing the ever-widening achievement gap in Connecticut with our new after-school programs.

Again, the content will vary depending on your organization, but the structure of the explanation should still be applicable.

Cultivation and Solicitation Visits

I lump these two types of visits together because they both presuppose previous contact with a donor and because the next chapter actually contains a lot more on face-to-face solicitation. So we'll postpone an in-depth exploration of that type of visit until then. The outreach and meeting set up will often mirror that of the cultivational visit, again, because you have already met with this donor. Again, as a reminder, the cultivation stage of the gift cycle can be and often is broad and can and often does require more than one visit. It's the time when you continue to explore and probe the donor's interests in the hopes of triangulating your organization's funding priorities with the donors' philanthropic passions.

How you reach out to donors for cultivation visits will depend on how your initial assessment call went. Here are some questions to consider:

- Is the donor more responsive to an e-mail or a phone call?
- Is the tone between you and the donor formal or informal?
- Will the donor respond better to a short or a lengthy e-mail?
- When and where did you meet last time? This will help you because you can propose the same time and location as the last meeting. After all, you know it was convenient for them in the past.
- Have you been in contact with the donor via phone, e-mail, or mail since your last visit? Has the donor received any type of communication in the interim from you or your organization?

You won't need to reintroduce yourself in your outreach, but be sure to allude to the last point of contact that you had personally with the donor or that your organization has had with the donor.

With cultivation visits, you'll want to bring along material or be able to speak to the interest areas you were able to tease out in your last point of contact. If you were unable to discern interest areas in your previous visit, come prepared to talk about your institution's most pressing funding needs along with the fundraising goals. The cultivation visit is when you begin to zero in on a more specific ask amount, a more specific area of interest, and a clearer timeline regarding when a solicitation is appropriate.

During this meeting, notice when the donor perks up or—equally important—if he doesn't perk up when you were hoping he would. Be a close listener and observer. When you present funding priorities, goals, and opportunities, how does he react? What gets the donor excited?

Trust that you don't have to leave everything to chance. You can ask very pointed questions as long as you do so diplomatically and tactfully, not forcefully or brazenly. It is okay for you to ask outright if a specific project that you're discussing is one that the donor would consider supporting in a systematic way. If the answer is no, the best follow-up question is, "What would be a project that would excite you?"

Challenges can arise during the cultivation process, if a donor's interests are somewhat far afield from your funding priorities. Sometimes, it is possible to find an altered fit or just to force the donor's wishes through to your institution. The negotiation process will often take place post-visit.

I will talk at length about negotiations in Chapter 11 when we discuss major gifts, as cultivation can often live or die based on your skills as a negotiator and intermediary between the donor and your organization. Until then, here's the short of it: when it comes to steering your donor into the corrals of your institution's funding priorities, begin by zooming out. At the broadest level, what motivates the donor to give? I'm talking big, fat, abstract words: social change, poverty, sports, human rights, animal rights, environmental justice. After you've established that, ask yourself where your organization dovetails with those philanthropic priorities. Sometimes it's an indirect fit; sometimes the gift will be designated towards something for which there is a need at your organization, even if it isn't the greatest priority.

Again, we'll talk much more about negotiations in Chapter 11. The overarching point here with respect to cultivational visits is that you want to continue the momentum achieved from the assessment call and walk away from the meeting with the ability to come up with a very concrete solicitation plan, or at least very concrete next steps, for this donor.

Your outreach e-mail could look like this:

> *Dear Amy:*
>
> *Greetings from Farmington Animal Shelter (FAS)! I hope you are doing well and have been enjoying the summer. The shelter has enjoyed a successful season full of great placements and heartwarming stories.*
>
> *I'm writing to you today because I'm planning on being in Litchfield at the end of the month, on the 30th and 31st of August, and I'd love the chance to meet with you. I'd love to give you a recap of the summer we've been privileged enough to enjoy here at FAS and continue our conversation that we began in the springtime with respect to our capital campaign and your potential involvement.*
>
> *If it works with your schedule, would you like to meet at the Starbucks at County Line Road and Bishop Street on the 30th? You are one of the first folks I am calling for this trip, so I'm pretty open on both of those days. Let me know what works best with your schedule and we can go from there.*

In advance, Amy, thanks for your time and consideration. I'm looking forward to your reply.

With my best wishes,

Jeff Stauch

PS – I hope it does not present a problem if I follow up with a phone call in the event that I do not hear back from you by the end of next week.

Individual vs. Group Visits

Now, let's divide visits into individual and group visits. We'll start with the tradeoffs of meeting with one person vs. a small group (when I say small, I mean two to ten).

An individual meeting gives you the advantage of getting deep into a subject that either you as the fundraiser wanted to pursue or that is of particular interest to the donor.

In group settings, control of the conversation is a little more up in the air, depending on the subjects the various members would like to discuss. Of course, if you have a few simple points you want to get across, then presenting them to a group does have its advantages.

Each time you take the time to visit with a donor or donors, your aim is to make them feel it is worth your time and their time to spend an hour (or twenty minutes, or two hours) to discuss your organization's work. You want them to walk away feeling special and inspired: special because you took the time out of your day to talk to them and only them, and inspired because you've delivered a great message about the work of your organization. This can be achieved in both individual and group settings.

Again, your ability to control the flow of the conversation is greater in an individual meeting than with groups, and you'll be able to tailor your planning and messaging much more specifically. You'll also be able to craft much more personalized and thorough follow up for an individual than you could for a group, which, as we'll read below, can have significant implications.

Certainly, at least for major gift solicitations, individual meetings are better, but there are even exceptions to this rule (which we'll discuss below). For annual giving, group settings can definitely be a call to action. Cultivation can certainly lend itself to group settings in certain situations. However, assessment will likely be less effective in a group setting, as it will be harder to get the intel you're hoping to gather on an individual's giving capacity and inclination.

From the donors' perspectives, sometimes group meetings can imply lower pressure. Donors can assume they won't be singled out for a solicitation or that the fundraiser won't be asking for a check in hand at the end of the meeting. It can be more comfortable to have other folks in the room, so consider that as well. There are prospects out there that are *terrified* of meeting with fundraisers, and the only way that they'll do it is in group settings, usually with someone outside the organization they know well.

But before we get too far ahead of ourselves, let me take a minute to clarify what I mean when I talk about groups, because the composition of one group to the next varies widely.

A group meeting is, at its base, any meeting composed of more than just you (the fundraiser), and your prospect. It can be a meeting with multiple family members (a husband and wife, parents and children, etc.). The group could be composed of a number of locally based alumni from your high school or college. It could be a group of steady, annual fund donors; a group of major gift donors; or a mix of both. It could also be you, your prospective donor, and a board member. Or you, a board member, and a number of prospects. The permutations are numerous.

The setting can vary as well, much like with individual meetings. You could find yourself speaking in a conference or board room to these individuals or at the home of the family you're visiting. You could be meeting over dinner or at your office's headquarters. All these decisions will be influenced by the intended outcome of the meeting and the composition of the prospects you intend to invite.

Group Meetings

So let's look at group meetings for a bit. With respect to group settings, be strategic about who you call upon. If your aim is just to communicate certain things about your organization to a given group of people, you can probably get away with simply calling your high net-worth individuals and have them meet at one of your prospect's office space.

However, certain situations necessitate a little more thorough thinking.

For example, if you want a meeting to, as we say in the industry, "set someone's sights" or "raise someone's sights," and you think you can achieve that with the help of either a board member or a particularly enthusiastic donor, you'd want to keep that meeting to the three of you, and you'd want the donor or board member to be in the know as to the point of meeting with this particular prospect.

Group meetings are useful in that respect: you can use social pressure or, speaking more diplomatically, feed off one person's enthusiasm in the hopes of getting a buy-in from someone else. A buy-in can mean increasing one's giving to your organization or convincing them to help out in a volunteer role. Your board members can fill in the role of the enthusiastic participant, but others can as well.

If you are going to be using a board member or another enthusiastic prospect strategically in the hopes of warming up some other, less eager prospect, you will need an already existing familiarity with the party whose help you are hoping to enlist.

The advantage to this kind of set up is that the enthusiastic donor feels like he is helping beyond just giving, which in turn makes him feel good about the impact that he is making on your organization. It empowers that donor and also increases the likelihood that the prospect will react positively.

The added advantage to you being present at that meeting as opposed to letting the two meet alone is that you have some control over the message and can ensure the enthusiastic donor stays on point and doesn't misrepresent your organization—which can happen. With a board member, this is less likely to occur, but it is good to be present if only so that you can listen in and tailor your follow up accordingly.

Prospects also tend to react positively to folks who are volunteering their time to talk about the organization. Yes, the hope is that they will also react positively to you. But you're *paid* to stir up philanthropic support. Someone who voluntarily meets to talk with a prospect about getting involved with your organization may have a different kind of credibility.

Sometimes this requires some coaching on your part. Share your goals with the person whose help you're enlisting, and spell out clearly how the conversation should flow and who will take which speaking role. Once the meeting begins, that could fly out the window based on what the prospect wants to talk about. But it is always good to have some preordained structure.

Here is a real-life example of a successful group meeting. It was a recruitment meeting, meaning that I was hoping to recruit people as volunteer solicitors who would reach out to five to ten people that they knew in the hopes of getting those people to make gifts to the organization that I represent.

In anticipation of that meeting, I called on one of them, Henry, who was already a volunteer. I explained that I was going to be in his city and wanted to do some recruitment. Would he be of help? Two of his colleagues were alumni and rising within the ranks of the company for which they worked. Both were pretty well connected.

One of those colleagues, Charlie, was a very enthusiastic supporter of my organization. He was a likely candidate to volunteer. The other colleague, let's call him Bob, was a higher net-worth individual and the prospect I was hoping to engage and cultivate. He was the one that was going to be hard to convince.

In short, the lunch consisted of the recruiter (me), a current volunteer (Henry), a likely volunteer (Charlie), and someone who was a bit harder to read (Bob). The conversation over lunch played out like this. I began by thanking them all for meeting me and explained my role as a professional fundraiser. I then laid out why I was meeting with them and the outcome I desired as a result of this meeting. After an explanation of the volunteer role for which I was recruiting, Henry was able to speak about his involvement, why he volunteered in the first place, and his positive experience so far as a result of his participation.

Charlie then asked pointed questions about the role while Bob more or less sat back and listened. By the end of lunch, Charlie said that he would sign up, that he was into the idea of helping out.

To which Bob said smugly, "Well, hell, I guess that means I have to do it, too. Fine."

Both ended up signing up as volunteers and doing great work in those roles.

Not every lunch goes as smoothly as that one did. But pay attention to the work that went into planning that visit. I had to get Henry to visit with me and get his buy-in to help me out. He then took care of inviting his colleagues out to lunch. Even so, prior to the lunch itself, we had several conversations about Charlie and Bob, their differing personalities, and their roles within the company.

The tradeoff between arranging a single visit vs. group meetings, of course, is that there is a good deal more pre-planning for groups, especially if the group grows beyond three, as illustrated by the above example. Another danger with setting up group meetings is that as soon as one person has to cancel, it's more likely that others will back out, too. And, as noted, the conversation becomes much more susceptible to unanticipated twists and turns as you add members into the conversation.

Group meetings can definitely be a good use of your time, and they can sometimes even be of better use than individual visits. However, I anticipate that more of your visits will be held individually so that you can have that twenty or thirty minutes or—even better—an hour of someone's undivided attention with which to discuss your organization and move them along in the gift cycle.

So that's a brief taxonomy of the types of visits you'll be making and a short meditation on whether to do a group or individual visit. Now let's take a look at how to get you out on the road and in front of your donors.

Trip Planning

Let's now focus on the actual planning of a trip. Again, here we'll assume that you're planning an actual trip that requires you being on the road. There is also the possibility, if your organization's donor base is locally concentrated, that you won't need to stay overnight. But whether that's the case or you go out for a week or more at a time, the basic planning points I lay out here will still remain the same.

Timing and Tips

Allow yourself, ideally, at least two weeks prior to a trip to begin planning. If your trip is local, you can get away with planning a week beforehand, but it's best to allow yourself that first week out to secure the appointments and the week before the trip to *plan and prepare for your visits.*

Here are some vocabulary terms that we use in the fundraising business.

Anchor: Your anchor visit (or visits), as the name implies, is the principal reason for your visit. Anchor does not necessarily mean solicitation. An anchor appointment can be at any point in the gift cycle, from assessment to stewardship and anywhere in between. Your anchor visit should be someone with very high potential or, at the very least, very good connections who can help both financially and also open other doors for you.

The anchor is someone who is ripe for the next step in the gift cycle (and yes, sometimes this step can mean assessment). She is someone who needs to be visited both because of her potential as a donor and also because of your institutional priorities (the two don't always align, remember, so beware!).

Filler: Again, the name should give it away. Filler calls are folks who you need to see but don't bear the same imperative that your anchors do. They are people that are worth the time to meet with on an individual basis but aren't necessarily in urgent need of attention.

Of course, any individual donor will fluctuate between the anchor and filler roles over time. You'll need to figure out which donors are at which points during your trip planning.

You should aim to have three to five visits a day. Less than three and it might not be the best use of your time to be on the road. More than five and you'll be too fried to keep the conversations straight in your head after the fact.

The joy of travel and of meeting donors face to face is that, of course, sometimes anchors disappoint us and sometimes fillers pleasantly surprise us. Examples abound. I'll tell you a few stories later.

When planning your trip, you should call on your anchors first. Always put out more calls than you have time for, because it is a rarity that everyone you want to see on that trip will be available to see you. And if that *does* happen, well, having a stuffed trip is always a good thing if you can make the logistics of it work out. If you do become overbooked, be honest with donors. You can reply by saying, "In the time between my outreach to you and your response, a meeting has actually come up for 10 a.m. on the 27th. Would something later in the day work? Or perhaps the day after? If not, please know I plan on being back in town before the end of spring," or something along those lines. Donors tend to be pretty understanding, or at least the ones who are worth your time.

You might note that in a number of the examples I've provided for your outreach I include a PS in which I tell them that I will follow up with a phone call. If you are contacting the person initially by e-mail, be prepared to follow up with that phone call or a second e-mail. However, it is good to change methods if you don't hear back.

If I allow myself enough lead time, sometimes I do one e-mail, resend it a week later if I haven't heard back, and then follow up with a phone call. Other times, it's one e-mail and one phone call.

The phone call can be more nerve racking, but it's just as efficient *if not more so*. Occasionally, when I am really pressed to put a trip together at the last minute, I do my initial outreach via phone. If everyone picks up the phone during your calls, you can have entire day or two planned out in a matter of half an hour.

If you get the person on the phone, that's great! Explain who you are, tell them your title, and explain your role *honestly*. Then explain the reason for your visit, just as though it were an e-mail.

If you are leaving a voice mail, keep the message under 90 seconds or even under 60 if possible. You won't be able to cover everything you would in an e-mail. But the strategy then becomes to leave a voice mail alluding to the fact that you're going to follow up with an e-mail immediately following the call, and then follow through on that promise. The follow-up e-mail will allow you to talk more in depth about your goals.

A typical voice mail could go something like this:

> *Hello, this is a message for Wendy. Wendy, my name is Jeff Stauch, and I'm a gift officer at Roslindale Community Theater. The reason for my call today is that I'm planning on being in the Framingham area in two weeks, on Wednesday the 5th and Thursday the 6th, and I'd love the chance to meet with you. I'd love to say thanks in person for your ongoing support of RCT and to give you an update on the productions that we're going to be putting up this coming year. Again, Wendy, my name is Jeff Stauch from RCT, regarding a possible visit with you on either the 5th or 6th of October. My direct line is 617-555-5555. Again, that number is 617-555-5555. I'm also going to send you an e-mail that you can respond to. I look forward to hearing back from you. Thanks, and have a wonderful day!*

That voice mail, spoken at a moderate pace, takes about forty-five to fifty seconds. It communicates who you are, who you represent, and it conveys the message that you want to visit with the person to discuss the work of your organization. It also provides the donor with your job title.

You should *always leave your number twice*. Speak it slowly. Pause after the area code and after the exchange. Say your name at least twice during the message as well as the organization's name and the proposed dates. *Don't forget to say your name!*

The e-mail that you send immediately after the phone call should allude to the fact that you just left a voice mail. After that, you can use one of the templates I set forth above.

Packing

Pack as lightly as possible, but not lighter than possible. I mean this both in terms of what materials you want to bring that represent your organization and in terms of attire, etc. If you're flying, try to fit everything into your carry-on baggage. First, it's cheaper. Second, when you're on a tight turnaround time between landing and meeting, not having to wait at baggage claim buys you extra time to get to your first meeting on time. And believe me, when you travel as often as I do and you already have to deal with delays and other airline-related snags, you'll want to have as much autonomy over your belongings as humanly possible. Granted, sometimes it isn't always possible, especially if you're on the road for more than a week. But do your best to travel lightly. Travel is stressful enough as it is. The less you have to carry, the happier you'll be.

To your initial meeting with a donor, err on the side of conservatism and wear a suit if they haven't told you explicitly that they're dressing down (which they often do: "I'll be casual," or "I'll be in jeans"). If it turns out that they're casual, you'll know for next time. It's never good to be more casually dressed than your prospect. Of course, there have been times when I've been greeted by a donor in flip flops and ragged jeans, or even snow pants once (she was going skiing immediately after our meeting), but those meetings are the exception rather than the rule. Err on the side of the formal rather than the informal.

Regarding what to bring from your organization, this is a matter of style. I have waivered in the past between bringing a lot information with me to provide the donor and bringing nothing, preferring to send it as part of my follow up (see below).

If you happen to know going into a meeting where a donor's interests lie, it's probably a good idea to bring along some sort of printed material if you have something readily available. We call these kinds of things "leave-behinds." The advantage of leaving something behind is that it gives the donor something to have and hold after you leave. It is something to pore over once the meeting is over. Most times, donors will appreciate you providing them with something to take away from the meeting. It's rare that it will backfire on you.

One thing you won't want to forget is business cards. When you hand the potential donor yours, they will hand you theirs. Business cards can shed light on potential donors' jobs and provide you with new contact information.

And yes: If they haven't made a gift yet this fiscal year, bring a gift envelope.

Follow Up: Where You Really Impress Your Donors

The heartbreaking part about travel is that your visit does not close the communication loop. Rather, it opens it up. You fill each of your days on the road with at least three visits and sometimes more, no one cancels on you, and all of your conversations go exactly as you had planned. That's a trifecta if there ever was one. You can fly home and take a week off, right?

Sadly, you'd be making a huge error. Timely, thoughtful, and thorough follow up is how you cement the relationship with the donors with whom you visit individually.

The scope and nature of your follow up will vary widely based on the type of visit that you had with the donor. Each step in the gift cycle, as I've stressed before, is usually a visit or a lengthy phone call / e-mail exchange, and each of those steps requires follow up.

In the assessment follow up, you are usually providing the donor with information on subjects around which the conversation focused. For cultivational visits, send information on the project or area of your institution around which your solicitation will likely focus. For solicitation visits, if appropriate, send that proposal! For stewardship, send reporting that demonstrates the impact of the donor's philanthropy.

You should also be sure to answer any questions that came up during previous communication. This can sometimes involve detective work on your part, especially if an inquiry comes out of left field. You had gone into the meeting to discuss a new after-school mentorship program and you got asked a nuts-and-bolts question about how long Alfred Jones has been on the Board of Trustees. Ask for help from the appropriate sources in your institution until you can get the answers. This can involve e-mailing or calling other departments within your organization, and can sometimes engender some frustration, but it is worth your time and your organization's time for you to do the digging so that you can provide thorough, accurate answers to the donor's questions.

For those inquiries for which you don't know the answer in the meeting, *admit that you don't know*. It's always a little tough to stomach, and sometimes a little embarrassing, but it is always, *always* better to admit that you don't know something than to make something up. You don't want to get caught inventing something and then have it come back to bite you on the tail later on. Be sure to make a note of those questions so that you can answer them thoroughly when you return.

There is always tension, when there is a lot of follow up to be done, between wanting to provide the information piece-meal as you come across it and waiting until you have all the necessary information needed before sending it off via e-mail or mail. This is a judgment call that you'll have to make based on your read of the donor's patience. I tend to compile everything and send it off in one shot if only for the simple reason that it is the best way that I have come up with to make sure I actually get to all the follow-up activities I need to do. This makes it less easy to drop the ball.

Given my own modus operandi, if I do things piece-meal, I inevitably forget at least one element of follow up. So I wait until I have all the information that I need before sending it. If you think you can keep track of all the various items, by all means, contact the donor as you complete each individual element of your promised follow-up. The advantage to that approach is that it gives you an excuse to have multiple contacts with the donor.

The potential downside is that it might feel like you're barraging them, depending on the number of items you have to follow up on. Trust your gut and know yourself on this one. Regardless of your style, be sure to take the time to do your follow up work correctly. I can't stress enough that your *follow up is what cements the relationship and what gains the donor's trust in you.*

On Note Taking, Again

So, how do you remember everything the conversation contained? At the end of the day, after three to five visits, it's hard to disentangle all the conversations that you've had. Did I talk about our volunteer program with Vincent or Ted? Did the question about corporate matches come from Cynthia or Patty? How do you keep everyone straight and the content of each conversation accurately summarized?

You take notes. Earlier, in the chapter on data and records, I made the case for taking good notes. Well, here we are again, revisiting that theme. You need to take notes in order to execute your follow up effectively. Remember the small notebook I alluded to earlier, the one where you can write down your goals for the conversation before heading into it? The good news is that you can use that very same notebook to capture the content of your conversation after the meeting, too!

Summarize the meeting immediately afterwards. Write it down. I've had colleagues that use Dictaphones and voice recorders. Given how terrible my handwriting is, I should probably consider that myself. It's seductive to think that you'll remember everything, but you won't. Trust me. And that can come back to haunt you. Include not only the content of the conversation but also your anticipated next steps and the time horizon involved.

You should type all of your notes up within six to twelve hours of the meeting and send them via e-mail to yourself, to your support staff if you have it, and to your supervisor. I might sound repetitive with the constant petitioning to take notes, capture information, and put it in a place centrally located and universally accessible, but it is key to the success of your organization's fundraising operations. Remember that dismal question of business continuity? What if you get hit by the theoretical Mack Truck next week? How will the next fundraiser know what the next steps are for a given prospect?

Tales from the Road

I'll provide you with a few tales from personal visits that will hopefully prove, if nothing else, that despite everything I've just told you there are instances in which you will have to be flexible.

Case Study 1: The Zero-to-Sixty Conversation

The first case study is one in which a conversation went from zero to sixty far more quickly than I was anticipating. It was, for all intents and purposes, a planned assessment call. Granted, this prospect was one of my anchors for this trip to Indiana, but it was more an exploration of her interest in a certain science fundraising effort we were undertaking.

I arrived at the meeting and was led in by her assistant. The company she worked for had recently gotten some pretty negative PR. She, as the VP of Marketing and Public Relations, was taking heat. I walked into her office.

Her first words: "I haven't slept in 72 hours. You have thirty minutes. Let's talk."

I outlined, in the first five minutes, the project about which I wanted to talk. By minute ten, she had already taken two phone calls and was visibly distracted. Fifteen minutes into the meeting, she said, "Okay, I need the bottom line. Why are you here, and how much are you asking for."

I wasn't expecting to have to show the gift pyramid for this particular project, but I did have it on hand, miraculously. I showed her the fundraising goal and explained that I envisioned her being at the top of the gift pyramid, hoping that she would consider a six-figure gift to the sciences revolving around this project.

"I'm in for something. I'll let you know. Have to check with the other half." And that was it.

Normally, for me to get from assessment to solicitation would have taken multiple visits, but here I was going from assessment to solicitation in twenty minutes. I wasn't very well prepared, and I was caught more than a little off-guard by the pace of the conversation. However, the one thing I did do correctly was, noting how little time I had and how frantic she was to get on with her day (and also the fact that I wasn't planning on making it back to Indiana for at least six months), that I guessed that this was my one shot to make the ask with this donor. So I did. I put the $100,000 figure in front of her, and she said she'd consider. This was *not* an ideal situation by any means. But I don't think I was too rash in fast-forwarding that conversation. She ended up making a smaller gift, but it was still a very significant increase to her donations thus far, and she did leave the conversation open as to whether there would be bigger gifts in the future.

Case Study 2: Static Records vs. Dynamic Interests

Here's an example of our records misleading me in terms of area of interest. A prospect of mine in Illinois was cited as someone who we should consider "A-List" for a basketball fundraising effort. We were hoping to endow the programmatic costs of the sport. We knew he still played avidly and still traveled to various parts of the country to play in fun and informal tournaments along with other alumni. My predecessor, when meeting him for an assessment call, noted that the capacity was there; the inclination was medium; and the timing, at least for the prospect to start making small to moderate sized gifts, was imminent.

So I walked into this meeting with the intent of cultivating this prospect for a gift to the basketball program. Again, all signs pointed to the fact that basketball was still a big part of his life and the college connections only reinforced that signal.

The only problem was that I was dead wrong. He was interested in unrestricted giving and said he didn't want to support athletics. He provided his reasons, and the conversation very quickly turned to a conversation on the importance of unrestricted annual gifts to the school.

Again, I did all the necessary preparation to discuss basketball and ended up having an entirely different conversation.

These stories not designed to scare you but rather to advise you to prepare and to trust your gut *and* be open to the conversation turning in a completely different direction. It's easier said than done, and it does require practice. And this is NOT a recommendation against preparing thoroughly for a visit. Rather, it is a reminder that fundraising is, at the end of the day, an exploration in human interaction, and humans can do funny things.

Mike Tyson famously said: "Everyone has a plan until they get punched in the face." In other words, do your prep work, but be willing to leave it behind if need be.

Of course, not all unexpected conversations go poorly. You'll recall in the chapter on records that sometimes we go into meetings thinking we're meeting with a B-list filler visit only to find out that they've changed their mindset and are looking to increase their support to your organization. Always be open-minded when heading to each meeting no matter what your research and your past interactions suggest.

In this chapter, we've explored the joy of trip planning, the types of visits that fill up a day or a week on the road, and how to follow up properly.

And now, the moment you've all been waiting for: the in-person solicitation!

The Ask

Exploring Face-to-Face Solicitation

So I've finally got to the solicitation, the "ask." What took me so long? The book is titled *Effective Frontline Fundraising,* after all. Why have I spent so much time on the back end, behind-the-scene stuff? I hope, if nothing else, that the amount of time that it's taken to get here proves that the actual solicitation is only one part in a much, much larger cycle, and that there is a good amount of preparation that should go into a solicitation of any size, especially a big one.

But at the end of the day, preparation and planning won't amount to much if you don't actually put your neck out there and ask for money. This chapter is dedicated to helping you make that face-to-face ask.

Rejection: A Way of Life

I might as well get it out of the way early and put it out in the open: you are going to get rejected. *A lot.* Really, it's part of your job. You will hear *no* much more than you hear *yes.* Get used to it. And get *good* at it. I don't mean that you should jump out of your chair and do a dance every time someone says no. When I say get good at being rejected, I mean get comfortable with it, work on not taking it personally, and learn how to be *unflappable*—that is to say unperturbed—in the face of rejection.

I said it earlier, but it is worth repeating: you are *not responsible for the answer you get.* You are responsible for making the strongest case possible, for doing your homework so as to come up with the right ask amount, the right timing, and the right interest area. But you cannot control how someone will respond when you actually make the ask. It's worth remembering this. And reminding yourself of it before each solicitation.

There are a lot of sports analogies in fundraising, some better than others. One that comes up often is in baseball. Hall of Fame baseball players will, on average, have a batting average somewhere around .300. They will only get a hit three out of every ten times at bat.

A .300 average in development would make you one of the best-run organizations in the country. In fundraising, you'll find that, on average, a stellar shop will have a .250 success rate. In other words, as I've discussed previously, you'll raise a quarter for every dollar that you solicit. You should aim to have a batting average of .200 to .250.

It's important to bear these numbers in mind as you begin soliciting. It's so easy to get frustrated when you get a number of rejections, but you have to keep trusting that there are yeses out there, that each meeting is worth every bit of effort you can muster. Hall of Fame batters don't get to home plate by thinking they're going to strike out. So too, fundraisers should not go into a conversation thinking that they're going to hear no.

Nor should fundraisers be surprised, hurt, or discouraged, though, when the answer is, in fact, no.

You're going to get rejected. It's a harsh truth about your job. The good news is that you're also going to get positive responses. And, those are more than a counterbalance to the rejections.

The Psychology of the Ask

People ask me what I do for work. I tell them that I ask people for six- to eight-figure gifts. The response is usually some combination of, "I could never do that," and "You must be really smooth and suave."

Both statements are not entirely correct. Anyone can fundraise. As I said earlier, you've negotiated a salary, you've interviewed for a job, and you've asked someone out on a date. It's a very similar skill set.

As for the second statement, about being smooth and suave: I'm not particularly smooth or suave, nor does one need to be. Sure, you need to be able to hold an intelligent conversation, and have a basic level of social grace, but you needn't be excessively smooth.

Comfort with Discomfort

When people tell me that I must be suave, I tell them no, I'm just good at making people uncomfortable.

Then I tell them, paradoxically, that a donor is more likely to make a gift when in their comfort zone.

Here's what I mean. Money, per se, is often an awkward subject. It can be a sensitive topic, and everyone reacts differently. Philanthropy is a deeply personal matter, and bringing that personal choice out into the open can cause a certain amount of discomfort. It is in this zone of discomfort that the fundraiser has to be most comfortable.

When the time is right, you want to challenge folks to think beyond what they're normally giving and raise their philanthropic commitment to the next level. Naturally, that creates discomfort as well.

But what about the donor's comfort zone? I've gone on about how you need to be willing to create uncomfortable situations. The saving grace to the conversation, though, and what ultimately allows the donor to regain his or her comfort is that, at the end of the day, *the donor is in the driver's seat.*

This is a fine point to balance: On the one hand, you have projects that are urgently in need of funding, and it is your responsibility to convey that urgency, that need, to your donors. On the other hand, though, you do not want the donor to feel *rushed.* Effective fundraising is, after all, *relationship building.* You don't want a series of one-offs. You want to link donors to your organization in such a way that they feel good about it and will hopefully be lifetime supporters. Rushing them, pushing them too hard will do nothing but push them away.

So, you need to cause a little discomfort in donors because of the *nature of the conversation*, but you need to leave the pacing up to them. That is what allows donors to return to their comfort zone.[1]

The ask is an act of getting your donors to envision themselves making a gift at the level that you're soliciting. If done correctly, it won't come out of left field, and yet it will cause them to think. And yes, maybe to squirm.

This isn't to suggest that you should be brazen and ask all people for a million dollars the first time that you meet them. Far from it. The point is that soliciting people for money, for the money that they earned (or inherited) can often cause some discomfort—and you have to be comfortable with that.

---

[1] This will become especially true when we talk about major gifts in the next chapter!

Here is one very important thing to keep in mind, one that is easy to over-look. If you have properly disclosed your job title and your role with your institution, it's already out in the open that you're going to be asking your prospect for money at some point. It therefore follows that at a certain point in the conversation, *the donor is expecting you to ask for money.* The ask is the elephant in the room. Both parties know that at some point, the fund-raiser has to pull a trigger.

I had a meeting with a prospect once where we met over lunch. His giving history suggested that he wasn't a particularly good prospect. He had cried poor during a few previous visits with other staff members. We ordered our food, and I gave him the latest news from campus, and the entire time he had this smug grin on his face. I decided to call him out on it, saying, "Something I'm saying is entertaining you. What is it?" He replied, "I'm just wondering when you're going to ask me for money."

This was more than a little unexpected, given how modest a donor he had been up until that point. I surprised myself a little bit when I shot back: "Well, when will you be ready to increase your annual gift?"

He laughed and said that it wasn't the right time. The conversation then turned to his business, how it was doing, and all the things that I was hoping to cover.

I bring up the story because donors, especially ones who aren't yet very well educated in their philanthropy, do often expect an ask on the first visit. And sometimes, there *is* an ask on the first visit, especially if the fundraiser is just raising annual, expendable gifts (as opposed to major or endowed gifts).

Even educated donors and philanthropists are expecting an ask at some point during the relationship.

So ask! Missing an opportunity to ask can actually be detrimental to the do-nor's relationship with your organization, as there will arrive a point at which they feel that their time is being wasted, or worse, that you're not doing a good job of representing the organization in the capacity in which you're be-ing paid.

It's so logical when you read it, but believe me: when you're sitting across from the donor that you're hoping to solicit, you begin to think about put-ting it off until the next visit. And it is really hard to convince yourself to be-lieve that the person sitting on the other side of the table is waiting for the solicitation. In a certain manner, you're both looking to get it out of the way. So, get it out of the way.

The Importance of Being Nervous

Let's talk about the meaning of getting nervous. New fundraisers often complain about being nervous when they're asking for money, especially as the amount of money increases. While being nervous isn't necessarily something I want to encourage, I want you, at least at first, as you gain competence and comfort (and you get more accustomed to rejection) to be at peace with being nervous going into a solicitation.

When I first started fundraising and expressed this to my supervisor, she put me at ease by saying, "That's okay. It's an indication that you care about the outcome of the conversation." And that was true. I did care. I did want the prospect to say yes, not just for my own professional success, but because I wanted the organization I was representing to get the philanthropic support it needed to achieve its goals.

So take my supervisor's message to heart: being nervous is an indication that the outcome of the conversation is important to you. It affirms that you want to help the organization you're representing.

Even veteran fundraisers get nervous, believe me. A former colleague of mine, who had over ten years experience, divulged that for each of his phone conversations, solicitations or otherwise, he rehearsed the call several times before dialing. Before going into a solicitation, I usually take time the morning before (or, if I'm driving to an appointment, in the car before I step into the meeting) to close my eyes and envision the conversation playing out from the first handshake all the way through to the solicitation and the ensuing silence. Some meditate. Some listen to music to drown out the nervous chatter in their heads.

One of the most interesting cases of getting over the jitters wasn't from a fellow fundraiser, but from a former professor of mine. She was explaining how nerve racked she would get when she first started teaching at the university where she was doing her graduate work. I asked her how she got over it.

She said, "I decided to tell myself that I was not a professor, but rather an actress playing the role of a professor."

I thought that was brilliant.

We all develop our own rituals to overcome the nervousness. You'll find your own in time, if you don't already have one. Just know, before you do, that being nervous is okay, it's natural, and it's a sign that you care.

Liberace or Bogart? The Question of Style

I am always struck, when I look at my colleagues, at how vastly different each one of us is in terms of our approach to fundraising in general, and the solicitation in particular.

If your team consists of more than one frontline fundraiser, line up some joint-meetings in which two of them are in front of a single prospect. One should lead the meeting, with the other one observing and chiming in when appropriate.

It is always good to learn from one another. Observing someone else in action is a great way to gain insight as to how to have an effective face-to-face solicitation. When you observe, you shouldn't be looking just for what you want to emulate in your colleague, but also taking note of your differences.

One of my mentors is an extremely effective fundraiser. I really do find myself in awe of how good she is sometimes. But I also acknowledge that her style is not one that I can pull off. I've gotten pretty good at what I do, and I have learned a ton from observing her, but not in the sense that I'm co-opting her style. Rather, I hear what she says and how she says it, and I then figure out how to deliver the same message in a way that is more natural for me.

You'll hone your own style with time, but do remember what I said previously about being smooth and suave. You don't need to be smooth or suave to be effective. Of course, you *can* be. It won't hurt, but it isn't necessary. A friend of mine who did similar work to my own mentioned the biggest gift that his organization received in its history came from a gift officer whom everyone on the team regarded as very awkward to the point of being creepy. Having never met the officer, I can't say for certain how true this is, but I trust my friend's judgment. Also, based on my experience at fundraising conferences, I can say that fundraisers with less, more, and equal experience than I run the gamut from definitely charming to just plain normal to strange duck.

One thing I will say on style is that *it is your job to represent your organization enthusiastically and effectively* first *and to be cool* second, *if at all.* Fundraisers are often called an organization's cheerleaders. The analogy is not just cute, but also accurate. Cheerleaders operate under the principle of hyperbole—they overdo things, with the purpose of drawing in the crowd and getting it excited.

High school memories (or fantasies) aside, cheerleading isn't exactly cool. Taken out of context, a cheerleader doing his or her routine can look downright silly. Sometimes, when I watch cheerleaders, my response is to feel badly for just how exaggerated they are: their large gesticulations, their unmoving smiles, their jumping at the least provocation. The purpose of cheerleading is to get the audience to rise to the level of enthusiasm of the cheerleader, to want the same outcome as the cheerleader, which is for the home team to win.

While there is such a thing as overdoing it, I'd suggest that if you think you're overdoing it, you're probably not. Prospects want to know that you enjoy representing your institution, that you're proud of the work that it does, and that you care very deeply about its programming. You're not just there because it's your job to ask for money. You're there because you have a legitimate interest in improving the organization you represent.

Conveying this care and passion for your organization can be carried out by, well, thinking and acting like a cheerleader. Of course, I don't mean bringing pom-poms and jumping on the table when the prospect says yes to your solicitation. What I do mean is that you need to exude positive energy surrounding the work that your organization does. You need to bring the donor to your level of enthusiasm.

If you can do this by being the smooth and suave Humphrey Bogart, go for it. If it's easier for you to do this by being flashier and showier, in the vein of Liberace (minus the outfits), go for it. As long as you are comfortable in your own skin and can deliver a message that is compelling, you're good to go. Don't feel the need to be cool, especially if it feels unnatural to you. People are good at picking up when an act is forced, and you don't want your style to seem contrived.

You'll find out what works best for you. The point is not to try to imitate a style that does not jive well with your personality. Get out there; try different things; visit prospects with other gift officers with an open mind. All these things will help you hone your image, your voice, and your style.

Prep Work: The Time, the Place, the Amount, the Solicitor

If I have driven home no other point so far in this book, I hope that I have at least made clear the importance of preparatory work and strategizing. This section will focus on getting you ready to walk into the prospect's office or to sit down at the lunch table to make the actual ask for money.

When

The first thing to bear in mind is that you don't want the ask to catch people off guard. You don't want the prospect thinking you're coming into his office solely to give him an update on the institution's activities if it's in your plans to solicit him. If you've met with this donor before, you should be honest and give him a heads up that, for this upcoming meeting, you're planning on pulling the trigger.

An outreach e-mail could look like this (again, bearing in mind that you will have your own tone and style of writing).

> *Dear Quinn:*
>
> *Greetings from Denton. I hope that you're doing well. Life here at the Writing Workshop is busy as always; our after-school enrollment program is looking strong again this year, and we have a wonderful roster of tutors and mentors to rise to the challenge.*
>
> *The reason for my e-mail today is that I'm planning on visiting with folks in the Fort Worth area during the second half of the week of the twenty-second. During that time, I would really love the chance to come by your office. It would be wonderful to share with you our goals here for the coming year and to follow up on our conversation from last month regarding a potential significant commitment to our rural outreach program from your family.*
>
> *I'm early on in the planning stages of this trip, so please know that I am happy to work with what is best for your schedule. It is my intention to be in Fort Worth on the twenty-fifth and twenty-sixth all day. If you let me know which day and time is most convenient for you, I am confident that we can carve out some time to discuss further.*
>
> *I thank you so much for all that you've done already for the Writing Workshop, and I look forward to hearing back from you.*
>
> *Sincerely,*
>
> *Jeff Stauch*

In this e-mail, I've stated that there has been an ongoing conversation surrounding a gift, and I'm hoping to close on it.

If you haven't met with the donor before, you should also be forthcoming about the purpose of your visit.

Such an e-mail might look like this:

Dear Peggy:

Greetings from Denton. My name is Jeff Stauch, and I work at the Writing Workshop in the development shop. My responsibilities revolve around building our individual donor program, which is pivotal in helping to support the work that the Writing Workshop does with helping elementary and middle school students improve their writing through after-school and weekend programming.

The reason for my e-mail today is that I'm going to be in Dallas in two weeks meeting with individuals, and I'd love to meet with you. I'd welcome the opportunity to thank you for your past support, and to discuss the possibility of getting you involved with our current campaign to expand our outreach into the more rural school systems in the county. We are currently reaching out to all of our steadfast supporters to have conversations about how they can help us with this exciting new initiative.

I'm early in the planning stages of this trip, so please know that I am happy to work with what is best for your schedule. It is my intention to be in Dallas on the twenty-fifth and twenty-sixth all day. If you let me know which day and time is most convenient for you, I am confident that we can carve out some time to discuss further.

I thank you so much for all that you've done already for the Writing Workshop, and I look forward to hearing back from you.

Sincerely,

Jeff Stauch

In this e-mail, I disclose my work for the Writing Workshop as well as my intention to discuss Peggy's giving in this meeting. Regarding the appropriateness of asking for money on the first visit: It will depend on the scope of your fundraising initiatives and the level of support you're asking for from a given individual. Timing will vary for every project and every donor. It is up to you, the fundraiser and strategist extraordinaire, to be able to determine when is right. Trust your gut, but don't be afraid to ask for advice.

Sometimes, your anticipated timeline can get thrown off. For example, I was planning on soliciting a prospect of mine who was sending hints that she was soon going to sell her company. Based on the company's estimated value and other research, I was planning on a six-figure solicitation. My plan was to go back to the city where she was and solicit her in six months, around the time she was expecting to have turned her company into cash.

In the interim, however, I went back to the city and had a meeting with another prospect, who happened to know this woman quite well. I shared with him that I was going to be back next quarter to visit with her. You can imagine my surprise when I learned in this meeting that her company had gone bankrupt, and she had moved to Oklahoma.

The timing of that gift conversation was, naturally, delayed.

Another example is a married couple that had long been supportive of the institution and had even helped open doors in the city where they lived and hosted events. They were great prospects and had been well cultivated by my predecessor before he left.

They were positioned for an ask within a year of me taking them on as prospects. They had had the proper amount of high-level contact for a big gift conversation to take place.

Then what happened? A very messy divorce. Another obstacle I had to wait out. After everything shook out, I called on them both and resumed the conversation, but the solicitation got significantly delayed.

One common, inescapable obstacle that has arisen in the last few years has been the big recession of 2008–2009. This has delayed many a gift conversation at all levels. Whereas going bankrupt and a messy divorce do, without doubt, have financial implications for a prospect, I would argue that you cannot assume that everyone was hit equally by the recession. Therefore, I would advise against assuming that you cannot have the gift conversation that you had originally slated to have this year or next. Of course, don't be naïve or surprised when someone tells you that the recession has hit her business or portfolio very hard, but don't assume that that's the case. Certain industries got hit harder than others, and certain investments continued to perform well. A surprising number of prospects of mine have reported that they escaped the worst of the recession.

The takeaway here is that you want to plan your ask for an appropriate point in the conversation. Sometimes, when you're simply trying to build out your donor base or increase your annual dollars raised, you can make the solicitation on the first call. Sometimes, though, the timeline is longer.

Where

Where is the right place to ask someone for money? Ideally, it is a combination of where the donor feels comfortable and a setting and ambiance that is conducive to having an in-depth conversation. In practice, it is often more so the former and hopefully at least a little bit the latter.

Again, this will be an exercise in knowing your donor and knowing yourself. It's usually best to let the donor choose the venue to have the conversation (this is true of your other types of visits, too, by the way).

Remember, you want your prospect in his or her comfort zone when asking for money. And his or her comfort zone may or may not be conducive to having that candid, uncomfortable talk about giving. How you hold a conversation in a closed-door office will be different from how you hold a conversation in an open-spaced floor. You will need to have conversations in offices, over meals, over coffee, over drinks, while walking down the street, in elevators and lobbies, in crowded noisy places and quiet places, at 7 a.m., at 9 p.m., and for any amount of time ranging from less than five minutes to more than three hours.

You will need to get comfortable having gift conversations in all of these settings. Here, you'll need to be flexible in your planning. If you were hoping for 30 minutes and the donor tells you up front that you have 15, well, you have 15 minutes to make the ask. You have to accept the fact that you're at the mercy of the prospect's schedule and that your pitch has to adapt accordingly.

How Much?

Whether it's $100 or $1,000,000, you need to have a dollar amount in mind when you go into the conversation. I know it sounds obvious, but it's easy to leave the amount open. Don't. You need to offer specific numbers for the donor to consider. Sometimes, a range is appropriate, but you should aim for specific figures whenever possible.

Donors' impressions of a "big" gift can sometimes be, to your organization's standards, quite small. The reverse is also true (and I definitely celebrate and love those donors). It is best not to leave it to chance; place an actual number in their head. If you're asking them simply to renew their previous level of support, or to double it, I would still say the numbers out loud. The truth is that quite often, donors simply don't commit to memory how much they've pledged or given to your organization in the past, and sometimes they cannot remember when they last made a gift. This is true of donors of all levels. I'm not making this up when I say that prospects of mine who have pledged $50,000 can't remember how much they agreed to give. So it is important that you have an ask amount in mind and that you say it out loud in conversation (and then follow up in writing to reconfirm the amount).

Who

Remember: Sometimes, the frontline fundraiser is NOT actually the best person to make the ask. Often enough, it will be the fundraiser, but there are a plethora of other individuals that represent your organization that should also be considered for the actual solicitation. Those individuals can include the executive director (or equivalent), board members, or volunteers. Which other individuals are at your disposal will depend on the type of work that your organization does. Be creative in thinking about who's best to make the ask. Granted, your frontline fundraisers are the default and are the best practiced in making the solicitation, but also keep in mind that sometimes donors don't respond to fundraisers very well. Or that sometimes they feel entitled to a visit from the executive director.[2]

You'll have to be the one to decide who should be making the ask. Again, most of the time, it is the frontline fundraiser, but once in a while the role falls to someone else.

Here's a tip: Make sure that if someone else is making the ask, they have been vetted and coached by you.

Pulling the Trigger: Tips and Tricks

And so you arrive at the actual moment of the actual ask. You've secured the appointment, your plan is to solicit, and you've gotten through all the small talk and other topics in conversation that you wanted to cover. There is nothing left to do but make the ask, to put it out there in the open, and solicit that prospect for money.

While every fundraiser will develop his or her own style and approach, here are a few beginner's tips for that imminent moment, when you're about to pull the trigger.

---

[2]Again, this will be especially true for major and megagifts.

End Every Sentence, in Your Mind (and ONLY in Your Mind) with *"Damn It"*

A strange tip, to be sure, but there's a very sound reason for it. One thing that tends to happen with speaking when people get nervous is that they *upspeak*. Upspeak is when a person begins ending every sentence as though it were a question. It's *really* annoying to listen to and, more importantly, it makes one come off as nervous and weak, thus undermining the donor's confidence. Ending every sentence, again, *only* in your mind, with *damn it* is a simple trick that helps to prevent that. Practice it! "I'd really like you to consider a five year commitment of twenty-five thousand dollars, *damn it*. That level of support would enable our institution to make huge strides in helping to end gang violence in Hartford, *damn it*." Just be super, super careful not to let it slip out when you're actually speaking to your donor!

Speak Slowly

When people get to the ask, they often want to get it over with as quickly as possible. It's a fair enough desire; the ask is often the most nerve-racking part of the fundraising process. People want to get through it with all due speed. However, when you make the actual solicitation, you need to speak clearly and confidently. The confidently part can be achieved with the ending of every sentence with *damn it*. The clearly part must come from practice in slowing yourself down. If you speak too fast, the prospect might not hear you, or worse, misunderstand you. A former colleague of mine once told me that he had meant to ask for $200,000 and, by accident, in a nervous fit, he blurted out the figure of $20,000. The donor said yes. To $20,000.

One good way to slow yourself is to check if you're breathing or not. I know it might sound silly, but when people get nervous, one of the first things they often do is hold their breath. It's the fight-or-flight response kicking in.

Acting 101 again: In a way, fundraising is performance, and stage actors are taught to exaggerate. It is better to be speaking too slowly at this particular juncture in your interaction with your prospect than too quickly. Consciously slow yourself down. Ask yourself—if you can in that moment—if *you* can hear and understand what you're saying. If you cannot, then chances are very good that the donor is also struggling to hear what you have to say.

Let the Silence Hang

Silence is golden. After you make your ask, *shut up*. This rule is just as hard to follow, if not harder, than speaking slowly and avoiding upspeak. Really, though, remaining silent after you make the actual ask with an actual dollar sign is a key strategy. Think of silent time as "thinking time" for your prospect. The prospect is thinking, considering what you have just proposed. As the amount goes up, the amount of thinking time might increase (although it might not). Staying silent can be excruciating, but remember that silence is not a sign that they are saying no. So don't interrupt. Let the prospect begin to visualize him or herself writing that check or signing that pledge form. You will have the urge to interrupt, apologize, clarify, or take it back. Don't do it.

Here are some things that colleagues or peers have reported doing while the silence lingers.

- Making shopping lists
- Singing songs by favorite artists
- Making general observations about the prospect (for example, large gums, small teeth, hairy hands, or, when nervous, blows hair out of eyes)
- Thinking of the first three things to do at home
- Composing poetry

Whatever it is that you need to do to prevent yourself from interjecting during this critical period, do it. Silence can go on for an uncomfortably long time. Sometimes it's a matter of seconds. Sometimes, it can last up to a minute... sometimes more. It will feel like an eternity. Let it.

Don't Make It Sound Weird

Here is another odd tip, one that you'll have to practice. But do practice it. The less weird you make the solicitation sound, whether it's an ask of $25 or $25,000, the less weird the donor will perceive it to be. You have to deliver your ask in such a way that you give the impression that donating a million dollars to your organization is the most natural thing in the world.

If you sound unsure, if you make the amount seem unnaturally high based on your delivery, you're doing yourself a disservice. If the delivery comes off as uncertain, the donor is also immediately uncertain of you and of the idea of giving that amount. Practice the delivery repeatedly, and practice with different figures so that you gain comfort with a range of solicitations.

I speak from experience. My first $10,000 solicitation happened completely by accident and therefore did not go terribly well. It was a phone call from a donor who was asking about making a $2,000 gift for the current fiscal year. Given the enthusiasm of the donor, I wanted to stretch the gift into a five-year pledge of $10,000. I knew from meeting her before that she had the capacity to do so and really had the inclination as well. All I had to do was make a convincing ask.

The problem? The actual words "ten-thousand dollars" had never come out of my mouth before in the context of a solicitation. So I stumbled, and I distinctly remember thinking to myself, *I can't believe I'm actually asking someone for $10,000* and then, immediately afterwards, *did I just ask her for $10,000?*

That is not the reaction you want to be having in your head as you're asking for $10,000. I'm confident that my delivery was subpar, and the polite decline to commit to five years at $2,000 was likely due, at least in part, to my delivery.

Don't Phrase It as a Question

I keep using the word ask, but it's actually a bit misleading in terms of how you should make the actual solicitation. *A good pitch will be 100 percent devoid of question marks.*

Phrasing the solicitation, or the ask, as a question implies uncertainty, and you want as little uncertainty in the room as possible.

Again, here the question of style arises. One colleague of mine, because he is able to pull it off in a way that I can't, tells his prospects, "You should just do it." While I myself am not quite that bold, I do use phrases such as

- I'd like you to consider a gift of …
- I hope that you'll consider a proposal of …
- I would be delighted if you got involved at a level of …
- I'm currently seeking out folks that our organization has targeted as being able to give at a level of … for this project.

You'll find phrases that work for you. The point is to avoid question marks if at all possible.

Overcoming Objections

Remember how I began this chapter? I told you that you're going to get rejected. This section will focus on dealing with the myriad of reasons donors have not to give. There are plenty of them, some of them more valid than others. Objections are a common occurrence in fundraising, so it's best to be prepared to hear them. The nature of the objections will vary based on your organization, but there are common reasons that people say no, not yet, or not that much, all of which can arise no matter the nature of the organization.

When you first hear an objection, your initial reaction might be to retract or to say something immediately. The panic button goes off and you want to escape the situation. You immediately begin to get down on yourself, feeling bad that you're about to go back to your organization empty handed.

Pause. Repeat what you think you heard the prospect say to yourself. Remember to breathe. Remember that rejection is part of the job. Ask yourself if you've heard this rejection before and if you have a response to it.

Before I look at specific objections, let's take a look at two background issues: anger and the nature of the no.

Angry Donors

Oftentimes, our biggest fear is that a prospect will be angry or disappointed with our organization and will berate us the whole time. To this fear, I say two things.

One: It does happen, yes. Donors are sometimes upset with an institution and often it falls to the fundraiser, one of the main public faces of the institution, to take the heat. However, angry prospects will likely make up a small minority of your pool or call list. It's part of the job to deal with angry people, but not the main part of your job.

Two: Angry and upset is actually not as bad as it first sounds. Once you get past the fact that the prospect is angry, you should turn the situation on its head and realize that the prospect is actually presenting you with an opportunity to win back their affection… and dollars! A colleague of mine said that she enjoys those heated conversations because, to use her words, "They become like puppies" if you do the hard work and listen to their grievances and can address them directly, completely, and efficiently, whether during the meeting itself or as a part of your follow up. She has a very valid point: the prospect is yelling at you because they see a problem and they want it solved. It is nothing less than an invitation to impress them. And if you are able to solve the problem, or at least steer the problem down a path towards resolution (if you yourself are not in a capacity to solve it yourself) by connecting the donor to the right folks in your organization, then you really do gain their respect and trust.

Anger implies passionate feeling. If they are angry at the organization, it is because they are emotionally (and, hopefully, philanthropically) invested in the work that you do and the affiliation that they feel as a supporter of the work that you do. If they didn't care about your organization, they wouldn't spend the time getting angry.

I tell new fundraisers that I would rather have five conversations in a row with angry donors than one conversation with a complete dud of a donor that says nothing to me the whole time (and I've had *plenty of both*). Personally, it is much more nerve racking when I'm in a meeting, making a pitch, and the donor just looks and doesn't say anything. Not getting a reaction is for me more difficult than getting a very negative one. I find it harder to read and harder to know where I stand with the prospect.

What Kind of No Is It?

As the number of asks you make increases, you'll be able to discern between hard nos, soft nos, and not yets (and also "not that much [money]!").

Let's begin with the easiest no, the hard no. This response is pretty unequivocal and unambiguous. And believe me, this can happen both on the first visit and after years of cultivational work. A hard no is donors telling you flat out that no, they cannot give at the level you asked for, that they cannot give to your organization—period, and that it isn't worth your time to call them again until well into the future (or never… which is never really never, by the way). If you get this response, you know that you can cross them off your list of calls for the next year (or maybe even two years). It's okay. Dust off and get back up again.

Soft nos are nos in which the donor says no, but after some deliberation and with a visible amount of difficulty. Some cue phrases to listen for are "I wish I could," "I feel really badly saying no," or some other phrase encapsulating this sentiment. When soft nos arise, close the communication loop by asking very specific, pointed questions such as the following:

- Is it the amount that's off?
- Is it the timing that's off?

- Is it the funding area that I pitched?
- Is it an unforeseen circumstance?

You can be so direct as to ask them when in the future a gift of the size that you just solicited might be more appropriate. It's better to be that plain in your follow-up question, so that you can create a clear set of expectations. You're not walking away from the no, and you're gathering intelligence for when that no might convert into a yes.

Now let's take a look at specific types of rejections that tend to come up often enough that I can hear them in my sleep.

Specific, Common Objections

I can't give that much / I can't give at the level I used to give at.

Remember how I kept insisting that you need to have a dollar amount in mind when making the ask? The one potential snag is that if the amount is untenable for the donor at the time, the risk becomes that the donor might feel that since they cannot give at the level solicited, he or she should not make a gift at all. While the logic is faulty, it happens often enough where the donor, unable to give at the exact level I was asking, then feels bad giving less than that and decides not to give at all.

An equally common occurrence is that when you go to resolicit donors for their annual gift at a certain level, they feel that since they cannot support your organization this year at their past giving level, that they need to cut their support altogether. For whatever reasons, giving less than what they used to give can sometimes bear a stigma.

Here, if the donor comes back with the "I can't give at that level," you need to reassure them that gifts of all sizes matter, and that you'd be doing your organization a disservice if you didn't treat gifts of all amounts with the equal amount of gratitude. Using the strength in numbers argument works, and it makes sense to do a little bit of research for this type of rebuttal. Look at your donor roll: what is the sum total of all gifts of $100 and under? $50 and under? $25 and under? You want to be able to tell that donor, "Did you know that all gifts of $50 and under to our organization added up to more than $75,000 last year?"

It is often this kind of argument that helps donors to see that even if they aren't able to support this year at $500, they should still consider participating with a smaller gift.

Avoid calling it a token gift. This can be seen as pejorative. It isn't in and of itself diminutive, but it can inspire a small amount of shame in a donor.

This rebuttal is also very effective when dealing with this objection: "My $25 doesn't really make a difference." Again, if you can come back quickly and say that all gifts under $25 to your organization last year totaled over $30,000, that's pretty compelling. You can say that if every donor that said they only had $25 to give decided not to, that's $30,000 that your organization would not have otherwise received. $30,000 allowed us to do X, Y, and Z.

When I was canvassing on behalf of the DNC in Boston, when I would talk to folks about the impact of their $10 gift, I would tell them a message along the following lines: on a given day on the streets of Boston, I stop about 20, maybe 25 people. If every one of those people gave me $10, that's $200, maybe even $250. Now, I have a team of 5 that are also out with me today. So all of a sudden, we're talking $1,000 or more. But keep going: there are over a dozen other offices across the country that are *also* out on the streets today building support, some with teams of 10 or 15 or more doing exactly what I'm doing.

All of a sudden, a $10 gift has snowballed into tens of thousands of dollars. Granted, the DNC has a huge fundraising operation, but you can still use the snowball or multiplier effect to make your case as to why someone should give *something*, even if they cannot give at the amount that you originally proposed.

I give to other organizations already and am all tapped out.

With any objection, you should be open to the fact that you might not re-but in a way that results in an immediate conversion of a no to a yes. The point of negotiating is, yes, ultimately to get a gift, but in the interim, to sustain the dialogue and to nurture the relationship.

With this particular objection, you need to see where their philanthropic dollars are going. What organizations are they currently supporting? If possible, find out at what dollar level they are supporting, too.

If you don't know the work of the other organizations, ask the donor what they do. Ask why the donor supports them. Ask them what about that organization inspires them to give. If you can, figure out how much.

Figuring out why they support other organizations is important because you have to listen carefully to figure out if there is a good fit for the work that your nonprofit does. Does your organization have a similar or complementary mission to what that donor is supporting?

If it does, then be sure to point that out explicitly, explaining how the work that the other organization does is valid and important, but that supporting your organization, due to the complementary nature of the work that it does vis-à-vis the other one, will help the overall mission of both nonprofits.

Also, be sure to let them know that you appreciate the fact that they are philanthropic generally, even if not to your organization specifically. You want people to continue to behave philanthropically, because relationships and wealth levels change over time. So encourage them, even if you really cannot get them to budge and give to your institution, to continue giving, as the act of giving now is a good indicator of giving in the future.

Earlier, I stressed finding out the level of support that that donor gives to other organizations. I did this because it may or may not be at a level of support that you were hoping to solicit. If, say, the donor boasts that he is giving $5,000 to another organization, you can tell that donor that he can get involved with your organization at a level that is comfortable for him, much like the previous set of rebuttals on not being able to give at the level for which you originally solicited.

I'm not giving because I'm upset with a decision that your organization has made recently.

I'm not giving because I'm disappointed with the leadership of your organization right now.

This one comes up a lot. The way to look at this one positively is that it means that you are dealing with a donor who is following the work that you do. Previously, I talked about dealing with the angry donor, and this is a variation on that situation.

The first thing you need to do is have the donor articulate in his or her own words what is upsetting and why. Don't interrupt. Just listen to the testimony, even if it takes on the form of a rant.

While listening, you need to have an ear towards how accurate his or her perception of the situation is as well as if he or she is putting the grievance into its proper context.

Sometimes, the act of listening is enough to calm people down, to get them back on your side. Oftentimes, asking them to articulate why they were upset diffuses the situation that they had been building up in their mind.

I had a prospect who had supported the institution for years and suddenly stopped giving. I visited with him and asked him why he had stopped. His initial answer was vague: "I don't like the current president or athletics director."

When I pushed him on why, he wasn't really able to come up with anything concrete: he just didn't like them. After realizing that he was just being somewhat petty, and after a discussion of what each person had actually accomplished in their positions, we were able to discuss getting him back on board as a donor.

Very often, an explanation of the decision-making process that resulted in the donor's ire will help. Even if the donor is still in disagreement with why a decision was made, explaining how your organization got to that decision can help. It makes the donor feel like an insider to have the process divulged to him or her. It also helps the donor to see all the stakeholders in your organization that were affected in that decision.

So ask questions, provide context, and, if the donor's perceptions are simply out of sync with reality, delicately and diplomatically explain that they are slightly off in his or her read on things.

The other tactic you can employ here is to refocus the conversation on the positive work that your organization is doing. Don't ignore the fact that the donor is upset. Acknowledge it; honor it. But then see if you can steer the prospect's attention back to the substance of your organization, of the work that you are doing, and why that merits support. In essence, you're asking the donor to hang up his or her hang ups and focus on the big picture: your organization is doing very important work that matters to society and should matter to the donor, and you need that philanthropic support in order to continue achieving your institutional goals.

Granted, there are a myriad of other objections that can come up. These are just some common ones, along with proposed rebuttals that tend to work. Remember that not every rebuttal will turn the conversation around immediately, but it does allow the dialogue to continue and allows you to prove to your prospect that you believe strongly enough in your work and your organization that you want to find a good philanthropic fit for the donor at a time and level that is comfortable for him or her.

So there it is: the ask, dissected and inspected from many angles. We started the chapter with a brief meditation on rejection, and it's my hope that you'll accept it as a part of the trade. I then spoke at length about how the ask will usually engender some level of discomfort, and that that's OK. If the donor is completely comfortable with the solicitation, you are probably low-balling her. I then outlined the various preparatory steps that go into the actual ask, and the considerations of time, setting, solicitor, and amount. We then took a look at some tips and tricks for you to use when pulling the trigger, and then spent some time dealing with rebuttals and how to deal effectively with a number of common ones.

Let's turn our attention now to major gifts and talk about how to ask for those gifts amount your top 20 percent.

Major Gifts

Big Money for Big Projects

Not to sound alarmist, but major gifts will make or break your fundraising shop. The long-term success and sustainability of your operation hinges on your ability to solicit and close major gifts. What's more, any fundraising campaign that you launch with a dollar goal will depend on being able to line up some heavy-hitting donors. This sounds intuitive, and you can set up a fundraising shop with the best of intentions to develop a major gift program. But when you hit the ground running and have to meet annual targets (which have significant budgetary considerations), it can be easy to sell yourself short and neglect your biggest donors.

The good news is that major gifts needn't be a stressful affair. There is a lot to major gifts solicitation that is very similar to soliciting regular gifts. And there is plenty that's different. Don't worry, though. We'll walk through the process of asking for these large, large gifts.

The threshold for major gifts will vary depending on your donor base. I would define it as your top 20 percent in terms of gift size. In this chapter, we'll focus on the top of your gift pyramid, the similarities and differences from the other 80 percent of your donor base, timelines, expectations, a reflection on major gifts since the recession of 2008, and advice on the actual solicitation. I provide an example of a major-gift solicitation in Appendix B.

What's the Same

Let's start with what is the same between major gifts and regular participation gifts.

When I was first recruited to do major gifts, a colleague in the major gifts department said, "It's just adding zeroes." And in some ways, that's a good departure point for beginning to think about major gifts.

So, what's the same? Well, for starters, you're still dealing with people. Yes, they're wealthier than your average donor, but at the end of the day, major gift prospects are just people. Yes, they sometimes get special attention and should get treated differently, but they're not royalty. You don't need to grovel. So that's the first point: it's still a human interaction, and these major donors are still regular people. They just happen to be a bit wealthier than average. There's a balancing act that will happen with each of your major gift prospects in terms of how much you need to stroke their ego.

Secondly, there's an actual ask, just like a participation gift. Granted, the time horizon is longer, but a day still arrives in which you must ask for a philanthropic commitment to your organization.

How you contact them won't change, either—you plan a trip and a call list in the same way you would to plan a trip based solely on participation and annual giving. In short, the first and last steps—the outreach and ask—happen in much the same manner as with any other prospect.

What's Different

There is, however, a good deal that differs in the solicitation of major gifts and the solicitation of participation gifts. The first big difference is the time horizon. On average, a major gift solicitation cycle will take twelve to eighteen months. I know, that sounds like a long time, especially when you're trying to raise money just to keep the doors open and the lights on. Remember, though, this is only for your biggest donors. There is a difference between a high-end annual participation gift and a major gift. (I should also state here that the high-end annual givers of today are the major gift prospects of tomorrow, and they also need special attention, but that's not the focus of our current line of discussion; it is important to note, however.)

Major gifts do take a longer time to close, and that's because you want those gifts to correspond with the core of your organization's goals. If you close a major gift that happens to support something for which there isn't currently a need at your institution, you do a disservice to both your prospect and your institution.

The way that major gifts impact your organization can vary in many more ways than participation gifts. Participation gifts often provide budget-relieving support to your institution in a limited number of areas. Major gifts can range from providing budget relief to creating new programs to transforming an existing program and bringing it to new heights.

It Takes Time

It is in part due to this potentiality that negotiating major gifts takes a longer time. You want the prospect's money, but you want it delivered in such a way that the donor feels good about the gift they are making, and that your organization can use this money effectively. It's of no use to you to close gifts that do little or nothing to enhance your organization's core programming.

This sounds like a no-brainer, but believe me, it can be tougher than you think. There is a burgeoning industry of philanthropic advising, in which companies advise and consult with extremely large foundations on how to effectively give away their money. As an industry peer said to me, as to why such companies exist (and thrive), "It's harder than you think to give away $100 million."

There are snags in major gift work that do not arise in soliciting annual gifts. By the nature of the size of the gift (and sometimes by the accompanying size of the ego), there is often the philanthropic equivalent of strings being attached. The donor will have preferences, and the capacity of your institution to honor these preferences may vary.

Beware the Naming Opportunity Minefield

Let's spend some time talking about naming opportunities, as this is something your institution needs to think about and plan for seriously. What naming opportunities are available for major donors, and what are the giving thresholds at which you will name something? You can name buildings, you can name programs. You can name rooms. You can name staff positions. This work will involve coordination with your stewardship/donor relations staff, as you will need to report on each named fund.

Establishing naming opportunities and thresholds will depend on your current donor base. It doesn't make a lot of sense to set a naming opportunity at $100,000 if you have nobody in your donor base that can give at that level.

On the other hand, naming opportunities do have the ability to raise donors' sights, even if they are not yet able to give at a certain threshold. It lets them know that donors already exist at that level, and that giving at that level would make them one of the top donors to your organization.

Sometimes, when I am reading through the program at certain performances or events and I get to the list of benefactors, broken down by giving level, I see something interesting. There are, as expected, a lot of donors at the lower levels, with fewer and fewer as the gift level rises. This is the gift pyramid playing itself out. Then, I'll see one or more levels at the very top that are *empty*.

It's an interesting strategy, one that I think has value. It's sending a clear signal to donors, most notably to those at the *current* top of the list, that your organization has aspirations to solicit individuals for even more than they are already giving.

Just so you don't think I'm speaking out of both sides of my mouth here, let me reconcile all of this: when setting giving levels, and thresholds for naming opportunities and giving societies, you are limited to the resources within your current donor base. However, this is not to say that you cannot create thresholds or societies for which you do not currently have any support. By doing that, you are revealing your philanthropic hopes and dreams as an institution, as well as providing your donor base with an idea of where your organization is heading.

What is more, your current donor base is ripe for further development. Chances are that a number of your top donors—as well as a good percentage of your mid-range donors—actually have the ability to give far beyond what they are currently giving. The professionalization of your development shop, and the creation of a robust major gifts program, will raise their sights and hopefully empower a number of them to begin giving beyond their already generous levels of financial support.

There will be a temptation, especially early on, to provide naming opportunities at the drop of a hat, and to make exceptions if a donor's giving levels are close enough, or even within reason. There is certainly a good justification for doing this—it keeps donors engaged, makes them happy, and strokes their egos.

But you set a dangerous precedent on two levels. On one level, you are selling yourself short with that particular donor. By making an exception once, you are undermining your donor's confidence in you. This is less of an issue if the donor does not know you made an exception, but it does tend to erode the relationship. Part of you will end up resenting either yourself or the donor for selling the organization short on a pre-established naming opportunity.

It is easy, years down the road, to look back at how you gave away the name of a program or a building for far too little. Assuming that the decision to "sell" it at a lower price doesn't come back to haunt you.

Believe me, when a donor asks how much it costs to name something, part of me, every time, wants to suggest a figure to which I know they'll say yes, even if it's far below what I should be targeting.

You're implicitly saying that it's okay for them to stay at the level at which they are currently giving. And for young nonprofits, it's rarely the case that a donor is giving at their full capacity. If you never ask for more than what they are currently giving, they will never be challenged to step up their philanthropic commitment to your organization.

Not every donor will turn into a major donor—some will stay at their consistent, high-end annual gift, but you at least need to present funding opportunities above their current giving level from time to time.

There is another level at which you sell your organization short: by cutting corners on funding opportunities. You send a bad message to the rest of your donor base. Again, you set a precarious precedent for yourself if word gets out that the price tag on a naming opportunity is negotiable. Whereas, if you go to your next donor and stick to the script, what would happen if the previous donor had been in contact with this one? If the first donor tells the second that he had something named after him for a certain price, how are you going to explain it to the next donor? Will you have to make a second exception?

It gets messy in ways that you can't anticipate. You can control how you communicate with your prospects, but you cannot control how prospects communicate with one another. And you simply can't know who is saying what about your organization. The smaller your donor base, especially your top donor base, the more likely it is that they converse with one another. Circles of wealth tend to overlap, and more so once you begin doing high-end donor events, since the network gets smaller (and the wealth more concentrated).

The final argument against making exceptions to pre-established funding levels is the simplest: there is a donor out there who *will* give at that level. So let the reluctant prospect give at a comfortable level, gracefully decline them the naming opportunity and/or find them an opportunity you've established at a more modest level, and go in search of someone else! It's hard to trust this fact, especially early on in your major gift work, but please believe that there are donors out there who can give you large amounts of money . . . and that with enough training and time, your team will have the ability to solicit these donors for the desired level of funding.

When Priorities Do Not Mesh

A tougher situation than naming opportunities can arise when your donor's interests and your organization's funding priorities do not mesh. At the annual giving/participation gift level, this is generally not a problem—you either have a budget category to which they can make a donation or you don't. But what if someone comes to you with a million dollars and there is no need for what that donor wants to support?

It becomes a bit like a chess match or a tug-of-war, depending on your personality and the donor's. Sometimes there is no match to be made. For example, if you are an organization that promotes the game of squash in poor, urban high schools as a gateway to help get these students into college, and a donor approaches you with a million dollars to build a new swimming pool at your facility for cross-training, chances are the proposal will not be well received.

But what if the situation is a little blurrier? When are you willing to bend for a donor? What if, say, your organization does environmental advocacy work and needs additional office space? A donor comes along who is willing to give you as much money as you need, but she wants to select a friend as the architect, someone not qualified in green design. What then? Do you take the building at the expense of betraying your ideals? Or do you turn the donor away?

The hope is that there is room for negotiation, and that you and your organization can make the case for employing a LEED-certified architect. But if the donor does not budge, what do you do?

This is an ethical question that has no easy answer. I am certainly not about to prescribe a formula that could damage your organization's relationship with a top donor. If there is this level of intransigence, it might make sense to get your governing board to weigh in, or to have a board member/trustee engage the donor or architect directly. Either way, as a fundraiser you need to weigh in on the matter, while also accepting the fact that you might not be the best person to be the ultimate arbiter of the situation. After all, your ultimate goal is to close gifts; you have an understandably skewed view of things. By the very nature of your work, you are more likely to side with the donor. That is more than acceptable; it's your job to do so. It's for this very reason that I'm advising you to kick it up the ladder when you are in the midst of a negotiation this intense. If you're in this situation, it is justifiable to delegate decision making to the higher powers.

While not every major gift will present you with a dilemma of this magnitude, and not every prospect will haggle about the price of a naming opportunity, these are issues that come up with major gift work that simply don't arise with participation gifts or annual giving.

Storytelling and Negotiating: The Essential Skills of a Major Gift Officer

Even if yours is a single-issue advocacy group, you shouldn't discount donors who are giving to other causes. Think creatively about the work your organization does and, if applicable, where you fit into the broader movement.

Here are some questions to help you frame your organization to a donor:

- What is your mission?
- What is the effect of your work?
- What kind of labor goes into creating that effect?
- Which way does your organization lean politically?
- Are there complementary issues to the ones that you are focusing on? For example, if you are an organization focused on increasing literacy rates, and the rate at which teenagers graduate from high school in four years, might you not seek partnerships with organizations focused on educational reform?[1] Have you partnered with other organizations in the past?
- How would the broader movement suffer if your organization were unable to carry out the work that it does?
- What is the profile of the average person affected by the work that your organization does? If you work for a group that helps teenagers cope with the stress of coming out, and a donor's interests aren't necessarily in LGBTQ rights, yet they enjoy helping teenagers overcome depression and suicidal thoughts, then your organization's work can dovetail with their interests. It all depends on how you frame the work that you do. This is one of the skills that a major gift officer must possess: *the ability to see latent connections between a donor and a nonprofit and tease them out, bring them to the surface, and initiate a robust conversation around a philanthropic relationship.* If your organization is focused on clean water and the preservation of lakes, rivers, and

---

[1] This is not an implicit suggestion to steal donors from other nonprofits.

streams in the Pacific Northwest, you probably have an audience among conservationists focused on forests or water-dwelling wildlife. It is up to you to figure out how the pieces fit together, and then how to narrate that in a convincing manner to the donor.

- Do you have any great spokespeople who have directly benefited from the work of your organization? Anyone famous, regionally or nationally?

In addition to these broad, sweeping questions, you also need to think about the minutiae of running your organization: how much does *everything* cost, from the salaries of your staff, to the rental of office space, to the electric bill, to the phone bill, to the cost of mailing printed material.

Tell a Good Story

The really broad questions, and the really small ones, should help you craft a narrative. So much of the work of fundraising at the annual giving level, and especially at the major gift level, is about crafting a compelling narrative, or being a great storyteller. The more details you can include in your story, the more likely you'll connect to a donor. The story should be constructed from the questions posed above, and it should be crafted in such a way that it answers the essential question on a donor's mind: *why should I support your organization with a major gift?*

Storytellers have to keep the attention of their audience, and each audience is different. Most of your major gift conversations will be happening face-to-face, on a 1-to-1 basis—one fundraiser in front of one prospect. You will need to tailor your story to each individual prospect, and this will depend on their history with your organization, their current interests, and, if it's revealed in a meeting, their anticipated future interests and their financial capacity to make philanthropic commitments.

Remember: you can do all the necessary homework and craft a beautiful story, only to have it crash and burn because you either misinterpreted the donor's interests in the past or the donor's interests have changed (and they do—believe me). I've labored over a narrative on athletics, only to have the donor tell me that they're less interested in supporting athletes than they are in supporting scholarships. And vice versa—I've had donors where I thought the conversation was trending towards a gift for financial aid, only to find out that what they really support is the idea of cultivating student athletes—even though the donor was not an athlete at the college.

This is a long way of saying you need to have more than one story at your disposal, in the event that your prospect's interests change.

We tell stories not just because they're interesting, but because they help invite a prospect into your organization; it's a peek behind the curtain. The better crafted your story, the more the prospect will be able to envision helping you, and the more clearly they'll be able to see the impact of their philanthropic relationship. Prospects do not want to feel uncertain about how their money is being spent. A well-told story will explain why you need their money, and also how their money will shape the future work that your organization does.

Take your various funding priorities. Construct a narrative around them that addresses the broader questions posed above. Create a different one for each of your institution's priorities, so that you're prepared for multiple conversations if the donor takes you in a direction you hadn't anticipated.

The Value of a Rough First Draft

Remember the points from Chapter 7 on crafting your written, e-mail, and telephone solicitations? The same elements are needed for a compelling major gift narrative—it's just that the elements are much more individually tailored.

If you're new to the major-gift story game (and I'm assuming that you are), invest in a dry-erase board or butcher block paper. You want to be able to toss down a lot of ideas, answer the questions posed above, and then string these answers together, using your own voice, to create the story of your nonprofit as being the little engine that could—with the appropriate amount of philanthropic support, of course. When writing the first drafts of your major gift narratives, you want to imagine and create freely. Get all the ideas down, even if you think they're half-baked—thus, the dry-erase board or butcher block paper.

When taking that first cut at your major gift narratives, it is a good idea to *overwrite*. Cram in more information than you think you need. Include every-thing that could be relevant, including the kitchen sink. Imagine that your donor is so infinitely patient and so incredibly intelligent that they can make sense of all the nonsense you're throwing down on that dry-erase board.

You don't even have to think in a linear fashion (i.e. in order to do X, we need $Y) when taking that first cut at your narratives. It's okay to think in flow-charts, diagrams, and shapes. Remember: this is brainstorming; this is the dream state; this is pre-verbal and pre-coherence. You'll have time to iron it into a neater form later on.

Let it sit overnight. Come back to it in the morning, and begin paring it down. I'm a firm believer in the value of overwritten and somewhat disorienting first drafts. It's not accidental that they're called "rough" drafts. Don't let your more rational filters get in the way during the rough draft session. Just throw it all down on paper (or the dry erase board). It doesn't matter if you come back the next day and think *what the heck was I thinking?!* For every moment like that, you will likely have one of glorious inspiration, in which you have succeeded in painting a beautiful picture for the donor.

Overwrite, be sloppy, get it all down on paper. It's a good exercise for you to reduce, organize, and distill that psycho-babble into a more compelling and powerful story with fewer words.

Remember: the great painters of yesterday did not go straight to the canvas with their oil paints. They sketched it first, and produced interim versions of the final product (smaller scale studies, pastels) before the final opus took shape. You must approach your narratives, especially at the major gift level, in this way. The great painters needed to produce work that was pleasing to their patrons. For you, as a development officer, your patrons are your prospects.[2]

Take this one step further: create different versions of each narrative for each funding priority. Create one long narrative, rich with examples to support your case. Then create an "elevator pitch" for each, which can be delivered in 90 seconds or less (ideally 60 seconds). Do you have a story that can be told in the time it takes to walk from your desk to the restroom?[3]

Let me expound on brevity, and creating a short narrative. It's important, because it's more difficult and more stressful to make the case for a significant philanthropic commitment when the clock is ticking. All of a sudden the pressure is on and you have to deliver a compelling case if you want this donor to write a check. If you have an hour, it's a bit easier to figure out where her interests lie, and you can build upon her enthusiasm as the conversation goes on. But if time is short, you can find yourself choking.

---

[2] Remember: for all my talk of this as an art form, don't forget that oftentimes donors will want quantitative data on the program they are considering supporting; and they may also want data on their fund once it is established (remember the chapter on stewardship). It is how you weave these numbers into your narrative that will enhance the case for giving.

[3] I have had times where I had to continue talking to a prospect while standing side-by-side at the urinal—no joke. If they don't think it's awkward, go for it. Also, don't call attention to the fact that it is somewhat strange to be pitching while relieving yourself.

So it really does behoove you to craft short pitches for a variety of your organization's funding needs, not only because you sometimes have only five minutes of a donor's time, but because, as you've seen, a donor might throw you a curve ball, and you'll have to speak about something else. What if this happens as the donor is paying the bill, or as you're getting up to leave? What if, as you're walking to the exit, she wants to know about something else that your organization does, and *really* perks up when you start speaking about it?

It's happened to me more than once, where, during a half hour meeting, despite numerous casts, I could not get a donor to bite on anything. I tossed out story after story on what I thought would interest them after doing my homework. I'm not exaggerating when I say that sometimes it is only once the elevator's been called, quite literally, that I mention a certain program in passing, just to kill time while waiting for the elevator doors to open, only to see the donor get really excited about the initiative. Needless to say, my follow up with these donors includes a lot of information on the program I covered in those last 30 seconds together.

To work on your shorter narratives, you have two great resources at your disposal: jokes and the short personal essay. Jokes are good to study because they teach you delivery, timing, and brevity. It's harder to tell a really long joke than it is to tell a short joke. Or you can think of it this way: over the course of a dinner, you have time for an entire standup comedy routine. But if you have only 90 seconds, you have to think of it more like telling a simple joke. Not that roping in donors by telling jokes is an essential skill; it's just that joke-telling is good practice for coming up with short narratives because it trains you to articulate and deliver a message clearly and succinctly.

For help with content and economy of words, you should turn to the short personal essay, which is a narrative form gaining prominence in the literary world, and with good reason. It is hard to pack an entire story into a single page, or even a single paragraph. It's worth reading a few of them, and studying the use of language, to come up with a compelling message. As with the study of joke-telling, be sure to spend some time looking at how the ending of each essay rounds out, or recasts, all that precedes it.

You want your stories to end similarly to these short, personal essays; you want the last lines of your story to force the donor to think broadly about how your organization makes an impact, how it fits into the larger movement, and why they need to get involved right now.

Here are some essays you should read to see what I'm talking about:[4]

- "Wallet" by Allen Woodman
- "Sweethearts" by Jayne Anne Phillips
- "In the Animal Shelter" by Amy Hempel
- "Morning News" by Jerome Stern (a personal favorite of mine)

Take a look at your "leave-behinds." Do you have supporting material for each of your funding priorities in the event that you don't get to talk about everything you were hoping to? Even if you do get to address everything, there is always the possibility that the donor will want something over which to ruminate. Do these materials complement or regurgitate the oral story you are working on?

The case for a major gift lives or dies on the strength of the story. When I first moved from annual giving to major gifts, a colleague, who became my mentor, pithily explained that "the conversations are more philosophical." And that's about as good a summary as I can give, not only for the work of a major gift officer, but also for the distinction between major gifts and annual gifts. Instead of hammering away at the message of participation and the bottom line, major gift conversations necessitate a certain abstraction, more of a bird's eye view of your organization.

Telling Your Story to a Group

Group meetings can be useful as well, especially if you have a group of prospects in the cultivation stage that you're looking to move along. Though most of your meetings for major gift conversations should happen on a 1-to-1 basis, group meetings, as noted earlier in the book, do have their uses.

For a group meeting,[5] you generally want to advise the audience in advance what the topic will be. You can't tailor the narrative to include everyone's specific interests, so you'll really have to focus on either the stories that most effectively highlight your institution's most pressing needs or a narrative that best captures the interests of the majority of prospects on your invite list.

When organizing a group meeting, if there is an invitation that goes out to prospects, it's generally good to have a title for your talk or theme, along

---

[4] Credit to author David Shields for introducing me to these wonderful essays.

[5] This kind of meeting is different from a simple social gathering. A group meeting is generally content rich as opposed to a more general mix-and-mingle.

with a quick paragraph on what you hope to talk about. The reason is to create a clear set of expectations for what the prospects will hear, and to create for yourself an audience legitimately interested in hearing about the given topic.

In these group meetings, be sure to leave plenty of time for a question-and-answer period. It will be up to you to decide how much time to leave, but you want the meeting to turn into a conversation, as opposed to a lecture. Yes, you want to deliver your points and make the case for giving, but the more you allow the group to ask questions, the more tailored the conversation will become and the more it will reflect their interests. And, of equal importance, you will acquire more information, which will enable quality, personalized follow-up.

When to Negotiate

Negotiating with donors when there is a misalignment between your organizational needs and their philanthropic priorities can be tough, and at times downright frustrating, but it is essential work for any good major gift officer. So let's talk about how to fit that square peg into a round hole.

Be prepared: sometimes the match—the fit—just isn't there. The more single-issue oriented your nonprofit is, though, the less likely that is to happen. I am guessing that most people reading this book belong to this type of organization, which focuses on one or two issues for which they advocate strongly.

Negotiations can take many forms. The simplest form is answering the donor's questions regarding the various aspects of the gift, from the timing of the gift, to the allocation of the funds, to the reporting, etc. Be up front with the donor, even if you think she might not like the answer. It isn't worth anyone's time to sugarcoat anything. Yes, an answer might turn a donor off, but it's better to be honest.

As soon as donors start asking questions, the tendency is to get nervous, feeling as though the donors are trying to punch holes in your solicitation. You fear that the conversation is heading downhill, toward rejection. However, this is not necessarily the case. Donors are often genuinely curious about how their gifts will impact the organization. Questions are a *good thing*. They indicate that a donor is interested, and looking for more information. While it's natural to feel uncomfortable when you're barraged with questions, you should take it as a good sign: you've inspired a response, and you have made them curious about continuing the conversation. When they are asking questions, they are beginning to envision themselves doing what you've asked them to do.

So why are storytelling and negotiations lumped together in the same section? Negotiations aren't necessarily born from the stories that you tell, but there's certainly a lot of ammunition from the crafted narrative that you can use. Especially when a short pitch invites a longer conversation, and when the negotiations turn into more than just answering questions.

Having stories at your disposal is the equivalent of having more arrows in your quiver—you will often find yourself drawing upon these narratives in order to build a case when a donor's interests don't align perfectly with your organization's goals.

The situation in which you'll most often find yourself is with a donor who has the capacity, and who has been supporting your organization, but whose philanthropic passion lies elsewhere. The prospect is reluctant to increase his giving because, well, his real interests are, on the surface, outside the scope of what your organization does.

This situation can be described in many different ways, but it will be clear when you're dealing with it because of the frequency with which it arises. The prospect considers himself to be a token donor, and the increased commitment is greeted with hesitation and discomfort.

It's generally my recommendation to zoom out when this happens, much like when you begin thinking of how to tell your story. Again, going back to what my mentor said, it's time to get philosophical and steer the conversation to the big picture, away from the specific solicitation (at least for the moment). If you start the negotiation process with too narrow a focus, on getting a yes or no, you'll be shooting yourself in the foot. Avoid positional bargaining. Positional bargaining happens when you become too focused on the outcome of the conversation—the bottom line, the yes-or-no resolution. If you worry too much about the ultimate "position" of the donor, you will likely walk away empty handed, leaving a donor who is none too impressed with your lack of finesse.

You need to start big and get small. This will involve talking about your core mission in the broadest way possible. Think about the "beating heart" of your organization, and render it explicitly for the donor. If your organization were a person, what would get it out of bed in the morning? Have examples of people who directly benefited from the work that your organization does: think about your poster children, the biggest success stories. Part of a successful philanthropic negotiation is inspiring an on-the-fence donor. Sometimes the inspiration is data-driven: the donor will want to learn about the successes of the program you're asking them to support through the numbers. Sometimes, the inspiration is case-driven: the donor wants to hear an example of a life changed. Sometimes the donor wants both. So, have both types of example at the ready.

Here's an example of a great negotiation from a colleague of mine. One objection that we often encounter with donors who are far from the campus is that the major gift prospect prefers to give locally, since their gift of $100,000 will have a more direct and powerful impact on their community than on some place halfway across the country. My colleague's rebuttal is brilliant. I'm going to do my best to reproduce it for you here, acknowledging, with apologies, that I'm messing up a few words here or there:

> *It's wonderful that you're so philanthropically committed locally, and there will always be a need for that type of support. The reason that I'm here asking for a major commitment to a place like [our school] is so that we can continue to educate the best and the brightest to produce the leaders of tomorrow, who will be able to directly address the societal challenges of the nonprofits you're supporting here in your hometown.*

A short, very sweet response to a very common objection when talking major gifts. A few things make this rebuttal stellar. The first is that my colleague acknowledges out loud his appreciation for the donor's philanthropy, even if it isn't towards our organization. You never want a donor to feel badly for giving money away. Other nonprofits need (and deserve) money just as badly as yours does. By making the donor feel okay with their other outstanding philanthropic commitments, my colleague is now well poised to continue a meaningful dialogue with the prospect.

Now look at how quickly my colleague zooms out, and talks about our organization at the broadest possible level. Without getting into the program for which he was hoping to raise support, without talking about dollar amounts, he focuses for a moment on the mission of our organization: to educate and produce leaders in society.

My colleague, with this rebuttal, has carved a new path in pursuing the conversation with the prospect. He isn't entrenching himself by being overly concerned with the ultimate dollar amount or the program supported. He has invited the donor to walk down a path with him, to see what type of program in our organization might, albeit indirectly, best serve the prospect's philanthropic interests.

Despite my praise for this brilliant rebuttal, I need to be honest and admit that I've never been able to pull it off in a face-to-face meeting. I'm hoping that with enough practice in the mirror I'll be able to use these lines successfully at some point during negotiations.

Negotiations take time, and, often enough, it takes more than one meeting, with no dearth of follow up in between. Much like storytelling, you're building a case for giving, but the difference here is that your audience is much more active and your story has to be more individually tailored.

If you're really lucky, the situation will be such that when the donor thinks that his interests are not represented by the work that your institution does, in reality there are programs that he simply doesn't know about. Then negotiations become easy, and you can let him know how the fit is better than he originally thought. However, this is often not the case, so you'll need to be more creative in making your claim.

Start by listening closely: where do the prospect's philanthropic interests lie? What is he passionate about? Look for potential opportunities for cross-pollination or, again, latent parallels or areas of overlap that you can tease out.

While the parallels will depend on your organization's work and the donor's stated interests, here are some categories that will help you think about how to frame the negotiations:

- Political affiliation or leaning
- General cause (environment and wildlife, education, human rights, athletics)
- Demographics served (age, gender, religion, sexual orientation, minority status, among others)
- Methods of outreach/engagement/effecting change
- Notable affiliate organizations—other nonprofits with whom your organization has partnered, or that do similar work

Once you've thought about these, inform the prospect of the relationship between his interests and the work that your organization does, focusing on the complementary nature of your work and what he is currently supporting. In helping your organization do its job, he will also be helping the work of the organizations he is already supporting.

What you're essentially doing here is using storytelling as a way of negotiating. You're constructing, whether on the spot or in your follow up, an alternate narrative to the original one you pitched. Your follow-up story, your revised, re-tailored narrative, is your offering at the negotiating table. You are finding latent connections, teasing them out for the donor, and then rendering them in an explicit way.

The broader goals of the movement will be achieved through the work that both organizations do, which means that both need philanthropic support.

Here are some examples, some of which you've read about before, of missions that aren't necessarily the same, but which complement one another:

- Organizations that deal with depression, teenage LGBTQ groups that support individuals during the coming-out process, and suicide hotlines
- Affordable housing organizations, homeless shelters, and poverty alleviation nonprofits
- Organizations that promote access to healthy food, soup kitchens, and poverty-alleviation nonprofits
- Nonprofits that concentrate on deforestation and broad-reaching environmental organizations
- Youth sports programs and educational nonprofits
- Civil liberties groups and 1st amendment activist groups
- Politically conservative nonprofits and religious organizations

These are just a few examples of like-minded organizations that might not work together directly, but which you, as a fundraiser, need to be coupling in your own mind as you engage your prospects and hear what interests them in terms of their philanthropic priorities. Again, to the donor these connections might be latent and implicit, but it is up to you as a gift officer to render them explicit.

The other situation that requires no small amount of negotiation, is when you have a major gift prospect who simply isn't terribly philanthropic. They'll give their $25 once a year, or once every few years, despite the fact that your research shows they could easily give your organization five-figure gifts every year.

There are many reasons why people aren't philanthropic: they weren't raised that way, they've never been approached, they simply don't believe in giving things away.

Negotiations become a process of educating the prospect on the importance of philanthropy, and just how critical a role it plays in keeping nonprofits afloat. Again, start broad and then get specific. Begin with a sweeping description of how philanthropic dollars are often the life blood of any major nonprofit, and a very important part of the smaller ones, too. You'll then want to get into the nuts and bolts of how philanthropy impacts your organization. What percentage of your organization's revenue comes in the form of donations? What would happen if that revenue dried up? What would happen if that revenue increased? How would it benefit your organization, and more importantly, how would it increase your organization's efficacy at promoting change, at carrying out its mission? What are concrete examples of how philanthropy affects your organization? Notice here that you've returned to the importance of storytelling.

Not every non-philanthropic prospect will be converted. But just because someone isn't giving now, does not mean that they will never give. I know I've said it before, but you never know when the timing is right until you ask.

Finally, a call for patience—both with the donor and with yourself. You are at the donor's mercy, so you need to be patient as she processes the narrative you have constructed. But you have to be patient with yourself, too. You won't be diving into this work as a master of negotiations. You'll learn through practice—and yes, by messing up a few times. It happens to everyone; ask any veteran of the trade. I'll be the first to admit to fumbling my first few major gift negotiations. You also need to be patient with yourself during the negotiation process because, as I've said before, you are not responsible for the outcome. You are only responsible for making the best possible case for giving. And sometimes, in fundraising, this just isn't enough. And that's okay. You did your best.

Challenge Gifts

One trick that you can use that, *when properly executed*, is a win-win for your annual fund and major gift team is to line up what we call a challenge gift. Challenge gifts can be structured in several different ways, and I'd caution against creating anything too complex. As I've noted before, it's hard enough to keep a donor's attention, much less ask them to do math.

Challenge gifts occur when one donor makes a big gift or pledges a big gift but does so in a way that engages and rallies your "base," which is to say your smaller-league donors. The two simplest ways to structure a challenge are as follows:

- The donor matches all gifts to your organization, dollar for dollar at a rate of 1:1 until the entire value of the pledged gifts from the major donor is drawn.

- The donor pledges a lump sum gift if your organization can clear a
  certain benchmark. Those benchmarks can include:
  - Raising a certain dollar amount by a certain date
  - Getting a certain number of donors by a certain date
  - Increasing the percentage of gifts by a certain amount by a cer-
    tain date

The situation is win-win because it makes your major donor feel very good
about increasing the level of support to your organization and because, well,
hopefully, you're getting new gifts or increased gifts that you wouldn't otherwise get.

The only drawback is that it does create work for your organization. You
want the challenge to bring successful results (and believe me, the donor
really does, too). Making it work will require increased communication from
your office to your donors and prospective donors. You really need to
hammer the message and structure of the challenge through aggressively,
but in a celebratory way. It will take your audience more than one communication to get the message. But it's worth your time, because there's a lot
of money to be had with challenges.

Challenges do work. But again, keep it simple. Put too many rules in place
and it will be distracting. Even more importantly, the data suggests that more
stipulations don't really help increase giving much. It's more the very exis-
tence of the challenge itself that motivates donors to step up and give. Donors give at higher rates and higher amounts when there is a 1:1 match, for
example, than without a match in place. However, there is not necessarily a
discernible increase in giving when the match goes from 1:1 to 2:1. Another
argument for keeping it simple, then: the marginal returns just aren't there.

As great as these gifts can be, it does add work to your plate, so do ask
yourself whether it is worth your time to issue a challenge, or whether it
makes more sense just to try to get the major donor to make a major gift
without all the fanfare. That decision will be up to you and will depend on
your organization's resources.

When it comes to solicitation of a major donor, it isn't the norm to lead
with a challenge gift solicitation. It takes a certain kind of donor and a certain kind of institutional motivation to make a challenge work. So don't go
out and pitch challenge gifts to all your major gift prospects. Just know that
it can be a useful tool for boosting participation towards special projects, or
just to giving you some fresh messaging.

Timelines and Strategies

Let's talk about the timeline engendered by major gift solicitations, which requires patience and more than a little bit of faith.

In Fundraising 101, you're told that major gifts tend to take 12 to 18 months to close. This is an average. It can take less time. And it can take more time. The 12 to 18 months indicates the time from your assessment visit to the solicitation. And sometimes the solicitation can hang there in the ether. Sometimes it gets an immediate yes or no, but it can also be received with silence for a long time.

That year to year-and-a-half requires constant work to reach a close. If your attentions are divided between doing major gift work and other things, expect things to take a bit longer.

You need to come up with a strategy for each of your major gift prospects after you've assessed them and deemed them viable prospects. Here are the questions that need to be asked when coming up with your strategy for a given prospect:

- When will you next visit this prospect face to face?
- Who else from your organization, if anyone, should be brought into the gift conversation?
- How many visits do you anticipate before solicitation?
- What will you communicate to the prospect between visits? What information should they be receiving?
- What areas of your institution do you anticipate this donor supporting?
- Will the solicitation be in person, a written/e-mailed proposal, or a combination of the two?
- Will the prospect be removed from regular solicitations while the gift conversation is going on?

You should keep a master list of anticipated solicitations and track them quarterly, to see if you are on schedule and on track or if adjustments need to be made (and they often do).

By the time you get to the solicitation, your prospect should know what's coming. You never want the major gift solicitation to be a surprise, at least not the timing of it. The donor should know, clearly, that you plan to discuss closing on a gift when you walk into that meeting. The solicitation, the actual ask, is much like a regular ask. What's different is the background work you've done, the cultivation, the months of follow up, and zeroing in on the right area to solicit. Asking really does become just a function of adding zeroes. It's the conversations up to that point, the philosophical level and the storytelling, and the case building that is different, and more elongated.

I'll close out this section with a reminder to practice saying the gift amounts out loud, so that your first time saying "$250,000" is not in front of your prospect. You'll trip or botch the delivery. And that is not the time to trip.

Trends in Major Gifts since 2008

The fall of 2008 saw the biggest financial collapse since the Great Depression. Many industries and individuals have recovered, but at the time of this writing the jury is still out as to how stable the global economy is. With the debt ceiling debate still fresh, and with the current turmoil the European Union finds itself in, it is hard to know if we are really in the clear.

The philanthropic landscape looks very different today than it did in 2007. The good news is that there are exceptions to trends, and you shouldn't leave this section feeling despondent.

There are two very noticeable trends. One is that it is taking longer to close major gifts. Prospects are more reluctant to part with their money, even if they have recovered their lost wealth. The uncertainty in the economy makes it hard for people to predict what their portfolios will look like in two years.

The other trend is that it is hard to get multi-year pledges. This can be problematic when you're trying to build a fund over a three-to-five-year period. But many folks simply aren't willing to sign pledge forms these days, for the same reason that they're not willing to give away what they once had no problems in relinquishing.

The positive thing is that this is not a secret to anyone. And since there has been so much news about how badly nonprofits have been struggling during this economic downturn, it is easier to make the case for why you need money. The other side of this though is that other nonprofits are likely knocking on a prospect's door with the same message.

In short, it's a tougher environment than it once was for major gift work. Your once reliable prospects might not be as reliable now. You may need to go deeper into your call list, digging deeper into the B list than you once had to.

But don't despair. I just want you to have a realistic idea of what you're up against. There are still prospects out there with money to give away, and lots of it. And eventually they will pledge a five-year commitment. It's just going to require a little more patience, a lot more digging, and really good storytelling.

Political Fundraising

Or, How to Get Yourself into Trouble in Ten Easy Steps

Campaign finance is an oft-discussed and equally oft-misunderstood topic. It's a hot-button issue and is sure to stir up the passions of everyone on both sides of the debate. It's not my job here to talk about what's wrong or right with the current system, but rather to do my best to help you understand what's at stake, and how political fundraising is very much the same and also very different from your average, run-of-the-mill nonprofit fundraising.

First, the Good News

The good news is that campaign contributions are viewed by the courts, thus far, as free speech, and therefore are protected by the First Amendment. This means that, as a political organization, you generally have the law on your side with respect to unhindered fundraising. That is one thing that has usually been consistent about campaign contributions, particularly from individuals, even if there are limits to what an individual can contribute to a party, PAC (political action committee), or candidate in a given year. With the demise of soft money contributions from corporations, gifts from individuals have been allowed, with limitations, for quite some time (although now, with the advent of "super-PACs," it remains to be seen whether soft money might make a *de facto* comeback). The legal history is rich and fascinating, and far too complex for me to do any justice in this chapter. Just know that It's easy to get yourself into trouble, either with your supporters or with the law.

In this chapter, we'll begin by talking about a few qualities of political fundraising that are distinct from the rest of the nonprofit world. We'll then move on to discuss fundraising strategies for parties, PACs, and candidates. We'll end with a meditation on what to do about the post-election fundraising hangover, which in essence is to take two aspirin, hydrate, and keep going.

What's Different from "Regular" Nonprofit Fundraising

Let's begin by discussing some properties of political fundraising that differ from the rest of the nonprofit world. We'll discuss the visibility of campaign contributions, the temptation involved with campaign contributions, the incumbent's edge in fundraising and exposure, and the pace of political fundraising.

Visibility

The most immediate difference in political fundraising is just how public the information is. Even though the posting of information is delayed, you can easily browse the flow of political contributions with a simple visit to Open Secrets (www.opensecrets.org). My one piece of advice is that you don't visit the site unless you have more than an hour. It's so easy to get lost in the wealth of information (in a good way, of course). The site itself is fascinating because of the level of detail. You can see how much an individual gave to the Republican National Committee, for example, as well as a detailed breakdown of a certain representative's donor roll. It's a wild trip, and well worth the time if you're considering raising money for a candidate, a PAC, or a local political party. This website will leave you with absolutely zero doubt that political contributions are public information, accessible to anyone who wants to see them (you cannot give more than $50 anonymously[1]).

---

[1] http://www.fec.gov/pages/brochures/citizens.shtml

Temptation

The potential for *moral hazard* is also much higher in political and campaign fundraising because of a little term which you should commit to memory: *quid pro quo*. Quid pro quo is your mortal enemy and should be avoided. For you non-Latin scholars, quid pro quo means, in short, something for something. I give you a campaign contribution so that you break the backs of unions in your district. I write your party a big check to alter its stance on gay marriage. It can be hard to prove that a political decision or action was quid pro quo, but if it is proven, you will get nailed. Have no doubt.

It can be tempting for any nonprofit to overpromise, but this is especially true for a political party, PAC, or candidate, and all the more so if a big gift is dangling in front of you. History suggests that, although it's somewhat fuzzy, a line does nonetheless exist between allowing a donor extra face time with you, and promising outright or at least implicitly suggesting that they will get what they want because of their campaign contributions. The general rule should be that if it feels even the slightest bit off, you'd better reject the gift, or say very explicitly (publicly and written down, so that it can be tracked) that you are in no way making policy decisions based on a political contribution. It's so easy to enter office with the purest of intentions. However, reelection is always a consideration, and with the need to amass funds for your "war chest," as it's often called, you may find yourself in a compromised position.

Velocity

It is hard to overstate how quickly a fundraising shop in the political world can start running at breakneck speed. While this isn't necessarily different from other charitable fundraising, it is exaggerated in political campaign fundraising. This is owed in large part to the pace of the election cycle. It is difficult to exaggerate how hard candidates work to raise money for their campaigns. This is on top of the other tasks that they have (public-speaking engagements, town hall meetings, strategizing with staff, and, for incumbents, actually participating in the political process). It's a grueling schedule, and one that's usually carried out only with the help of competent staff who then in turn delegate to vetted volunteers.

The Incumbent Advantage

It might interest you to know that the majority of contributions from PACs, lobbyists, and lobbying organizations aren't necessarily partisan in nature.

Rather, the incumbent candidate or party enjoys a severe fundraising advantage. What this means for you if you are a candidate challenging an incumbent is that you are faced with a unique set of obstacles in raising money—you are immediately disadvantaged by virtue of your status as an outsider. That isn't to say that it is impossible to raise money with equal efficiency, just that you're going to have to work a little bit harder (or maybe a lot harder).

You should feel free to use this fact in your appeals to your donors: you face an uphill battle against the incumbent, who already has a fundraising machine in place. It's common enough practice to compare the size of your "war chest" to your opponent's. The underdog message can really sell.

Incumbents, or newly elected officials, you can expect this fundraising edge to bring with it the temptations I mentioned above.

Of course, certain lobbies make contributions to both sides of the aisle as a way to hedge against unfavorable outcomes (again, you can check out Open Secrets if you doubt this). The implication here is that there is the hope, on the part of the donor, that campaign contributions do influence policy decisions. Even smaller donors hold on to the belief that if enough of them give, they'll form a powerful base of support which must be heeded by policymakers. A look at the 2008 Obama campaign suggests that his marketing team understood this. (While he did raise a ton of money from small contributions, his campaign was not lacking in larger contributions. Nor was the Democratic National Committee.)

Again, I can bark at you all day on how important it is to retain a healthy knowledge of this, but it's easy to forget and easy to get greedy when you see your opponent out-fundraising you.

Thus, to a degree much more pronounced than with other nonprofits, you need to communicate clearly what donating to your campaign will *not* do for interested lobbies, individuals, and other groups. It is better to leave money on the table than to compromise your integrity (or break the law).

Recognition in the Marketplace

The second advantage of an incumbent is in the competition for exposure and name recognition. As noted, incumbents have a significant advantage in terms of their ability to fundraise, and the statistics for the reelection of incumbents who have served at least two terms are pretty discouraging for challengers. What's more, the incumbent already has the name recognition that an unelected challenger doesn't, and has a policy record (which, admittedly, could be good or bad).

Even in open elections, though, when an incumbent steps down and all parties are new to the game, it is hard at first to get any sort of name recognition. Then after that, it is hard to communicate your platform in such a way that people understand what you would do if elected.

The good news in US politics is that the two-party system, at least in many districts, makes it somewhat easier for folks to decide how they're going to vote. The two main political parties that we have here in the US, as imperfect as they might be and as imperfect as the two-party system itself might be, do help voters order their priorities. The party system provides them with a calculus on how to vote without doing significant research into each candidate.

This of course raises the question of whether raising money is important at all, and whether or not it's necessary to maintain the breakneck pace of campaign fundraising just to keep up with your competition. Let's assume, boldly, that fundraising does matter, so that we can focus on how to do a good job of it come election season.[2] (And, by the way, it's *always* election season.)

Getting recognized is a herculean task, to be sure. Even if the two-party system does help you with the general elections, you'll still have to win the primaries, and before that you have to get on the ballot. These steps require a concerted effort at putting yourself out there, both to get exposure and to get money.

One final way in which campaign fundraising is distinct from other nonprofit fundraising is the zero sum nature of it. Whereas raising money for a women's shelter does not preclude the same donor from giving to, say, PETA, giving to one candidate usually does imply that a donor won't be making a gift to the opposing candidate. Taking that to the next level, whereas the success of the group that promotes healthy after-school activities does not preclude the success of the group that helps raise awareness about college among high school students, the election of one candidate does preclude the other candidate from holding office. In other words, there is a more heightened sense of competition.

Thus, when crafting your message to potential donors, you need to be able to tell folks not only who you are and what you represent, but also how you are better than the other candidate.

---

[2] Some data suggest that the general public puts more weight on how much a party or candidate raises, and less importance on how a party or candidate spends that money.

Canvassing: Because Every Army Needs an Infantry

Let's spend some time now discussing the slow, arduous process of getting name recognition, how to get it and how it segues into asking for money.

When I was fundraising in Boston, I had the privilege of having former Massachusetts State Senator Jarrett Barrios speak to my team of fundraisers, and he offered some inside advice on how to run a successful campaign.

It might not come as a surprise that the most effective way to raise awareness and to get money and votes is also the least efficient: going door-to-door. The most effective person for this job will also find it a strange use of time: the candidate himself or herself. It's very simple: candidates can best speak for their decisions or platform, and can most easily dispel rumors and put a prospective donor or voter at ease. Controlling the message becomes exponentially more difficult as the chain of communication gets passed from full-time staff, to paid canvasser, to volunteer.

If you're a candidate, investing in a door-to-door campaign effort can seem, on the surface, to be a bad use of your time and limited resources. But it makes sense to go door-to-door or to place yourself in busy sections of town to stop folks and have face-to-face conversations, especially at the local and regional levels. More than in other nonprofits, the practice of *movement-building* in campaign fundraising, particularly the direct action type, must be adopted.

Movement-building—what a broad, sweeping term, right? How do we go about building this movement of support? The answer is as simple as it is frustrating: you have to have one-on-one conversations with as many people as possible.

While this can be achieved in part online, via mail, and via phone, there is no substitute for a face-to-face conversation. This is a very annoying, hard to accept truth, but it is a truth nonetheless. Especially in this day and age, in which people's inboxes are so inundated with e-mails, and, more often than not, your phone call will be screened, the face-to-face conversation may be the only time you'll have someone's undivided attention.[3]

Yes, you can contact more people by phone or e-mail in a given hour than you can by standing at busy intersections or knocking on doors—but a call or an e-mail is also easier to ignore.

---

[3]Again, this is why most major gift conversations happen face-to-face and not over the phone or via e-mail.

Let's look at recent history, and turn to one of our nation's better modern organizers. César Chávez was the civil rights activist who founded what would become the United Farm Workers. The story goes that a student once asked Chávez how he organized.

His response: "First, I talk to one person. Then I talk to another person."

The student objected, saying, "No, how do you *organize?*"

Chávez responded again: "First, I talk to one person, then I talk to another person."

Given his success at mobilizing, I think we can feel safe in heeding his model. Talk to one person, and then talk to another.

In the modern political fundraising campaign, your canvassers are those interlocutors, your conversational infantry who are out on the streets or going door-to-door talking to people about your campaign and, yes, ultimately building financial support for it.

I spent some time at the very beginning of the book explaining how the financial model of canvassing works, but it makes sense in this particular conversation to take a second look at how and why it works.

If you have the resources to do so, it makes sense to pay your canvassers. It increases their incentive to do a good job, plain and simple. Incentivizing the pay scale such that the top 20 percent of your canvassers get paid more can sometimes make sense, but then you invite cheating. There's a fine balance between providing incentives to raise a ton of money and inviting questionable practices among your canvassers. Of course, if you simply don't have the resources to pay canvassers, you *should* be able to staff your canvassing corps with volunteer labor. The young and the old usually have the time and gumption to get out there to help during campaign time.

When it comes to recruiting, either volunteers or paid canvassers, you have to be aggressive to the point of being ruthless. You need to place recruitment posters everywhere that it's legal to post them, you need to be online, both via your website and via Craigslist, as well as other local services and social media (Facebook, Twitter, etc.), and you need to have someone available to answer phone or e-mail inquiries for as many hours of the day as you can. Get them in the door as quickly as possible, and get them hired as quickly as possible.

This might come as a shock, but the financial model of canvassing presupposes that your door-to-door and street operations will very likely lose money if you pay your canvassers. At the movement-building level, the first solicitation is an investment, not a money maker. So why do it?

Granted, you want your paid or volunteer canvassers to bring in as much money as possible, but more than that, you want contact information. Any contributions that you get during the information collection will just be to help offset the costs of the canvasser's pay if they're paid. If they're not, well, then it is a money maker.

The fact that a paid canvassing operation often loses money is an unglamorous truth, and it might not please your canvassers to know this. I wouldn't recommend being too public about this, although do of course tell the truth if asked. And if you are asked about it, please take the time to explain the context, the canvassers' role, and their importance.

You really do want to push your canvassers to not just take money, but also get phone, e-mail, and mailing information. Why? Because this information will be needed for the follow-up solicitation, which is much easier to do and will be where you really start making money.

The contribution form should be an entire 8.5 x 11 inch sheet, so that there is room to write large and legibly, and it should include a credit card form if your office has the capacity to process credit cards (it should). As quickly as is humanly possible for your office, you want the contact information entered centrally where it's easily accessible (but secure, to be sure). This is both so that you can thank your donors as quickly as possible, and also so that you can begin implementing stage two of building your movement/following: the follow-up phone and e-mail solicitations.

Before we visit the topics of phone and e-mail solicitations, let's round out this section by asking you to train and empower your canvassers to be compelling spokespeople beyond the act of asking for money. You need them to be able to articulate your stances on certain hot-button issues and have adequate ammunition to defend those stances. Take time with them; listen to their grievances, and ask them to give you feedback from the road. After all, they are in the trenches every day on your behalf.

Campaign Messaging: What's the Same, and a Defense of Simplicity

We've covered how to write effective phone scripts and e-mail solicitations in previous chapters, but I want to again stress just how quickly you have to move in a campaign setting. It's hard to exaggerate just how fast the pace in a campaign office is. The good news is that there's plenty of young talent out there looking for campaign experience, plenty of folks who have retired and have free time on their hands, and no dearth of good souls who just want to help out.

When crafting your messages for canvassing, e-mail, and phone, you need to find the right balance of communicating your own agenda and juxtaposing it with the inferior agenda of your competitor. (Remember, campaigns are a zero sum game; if your challenger wins, you lose.) It's so easy to get too negative, and I'd advise against it. Focus on how you're better instead of how the other candidate is worse. This is a subtle but important distinction. You need to have these scripts and templates written before your campaign starts; you'll simply run out of time if you're trying to compose them after you've started fundraising on the streets and in your local neighborhoods. Have them canned in advance so that once you have the data entered from your canvassing operations, you can immediately begin your followup contacts.

Whereas with other types of nonprofit work you want to avoid overcommunication lest you alienate your donor base, with political campaign fundraising, I'd argue that you can get away with a little more frequent contact given the very small window of activity. Whereas calling every day might alienate your base and cost you votes (and money), you will be able to e-mail often. Every e-mail that you send should include a solicitation, but you won't want every e-mail to be only a solicitation. You should include quick, brief reports on the campaign, where you are relative to your competition, public speaking engagements you'd like them attend, and so forth.

Political campaigns, because they are deadline driven more than any other nonprofit fundraising work, will see a huge groundswell of activity followed by a very quick dismantling of the shop afterward. This is a continuation on the theme of just how quickly you need to be able to move, how many hours a day you need to be putting in, and how you need to be able to adjust from an office of you and a handful of staffers to an entire cadre of paid or volunteer fundraisers that is bulging at the seams, outgrowing your original office headquarters. This is to say nothing of the rest of your political team, which you'll also need of course.

It's a strange cycle. Because of the increased competition for dollars and attention, your constituency is inundated with messages from both sides. Thus, it's best to keep your campaign messages simple. Again, a look at recent electoral history, particularly with the presidential elections, demonstrates just how overly simplistic those messages become, to the point of becoming little more than platitudes. In 2004, President Bush won on the theme of "America is safer." In 2008, President Obama ran on the themes of *change* and *hope*. Of course, those are little more than empty words when it comes to the actual political process in Washington, DC, but that's not the point. The point is that their themes were actually driven into the heads of American voters. In contrast, can you recall John Kerry's message in 2004? Or Hilary Clinton's during the Democratic primaries in 2008?[4]

Remember in the chapter on crafting your message how I distinguished between times when you have to keep it simple, and times when it makes more sense to expound upon your organization's mission? The same applies here: your campaign posters and yard signs need to be mind-numbingly consistent and simple. Save the explanation of your platform for debates, speeches, one-on-one meetings, fundraising, and get-out-the-vote phone calls.

Oh yeah, remember that other thing I said even earlier in the book about hanging up your guilt and shame? That effective fundraising isn't about being cool, and in fact engenders a certain level of discomfort? No better place does that apply than in the context of politics. You're more likely in this type of fundraising work to feel like you're being too pushy, like you're being a little too over-the-top in your frequency and enthusiasm, and that your staff is, too. I'd say that's normal—you are, after all, soliciting with a far greater frequency, directness, and urgency than a normal nonprofit (the exception being when legislation or a certain watershed event is presenting a very clear and urgent threat to the work of a specific nonprofit).

The overarching point is that you need to be aggressive and ethical—a very fine, nearly impossible balance. The good news is that in our current political system, your audience is preconditioned to assume that you're going to ask them for money, which makes it that much easier to put out your hand and ask for help.

An interesting thing to note here is the paradoxical nature of building up a huge war chest. Your ability to fundraise is an indication of your success at running a good campaign and therefore of your viability as a candidate (I dislike the term "electability"—there is very little reliable data that can reveal any identifiable notion of electability). The irony is that spending that money can be seen as a sign of weakness, of an implicit admittance that your campaign isn't going too well, and you need to do a media blitz to boost the numbers again. The research on the subject is imperfect, but there is the suggestion that if it's clear that you're spending down the reserves, your constituency's confidence in your ability to win diminishes. The bad news is

---

[4]Once, when on business in San Francisco, I observed a candidate trying to gather signatures to get himself on the ballot. He was standing outside a BART station, canvassing for himself. He said three things: 1) his name, 2) that he was trying to get on the ballot, and 3) that he was against the death penalty. Oversimplistic? Maybe, but how else are you going to stop rush hour pedestrian traffic other than with simple sound bites?

that I'm not qualified to tell you how to spend your money strategically. I can only tell you how to raise it.

The takeaway message from this section should be that the fundamentals of political campaign fundraising don't differ all that much from other nonprofit fundraising in the strategy, the messaging, and the need. What do differ are the intensity, the pace, the volume, and the aggressiveness with which it is carried out.

Parties, PACs, and Candidates: How the Strategies Vary

The basics of how to solicit for a party, PAC, or candidate, in terms of how to craft your message and build your base, are similar to those of the strategies laid forth for other nonprofits. And the differences between fundraising for parties, PACs, and candidates aren't huge, but there are a few things I'd like to highlight nonetheless.

If anything, PACs and single-issue political groups probably overlap the most with other nonprofits in that they are often focused more narrowly than political parties or candidates. Even if a candidate is making a name for himself or herself on a single issue, he or she can't escape the fact that governance is about more than just any one thing. You can treat fundraising almost like that of any other nonprofit, with the preceding caveats on pace.

The candidate and party face messaging challenges that single-issue political groups and PACs do not face. The tension is in how to cover all of your bases without diluting yourself completely. On the one hand, you need to have a stance on all the issues so that you can appeal to as many people as possible. On the other hand, you want your image and message to be simple, clear, and digestible. Again, this is part of why the two-party system, for all of its problems, does actually serve a very good purpose. The Democratic Party and the Republican Party both have official stances on most issues. Unless you, as a candidate, are extremely vocal about bucking the trend on a given issue, it's likely that voters and donors are going to conflate the party's stance with your own views.

However, you'll need to do some research to figure out the issues on people's minds and really amplify your stance on these issues vocally. As I've said, the competition for people's attention spans, particularly surrounding politics, is very steep. You can't waste your time talking about where you stand on everything. You need to concentrate what limited resources you have for hammering through a message to an audience with very limited time to listen to politics. This data can be gathered by your own staff, or by listening to the news. Be careful, though—every survey has its own imperfections and biases. You can rely on data to help you steer your messaging and winnow down the myriad of issues or themes out there to a select few upon which you should concentrate. (Clinton era: economy. G. W. Bush era: security. Obama 2008 election: change.)

When it comes to your general messaging, again, err on the side of oversimplification. There is such temptation to address everything, to say it all, to let people know that you have clearly thought out justifiable stances on everything. There is a time for that, at public-speaking events, large gatherings, and one-on-one meetings held either by you directly or your staff. But when you're crafting appeals, you want simplicity and consistency. You want the scripts of your canvassers, your telephone fundraisers, and your e-mails to overlap significantly. It will seem *very* repetitive to you, but believe me, *the public spends such little time thinking about it that they will hardly notice.* With so much going on in people's lives, and so little time to devote to thinking systematically about politics, when it comes to political fundraising and message, they want the bottom line.

In 2006, when I was fundraising on behalf of the DNC (Democratic National Committee), every canvasser was given a script, or a rap as we called it. While each canvasser had their own style and delivery, we did ask them to stick to the rap as much as possible.

The telephone scripts, in turn, repeated and complemented the content of the canvassing rap. In fact, since all of the gifts are coded so that you can track the sources from which they came, there was a specific part in the telephone script for donors who had given to canvassers. The e-mail appeals also displayed a very clear continuity. The donor can be thanked for giving to a canvasser, to a telephone fundraiser, or for giving online, before delivering the message.

Controlling the message is extremely important, particularly in political campaign fundraising. It can also be an impossible task once you have delegated your fundraising operations to paid canvassers or telephone fundraisers, or to volunteers. At some point, you relinquish having 100 percent control, but you can take steps to assure that your fundraisers don't turn into loose cannons.

Take the time to train them up, provide them with the script, and explain the importance of staying on-point and on-message. Explain that you want consistency, for the preceding reasons laid out for you.

Spend time with your fundraisers. Thank them often. And be sure to answer their questions on matters outside the script, so that they can feel like confident spokespeople when questions do arise beyond the scope of the script.

A reminder: *Take your fundraisers' feedback seriously.* They are the ones getting in people's faces every day, hearing what's going on, and getting the opinions of your voter base. Nothing will get a person to speak their mind on political matters like asking them for money. Many of us can be reticent to share our political opinions, but when asked to support a campaign, a party, or a candidate, we take it as an opportunity to vent about everything that's wrong with the system, the candidate, the opposition, and so on. So empower your fundraisers to listen carefully to what the donors are saying, and take it into account. Don't be dismissive. They're doing the hard work for you.

Of course, you as a candidate will have to do a good deal of fundraising on your own, especially for the larger gifts. This can be accomplished both by individual calls or visits and in group settings (dinners, etc.) where there is a very clear indication that the group will be solicited (or charged ahead of time). You can refer back to the chapter on major gifts for tips on how to approach these higher-level conversations.

Given this allusion to major gifts, I want to end this section with a reminder about the legal issue of *quid pro quo.* Remember, this is a book about philanthropy. You want donors that are giving to you out of goodness and out of a desire to help your cause, your party, or your campaign. You do not want donors that are giving with the expectation of getting anything in return (except, of course, a nice thank you note).

Political campaign fundraising can be harder than any other type of fundraising to keep clean. Donors don't even enjoy a tax break, so there's even less of a tangible benefit for their giving. You will get people who offer you varying sums of money to change your stance on this or that.

You will need to remind these people that your office is not for sale, nor are your policies. And yes, from an ethical standpoint, you need to turn that money down.

Other times, it won't be as explicit as a demand like that, but if it even begins to feel questionable, err on the side of caution. Take the high road.

After the Election ...

Once the election is over and your shop closes up, you either jump for joy at being elected, or get to reflect the morning after on what you could have done differently. You dust off, carry on, and forget about fundraising, right?

Incorrect. I was fundraising in Boston for the 2006 midterm elections, on the streets during the summer and door-to-door in the late fall. After the Democrats won both houses of Congress, my colleagues were understandably ecstatic—but we also knew that there was little time to rest. The day after the elections, the Republican National Committee was aggressively fundraising, building toward 2008. Foe though they might have been, it was exemplary, *inspirational* even. They had just lost, and they were out there within less than 24 hours with the clear message that they were not giving up on their long-term hopes.

The week after the elections, the organization I worked for had a retreat in Washington, DC. While we were all happy and the retreat was one of general pride in the work we had done, it was without question a working retreat, in which we spent many an hour in groups working out how to craft the next message, which was very different now that the left held the majority in both the House of Representatives and the Senate. We had to rewrite our scripts, and had to acknowledge that in a way, fundraising for the DNC would actually be a little more difficult than it was in 2006, especially before the 2008 primaries determined who the Democratic presidential candidate would be. All of a sudden, the message was a little more abstract, a little more intellectual than the basic gist of our midterm message, which had been "We need to control the House and Senate."

If you win the election, as we did in 2006, after thanking your donor base for making the victory possible, you do need to restart. This means thinking critically about your new message, which will be different and difficult now that you hold office, and cautiously but not timidly beginning to resolicit for the next election cycle. With only two years between certain types of elections, there really isn't all that much down time.

If you lose the election and are even half-serious about running again, you'd best follow the example of the Republican National Committee in 2006 and get right back on your feet to start asking for money for the next challenge. A certain amount of rebranding might be necessary, given that your current image/message/platform wasn't as effective as it could have been (after all, you lost), but what won't change is your need for funding. As I said above, the victor in this case will have an edge over you when it comes to receiving money from sources such as PACs and lobbies, so you'll have some catching up to do and will have to get creative to compensate for that gap.

For all I talk about aggressive approaches to political fundraising, I want to remind you to think about stewardship during the postelection hangover. It is a little easier to forget about this important piece of the pie when you're running a round-the-clock fundraising shop on a shoestring budget.

Whereas really stellar fundraising establishes a relationship between the donor and the organization that is founded upon, but not exclusive to, the monetary realm, I'd argue that in political fundraising, it's really hard to build upon those relationships at the grassroots level. Be extremely careful not to have the only contact with your donors be a thinly veiled resolicitation. I know that's somewhat contradictory to what I said earlier, but once the tunnel-visioned, adrenaline-filled rush to election day is over—in addition to taking some time to strategize, reconstruct, and eventually get back out there—you need to build in some time for some substantive stewardship.

The reason is the same as for any other nonprofit. You are in a much better position to resolicit come the next election cycle if you do a good, thoughtful job of thanking the folks that either helped you win, or helped you put up a good strong fight to the finish. And you'll need to resolicit them sooner rather than later, so you need to thank them sooner rather than later, too!

Charity, Advocacy Group, or Both?

Some Technical and Legal Considerations

Let's close by focusing on more technical and legal elements that you'll need to consider, for example where your organization fits into the greater world of the nonprofit kingdom, doing your homework with the IRS, and what to do when the tax code is not on your side.

I am somewhat loath to create an entire taxonomy of strategies depending on what niche in the nonprofit universe you inhabit, as I run the risk of creating unnecessary confusion, not to mention the risk of becoming quite redundant.

The truth of the matter is that a majority of the principles that I laid forth in previous chapters regarding strategies on crafting messages, travel, etc., will apply no matter what type of organization that you happen to represent. This will therefore be a somewhat shorter chapter than the previous few.

This chapter will begin by taking a look at how the pie of philanthropic dollars is divided up. I'll then spend some time exploring the jungle of the IRS's definitions of various 501(c) organizations. I will then discuss what happens when contributions to your nonprofit are not tax deductible (hint: not too much will change). I'll round out the chapter by revisiting some basic principles that will apply to all types of nonprofits, regardless of mission.

Who Gets What

Let's begin by taking a look at where philanthropic dollars went in 2010 in the US, to give you an idea of where your nonprofit stacks up in terms of the competition for charitable gifts. Table 13-1 gives you an idea of the distribution of philanthropic dollars in 2010.

Table 13-1. Distribution of US Philanthropic Dollars by Industry in 2010[1]

Recipient Organization	Percentage	Dollars (in billions)
Religion	35%	$ 100.63
Education	14%	$ 41.67
Foundations	11%	$ 33.00
Human Services	9%	$ 26.49
Public-Society/ Benefit	8%	$ 24.24
Health	8%	$ 22.83
International Affairs	5%	$ 15.77
Arts, Culture, Humanities	5%	$ 13.28
Environment/Animals	2%	$ 6.66
To individuals	2%	$ 4.20
Unallocated	1%	$ 2.12
Total	100%	$ 290.89

In short, it's great to be a church, a mosque, a synagogue, or a school. Almost half of all philanthropic dollars went to these types of organizations. Granted, within those groups, you have plenty of subcategories, but if your organization falls within one of the other categories mentioned, well, you lack the comparative advantage of religion and education. The good news is that even if you're working for an arts nonprofit, there's still, in absolute

---

[1] Source: Giving USA Foundation 2011 Executive Summary (www.givingusareports.org/)

terms, a ton of money to go around. You just have to get out there and get it. However, you might have to work a little harder than a college, a foundation, or a church.

I included this section not to discourage you. It's educational and sobering to know where you stack up and to realize that regardless of where your organization stands in this arrangement, that there is still plenty of private funding for your nonprofit, allowing you to secure gifts of all sizes regardless of your stated mission.

The Wonderful World of IRS Definitions

It makes sense to spend a little bit of time talking about whether or not you should be filed with the IRS as a 501(c)(3) or a 501(c)(4). It is not necessarily the easiest thing to understand. It is possible that your organization has already done its homework and done the appropriate research and filing, but in the event that it hasn't, this section will provide you with the information you'll need to keep the IRS happy.

501(c)(3)s are defined by the IRS as entities that are organized exclusively for one or more of the following purposes:

- Religious
- Charitable
- Scientific
- Testing for public safety
- Literary
- Educational
- Fostering national or international sports competition (as long as the activities do not include providing facilities or equipment)
- Preventing cruelty to children or animals

501(c)(3) organizations qualify to have their charitable gifts deducted from their donors' federal income tax.

You can find out if your organization is listed as exempt under 501(c)(3) by visiting the IRS's web site. If you are not, you'll need to file IRS form 1023, along with the appropriate filing fee.[2]

501(c)(4) organizations have a much narrower definition: this designation is generally reserved solely for organizations that promote social welfare to

---

[2] Fees are $850 if your organization expects to average yearly gross receipts of more than $10,000 and $400 if you expect it to average less than that (www.irs.gov).

benefit the community. The organization's earnings must be devoted "only to charitable, educational or recreational purposes."[3] Examples include civic associations and volunteer fire companies.

For these types of organizations, with the exception of volunteer fire companies, charitable donations *are not tax deductible* for federal income tax purposes.

There are actually a whole host of other 501(c) sub-categories out there. For example, your organization might be a 501(c)(19) Veterans' Organization, in which case contributions to your organization are tax deductible. However, I am guessing that if you are reading this book, your organization will likely be designated as either a 501(c)(3) or a 501(c)(4).

If you are interested, the IRS's web site is actually quite user-friendly. If you're unsure of how to define the work that you do within the strict (and pretty well defined) parameters of the IRS, it makes sense to jump online and take a look.

Verboten! What Activities Are Off Limits

501(c)(3)s are not allowed to participate in elections or political activities. The IRS web site dictates that

> If any of the activities (whether or not substantial) of your organization consist of participating in, or intervening in, any political campaign on behalf of (or in opposition to) any candidate for public office, your organization will not qualify for tax-exempt status under section 501(c)(3). Such participation or intervention includes the publishing or distributing of statements.

> Whether your organization is participating or intervening, directly or indirectly, in any political campaign on behalf of (or in opposition to) any candidate for public office depends upon all of the facts and circumstances of each case. Certain voter education activities or public forums conducted in a nonpartisan manner may not be prohibited political activity under section 501(c)(3), while other so-called voter education activities may be prohibited.[4]

---

[3] IRS, "Other Section 501 (c) Organizations," www.irs.gov/publications/ p557/ch04.html#en_US_2010_publink1000200291, 2010.

[4] IRS, "Section 501(c)(3) Organizations," www.irs.gov/publications/p557/ch03.html#en_US_2010_publink1000200036, 2010.

It gets trickier, of course, when we get into lobbying, because 501(c)(3)s are allowed to lobby (*unless you're a church—then no lobbying for you*). It gets somewhat technical, so if your organization does plan to participate directly (or really, even indirectly) in the business of influencing the political process, you'd be wise to check out the IRS's rules and regulations on permitted lobbying activities and expenditures for 501(c)(3) organizations. The rules can be found by visiting this link on the IRS web site: www.irs.gov/publications/p557/ch03.html#en_US_2010_publink1000200036.

With 501(c)(4) organizations, the law is similar, but if you can submit proof that your organization is organized *exclusively* to promote social welfare, you "can obtain exemption even if it participates legally in some political activity on behalf of or in opposition to candidates for public office."[5] Of course, the contributions to the organization still aren't tax deductible.

When the Tax Incentive Disappears

When contributions are not tax deductible, another hurdle for donors is raised. Certain nonprofits do not qualify—which isn't to say that they're not allowed to fundraise. Their donors just can't deduct the contributions from their taxes. Again, for a very thorough run-down of what types of organizations qualify to have their charitable contributions count as tax deductible, visit the IRS's web site: www.irs.gov.

So what happens when that tax deduction disappears? Do donors run and hide?

One thing you will likely lose if your organization is not tax exempt is the benefit of contributions from foundations and matching gift programs from most corporations that have such a program set up.

With respect to individual contributions, though (which, again, make up the vast majority of charitable gifts every year anyway), I'll concede that it's a hurdle, but I'd argue that it's a somewhat low-lying hurdle. To give you an idea of how much people can give to political parties, PACs (political action committees), and candidates, consider this information taken from the web site of the Federal Election Commission (FEC). An individual may give a maximum of

- $2,500 per election to a Federal candidate or the candidate's campaign committee. Notice that the limit applies separately to each

[5] IRS, "Other Sections 501(c) Organizations," www.irs.gov/publications/ p557/ch04.html#en_US_2010_publink1000200291, 2010.

election. Primaries, runoffs, and general elections are considered separate elections.

- $5,000 per calendar year to a PAC. This limit applies to a PAC that supports Federal candidates. (PACs are neither party committees nor candidate committees. Some PACs are sponsored by corporations and unions—trade, industry, and labor PACs. Other PACs, often ideological, do not have a corporate or labor sponsor and are therefore called nonconnected PACs.) PACs use donor contributions to make their own contributions to Federal candidates and to fund other election-related activities.

- $10,000 per calendar year to a State or local party committee. A State party committee shares its limits with local party committees in that state, unless a local committee's independence can be demonstrated.

- $30,800 per calendar year to a national party committee. This limit applies separately to a party's national committee, House campaign committee, and Senate campaign committee.

- $117,000 total biennial limit. This biennial limit places a ceiling on a donor's total contributions, as explained below.

- $100 in currency (cash) to any political committee. (Anonymous cash contributions may not exceed $50.) Contributions exceeding $100 must be made by check, money order, or other written instrument.[6]

$30,800 a year without a tax break? Nonsense, right? Nope. People give that much, and more. If there's a $117,000 biennial limit, that supposes that people are giving not only the max to the political party, but also maxing out on other types of political contributions.

When I was canvassing on behalf of the Democratic Party in 2006, I had more than one instance of canvassing someone only to hear them say, "I've already maxed out this year," or "I've given the maximum already this year." When I took the time to clarify that I was raising money for the DNC itself, not a candidate or party, they would say, "Yeah, I know. The limit's $26,000 or something like that, right?" At the time, it was $26,700.

So I met, in my few months canvassing on the streets of Boston, more than one individual who gave over $25,000 in a single year to a political party

---

[6] Federal Election Commission, *Citizens' Guide*, http://www.fec.gov/pages/brochures/citizens.shtml, February 2004 (updated February 2011).

without a tax deduction. I wasn't the only canvasser who ran into that situation in Boston—and Boston wasn't the only team that reported back that they had had such conversations.

In 2009, a non-election year, the Democratic National Committee raised $37,412,427. Of that, nearly $5 million was from contributions at the maximum permitted level (in 2009, $30,400). The Republican National Committee raised $45,695,088.[7]

In that mid-term election, the largest gift I received was $2,000. It was also my first gift, which, while frustrating, did not disappoint me too much (it was one of the largest contributions from my office for the entire summer, after all). There were a few other $2,000 gifts that summer in my office, and across the country, we did receive a few five figure gifts. These gifts came from hired, outsourced canvassers who were meeting complete strangers on the streets or on doorsteps and asking them for one-time contributions.

Tens of thousands of dollars to an organization without as much as a tax break. I'm going on at such length to drive home the fact that while the tax break is nice, it is by no means necessary to raise significant funds. So, if charitable gifts to your organization do not qualify for a tax deduction, don't sweat it. You can still raise plenty of money.

In this way, philanthropy can seem irrational from an economics perspective. But give someone a good, clear, convincing message as to why your organization deserves your support, and they'll write you a check, deduction or not. As I've said before, philanthropy is a deeply personal choice, and sometimes those deep personal convictions go beyond the more rational explanation of tax code, selective incentives, etc.

Different Groups, Same Rules

Regardless of your mission, regardless of how the tax code will treat charitable gifts to your organization, you will not be able to raise any money at all if you are not able to inspire.

Harking back to Chapter 7, I want to reiterate that inspirational messaging will always contain some combination of the following:

- Your organization's name and mission

---

[7] Federal Election Commission, *Sources of Receipts for National Party Committees Through June 30 of the Non-Election Year*, www.fec.gov/press/summaries/2012/ Party/6mthSummary/ 4dncrncsummary2011sixmonth.xls, July 2011

- The problem
- The solution
- A sense of urgency
- A call to action (i.e., an ask)

You need to position your organization as a solution to a big societal problem; if you don't secure the philanthropic support of your donors, then your work will be compromised, and the big societal problem will continue to be a big societal problem.

With the DNC fundraising in 2006, we were able to raise money because there was an election and we were delivering a message, day after day, in about 60 seconds or less, that contained all of these points.

As a paid fundraiser working on behalf of the DNC, this was my spiel: the problem (from the left side of the aisle) was that the Republicans in the House, Senate, and White House were taking the country in a very bad direction, were corrupt, and had us in the middle of two wars overseas. Also, they were in the pockets of big business. The solution was to take back the House of Representatives and the Senate, so that we could get America back on track. The urgency was that we were just a few months away from election season and the RNC was doing an equally good job of fundraising. (Their message would have been just as incendiary and emotional, and whatever it was, it worked well.) The call to action was asking for a contribution of $100, $200, $1,000, or other amount depending on the person's perceived inclination, so that we could help get Democratic candidates elected across the country.

It worked at a rate of about 20 percent, which is on par with the average fundraising organization. Again, all that was delivered in 60 seconds.

If you're representing an organization that needs money to raise awareness, provide treatment and counseling options, and also help promote research of a certain type of illness, your message will contain all those same elements. These are the questions that you should answer when crafting your messaging, both for your mass written appeals, and for your higher-level conversations: What is your organization's name? What is the illness's effect on society? How many people perish each year or are hospitalized as result of this illness? How are the families affected? What does your organization plan to do to address the problem *but cannot currently do because of lack of funding? Or, what critical programs will your organization have to cut if it does not continue to receive philanthropic support?* Why can the donor not afford to wait? What is on the line? How much are you asking the donor to give?

Here is another question that your organization needs to consider: *why should a donor give money to you and not to another nonprofit?* What makes your organization uniquely deserving?

Political organizations, you can use the same formula. Professional organizations, you, too. Educational nonprofits? Yes, you, too. It shouldn't make too much of a difference; these basic elements of building your case will remain the same, because, again, philanthropy happens out of inspiration. Yes, there can be a rational side to it, such as a tax deduction, and yes, donors want to know that your organization has its shop in order and that their philanthropic investments are "performing well" (cue the Stewardship Department!), but getting people to take out their checkbooks and their credit cards will only happen if you *inspire* them. Your organization has to tug at something deep within your donors. You can't just reason with them. You have to motivate them. You need to tap some part of them that they can't explain. If you think about it, giving away $100,000 that donors could otherwise be spending on themselves doesn't, at the surface, seem like a good idea. But if you, as a fundraiser, can make that feel terrific—through your skills as a storyteller, as a preacher—then writing that six-figure check is the best idea in the whole wide world. Everyone feels good; everyone is helped.

If you think about your fundraising as a performance (and, as I've stated earlier, that metaphor is actually a fitting parallel), you don't just want a cathartic response at the end. You don't want just applause. You want a standing ovation, and a demand for an encore.

So that's it. The takeaway point here is that no matter what type of organization you are, whether your organization is politically active or not, and whether or not charitable gifts to your organizations are tax-deductible, the same basic principles of constructing a compelling fundraising message apply. While you will have to tailor your message so that it resonates with your audience, there is a formula that you can follow. And don't forget to check to see if you've filed the appropriate paperwork with the IRS.

Let's turn to the conclusion now, where we'll revisit some of the major themes covered in this book.

Get Out There and Start Asking

It's been a long, wild ride. The goal of this book was to walk you through the process of transforming your fundraising operations into a professional operation, from how to recruit qualified candidates for the necessary positions to have a stellar shop to how to solicit gifts of $25 all the way up to $1 million—and everything in between.

I'd like to leave you with some final thoughts, some meditations on recurring themes that we've dealt with up to this point.

Rejection

First: remember that you are going to get rejected. A lot. More than you might think. As a reminder, you will get $0.20 to $0.25 for every dollar you ask for. Whether you're scrapping for $10 participation gifts or soliciting a major donor for $100,000, this ratio will hold over the long term. Again, this can mean that for every $100,000 solicitation you make you get one person in five who says yes, or five people who give you $20,000 in response. It almost always averages out to 1:4 or 1:5.

Do not take the rejections personally. You can't afford to. You need to develop a thick skin and divorce yourself from the *outcome. That isn't to suggest that you should also divorce yourself from the preparation* that goes into the solicitation. You might be asking why you should bother putting in the effort of coming up with a solicitation strategy.

Preparation does matter, even if, despite your best efforts, you're looking at 1:4 odds in the best of situations. You should enter every gift conversation assuming that you're going to hear yes.

Remember: there are hard nos and soft nos. There is also "not yet," "not that much," or "not this time." *No is not a permanent state.* Rather, *it is a response to a singular appeal at a given moment in time.* If someone says no this year (or quarter), that does not preclude him or her from giving later. The flip side, of course, is that just because someone gives now does not necessarily mean that he or she will give later. Take no donor for granted, and don't take "no" to mean forever.

Recently, when interviewing a candidate for a major gift position, a colleague talked (accurately, for the record) about how we divide our prospect pools into thirds. You have your top third: the people you can always rely on to be consistent and generous, those you can turn to in times of crisis or campaigns to step up their giving. Then you have the middle third: the people who give when they're asked to give, not always the amount that you'd hoped for, but people who can be prodded. Then you have your bottom third, your C list: the people who never get back to you or rarely respond, and are terrible donors relative to their capacity.

I was quick to qualify. Those thirds are malleable, moving targets. Someone in your top third today can very easily drop to the bottom third, and someone who has never given might finally see the light and begin writing checks and taking your calls. You just never know when they'll convert, nor will you necessarily be able to predict why. So you have to get out there, see as many people as you can, and solicit as much as possible at all three tiers of your prospect pool. The gritty work will pay off.

And, seriously, don't take rejection personally. Remember: you are not responsible for the outcome. You are responsible only for making the best possible case to the donor. Once you've made the solicitation, you don't control the situation.

Staffing

If you're the executive director of development, take heed: you need staff members. It's so hard to stomach the initial startup cost of paying another staff member, but believe me, in fundraising, staff members are a wise investment. *You leave money on the table for every aspect of the gift cycle that you leave unprofessionalized.* With some positions, it will be obvious. Frontline fundraisers are usually going to raise more than what they are paid. At least that's the hope, under normal circumstances. So that's a no-brainer. But what about your research staff, your stewardship department? Then, the argument becomes more indirect, a bit tougher to argue. I will argue for it, though. Granted, you want optimal efficiency from every hire, but you want a fully staffed shop. The more overstretched you make your employees, the more you ask them to do beyond their specialized role, the more you begin to sacrifice quality.

A mediocre stewardship report can be more harmful than none at all, for example. You don't want half-baked products coming out of your office, whether it's an invitation to an event or a million-dollar proposal. You therefore want to take the time and trust in the investment to hire an entire development staff. Start with your fundraisers and then move on to support staff (they, after all, keep the front liners' heads screwed on straight), researchers, donor relations, etc.

Fully staffed shops are good not just for efficiency but also for morale. You can build a team that thrives on the collaboration required to close gifts of all sizes. Put too much work on any given individual, and you run into troubles of attitude and stress. You also run the risk of burning out the few staff members you do have, which will leave you in a very bad place.

The Fundraiser's Place

The development shop's place within an organization can be strange. The buy-in among other constituents within the organization isn't always immediate, nor guaranteed, especially if you're just beginning to make the operation more professional. While still part of the nonprofit world, your operations mimic some for-profit business practices, since your work has very significant implications for the bottom line. Depending on how your nonprofit is doing, you might be fundraising just to keep the lights on at first.

On the one hand, your operation is mission-driven: you are asking for money to support a particular mission in which you believe strongly. On the other hand, you're a pragmatic, bottom line–driven operation: if your work isn't successful, the organization suffers.

The point is that a professional fundraising operation, when it's first set up, can raise some eyebrows. Even well after it's set up, it can continue to raise eyebrows. The development shop can often be perceived as a shadow organization within the organization. Your work can make others in the organization uncomfortable, as though somehow you're going to alienate their already small and fragile base of support.

I'd say that the aversion toward your work within your own ranks comes from a misguided understanding of what you do as opposed to an *actual* dislike of the operations. The discomfort that you can, and often do, cause is ill-founded, and can be easily ameliorated if you address this issue straight on.

In the early stages of setting up your operations, it makes sense to educate the rest of the organization on the work that you do and why you are doing it. Take the time to explain how they can partner with you, how you are part of the team, how sometimes they might actually be better poised to solicit a prospect than you, depending on the donor. Explain how your success has implications for the programs that the other departments oversee.

Ask them what they would do with additional funding. Have them be a part of the conversation early, to help them realize that partnering with the development shop is actually a great idea.

In short, engage the other departments within your organization, and more than anything, be transparent about what you do and how you do it. Be sure to report internally on your successes: circulate news of significant accomplishments, and narrate which programs those philanthropic dollars will be affecting.

Why We Do It

This applies to the entire development shop, but most specifically to the frontline fundraisers: you have to believe in the mission of your organization. I know this sounds mind-numbingly obvious. But it isn't always the case when someone is brought on board to fundraise for your organization with either a limited understanding of or a limited appreciation for your mission. The understanding side can be ameliorated, but the appreciation factor is harder to inspire. An employee is either delighted and proud to represent your organization, or he or she is not.

You need passion for the mission because fundraisers, in many cases, are the most public face of the organization. You're meeting people at events, at the office, on the road. You cannot afford to have a less-than-enthusiastic employee among your ranks. If you are misrepresented or underrepresented, there will be a huge mess to clean up or, worse, a relationship that is irreparably damaged.

To prospective fundraisers: work for the causes you feel good about. Don't take a job at any nonprofit just to pad your résumé. You will burn yourself out and do a disservice to yourself and the organization you're representing.

We fundraise for nonprofits because we believe in the mission of the organization, its leadership, and the outcomes that the organization helps to produce in society. We fundraise to allow the organization to expand the scope and depth of its operations, and to take the pressure off nonqualified or not-as-qualified individuals from having to raise money, allowing them to concentrate on what they are best suited to do.

We fundraise to validate the mission of the nonprofit by building a core of supporters who will consistently make gifts of $5 all the way to $50,000 or more. We fundraise because it raises awareness of the worthy cause and helps to build a movement of socially aware citizens. By asking for their philanthropic support, we are asking our donor base to join our mission, to be a very real part of it.

We forge the essential relationships between the public and the organization. We communicate the mission in a way that engages an audience beyond the scope of the employees and the directly affected constituents, and we make an honest call for action, a humble request for support. We are asking people to partner with the us, to help us walk the road to progress together.

Our job is to connect the dreamers and the doers with the supporters.

Your Donors

The majority of this book has been focused on how *you* should do your job. It's easy to lose sight of your audience, to cease to consider them as anything but dollar signs, new gifts, and a source of cash to underwrite your budgeted expenses. Do so at your own peril.

Behind every gift is a human being. This might sound very elementary, but remember, we are in the business, above all, of *relationship-building*. We build relationships with people, not with checks or research dossiers.

I talked about how our prospect pool can be divided into thirds: your all-stars, your stable donors who do just as much as you ask, and your duds. While this is generally true, you have to treat each conversation with every donor as though he or she is the next million-dollar support of your organization. Even the duds.

We must work hard to avoid having our view of donors turn adversarial, as if they are a problem. Yes, they can be tough, yes, it's a letdown when they give us $1,000 instead of the $10,000 we had asked for, and yes, it's frustrating when a gift conversation drags on for months—or years.

I'll be the first to admit I have my favorite prospects and my least favorite prospects. At times, I downright *dread* calling one to set up an appointment, or knowing what I'm in for, I have to steel myself before certain visits.

It's natural. *And it's not good business.* We really have to appreciate every donor, every prospect, even if the wealthiest prospect in our pool is undergiving by a lot. You really have to go into every conversation with every prospect thinking the following:

- I like you a lot.
- You are going to give me exactly what I ask for.

It can be hard, especially after you figure out that you rarely get exactly what you ask for. However, your *mind-set* plays a huge role in how you carry yourself even if you don't know it. I can't describe exactly how it will change your posture, your delivery, and your enthusiasm, but it will. If you go into a phone call or a meeting and think that you're wasting your time, well, then, you're probably going to end up wasting your time. And your donor's time, which is even worse. It becomes a self-fulfilling prophecy.

You can be pessimistic after the meeting, but please, do yourself a favor and be delusionally optimistic every time you speak with a donor.

The point is that bad eggs aren't always bad eggs. You never know when someone's circumstances change, when they finally decide that they need to start giving away more, when they finally let go of some longstanding grudge that they had with your organization. You can't predict it. You can only influence it with *consistent contact, constant gratitude, and an unflaggingly positive outlook* on converting that prospect. I know that I've already regaled you with tales of donors who for years had been pegged by my predecessors as people to put on the B list on good days, the C list on others. Would probably never be big donors. Then, through no magic of mine, I go into a first meeting with one such donor, and she told me she was going to give me a check for $20,000, which is five times her biggest gift to the organization ever. I repeat, *I brought nothing special to the conversation*, save a new face and fresh energy. The donor herself, though, had concluded she was ready to deepen her philanthropic relationship with the organization.

Now, notes up to that point had never suggested that I would be entering a conversation in which $20,000 would come up as a figure. The file on her suggested that the meeting would be cordial, that she would talk about how she prefers to give more to her prep school, and that she would hedge if asked to consider increasing her giving beyond $4,000 a year.

What I did right in preparing for that meeting was acknowledge the obstacles but *not let those obstacles define the conversation.* I went in there with a positive mind-set, and took stock of the fact that it had taken *more than a year to secure this appointment,* and I could not afford to waste this opportunity. She travels a lot for her work, so after four trips to Texas and almost 18 months of attempting unsuccessfully to see her, we finally intersected. She had only a half hour, so I knew I had to go in there and make the best use of limited time. And I was fortunate that she was positively predisposed to talk about increasing her giving.

Remember: until they say no, we assume that the answer is yes. There are plenty of yesses along the way until we get to the solicitation. Yes, I will visit with you. Yes, I will answer your questions about my current philanthropy, family situation, etc. Yes, I will see you again. Yes, I will consider a proposal. Count each one among your victories.

And also remember: there are hard nos, soft nos, not yets, not that muches, and not this years. In relationship-building, nothing is permanent, and everything is mutable.

The flip side, of course, the less-fun side, is that good eggs aren't always good eggs. For whatever the reason, sometimes people just stop giving to your organization. Or they start giving less.

Leave nothing to chance and assume nothing. Engage the donor. Ask: Why did you stop giving this year? What would have made you continue your support?

Again, how you choose to view someone from your A list who suddenly stops giving will influence the outcome of the situation. If you view having to get a donor to re-up his support or asking him pointed questions about how to get him back on board as an annoyance, both parties are likely to leave the conversation annoyed, and you aren't likely to get the information you need to reconvert.

If, however, you view the interaction as an opportunity to engage meaningfully with someone who already has a pre-established relationship with your organization, and to have a conversation with him about his priorities, well, then it's much more likely that you'll both feel good about the short term, and will have a clearer idea of the donor's intentions regarding his philanthropic relationship with you in the future.

People stop giving for many reasons. It just happens. Sometimes, it's out of your control. Other times, it isn't. Do damage control for the ones you can without selling the integrity of the organization. Address the problem or concern directly and quickly insofar as you are able.

For the ones you can't control: keep them on your list, and keep them connected through nonmonetary means until they're ready to reestablish their philanthropic relationship with you.

Here is a partial listing of reasons people might stop contributing to your organization:

- They moved away, and your organization is locally based.
- They have chosen to focus their philanthropic commitments on a different cause.
- They are upset about something that your organization has done or dislike the current leadership.
- They are now married, and their spouses aren't into philanthropy.
- They lost their jobs.
- They just forgot to give this year.
- You *forgot* to ask them to give this year.
- They died.

Again, don't make assumptions about why they didn't give this year. Ask them.

The thing to take away here is that *our donors are human beings*. They are more than their net worth on paper, more than the checks that they send in. They have their own lives, their own priorities. *The brutal truth is that your average donor, even your above-average donor, spends very, very little time thinking about your organization, and even less time thinking about giving to it.* Whereas our job as fundraisers is to think constantly about the nonprofit that we represent, its actions and policies and how to craft solicitation language for that. So we are constantly steeped in the inner workings of the organization. We're lucky if our donors think about us more than once a month without the aid of a phone call, an appeal, or a visit.

This is a good thing and a bad thing. The downside is that it's just hard to stay relevant on people's radar. They're busy, and other nonprofits are vying for attention. The good news is that we often underestimate people's patience with our check-ins, whether in the form of visits, solicitations, newsletters, etc. Most of the time, we just get ignored, so repeated attempts are okay. Now, there is a point at which you are being too aggressive (as we discussed in Chapter 6, when we talked about planning), but it's likely to be a few points of contact beyond what you initially think.

Beyond the fact that donors live most of their lives outside the realm of giving money to your organization, remember philanthropy is a deeply personal choice. You want a good match between your nonprofit and the donor. Remember: timing and personal circumstance can prevent a donor who is extremely wealthy on paper from making a gift commensurate with his apparent net worth. It is fair of you to ask why, knowing that you might be diving into very personal waters. I recently met with a donor in Chicago who looked very promising on paper, and seemed to be engaged with my organization. When asked why he wasn't giving more than he was, he replied that although he wanted to, he was currently spending a significant amount of money on his ill mother's medical expenses. He acknowledged out loud that he was not giving in proportion to what he might look like on paper.

In sum: do your homework, be open to the conversation taking unexpected turns, and take no donor for granted. Love your donors. You need them.

Butterflies vs. Fearlessness

I began the chapter by telling you that you're going to get rejected. That wasn't very nice of me, but I want to give you realistic expectations. What I did not do at the beginning of the chapter was tell you how to deal with this level of failure. I said not to take it personally, which is true. I said that you need to do your prep work, but you cannot control the response, which is also true.

When you mail a written appeal, send off an electronic solicitation, or dial a donor to ask for money, you don't want to come off as nervous. I gave you tips in Chapter 10, on face-to-face solicitations, for how to come off as calm, cool, and collected. You want a façade of fearlessness, of being unflappable, to gain the trust of the donor but also to keep the conversation comfortable. Appearing ill at ease will put the donor ill at ease.

But the butterflies in our stomach—what do we do about those? Why are they there?

They are there because we care about the outcome. They are there because we are genuinely invested in the mission of the organization that we are representing, and want very much, very sincerely, for the answer to our solicitation to be yes.

I still get butterflies when I'm soliciting someone for any kind of gift. Heck, I still get butterflies when calling prospects to set up appointments. It's natural.

It doesn't make sense for me to tell you, don't get nervous. What I will tell you is that you will get nervous, that it's natural, and that as it's happening, take notice of it. Listen to yourself, and make sure that you can hear the words you are saying. *Remember, if you can't understand the words coming out of your mouth, then it's unlikely that the donor on the other end of the phone line or across the table will.* Listening to yourself forces you to slow down.

You'll develop your own strategies for conquering or at least working through getting the butterflies. I want to end by saying that the stirring in your stomach is a good thing. It means you want to succeed. It means that you want your organization to succeed. And that you want the donor to be a meaningful part of that success. And those are all very good things.

So get going. Set your goals. Make your plan. Write your appeals. Call your donors. Visit with them. Ask them for a gift. Steward them well.

Have a positive impact upon the world.

Additional Resources

While it's best to spend what limited time and resources you have out asking potential donors for money, it can't hurt to have some supplemental guidance along the way in addition to what you've read in this book. Here are some recommendations for your reading/viewing pleasure:

Books

- Ahern, Tom. *How to Write Fundraising Materials that Raise Money: The Art, the Science, the Secrets.* Medfield, MA: Emerson & Church, 2007.
- Burnett, Ken. *Relationship Fundraising: A Donor-Based Approach to the Business of Raising Money.* San Francisco, CA: Jossey-Bass, 2002.
- Burdenski, Robert A. *Innovations in Annual Giving: Ten Departures That Worked.* Washington, DC: Council for the Advancement and Support of Education, 2003.
- Burk, Penelope. *Donor-Centered Fundraising: How to hold on to your donors and raise much more money.* Hamilton, ON (Canada): Cygnus Applied Research, Inc., 2003.
- Fisher, Roger, William L. Ury & Bruce Patton. *Getting to Yes: Negotiating Agreement Without Giving In.* New York, NY: Penguin Books, 1991.

- Levy, Reynold. *Yours for the Asking: An Indispensable Guide to Fundraising and Management.* Hoboken, NJ: John Wiley & Sons, Inc., 2008.
- Panas, Jerold. *Mega Gifts: Who Gives Them, Who Gets Them.* Medfield, MA: Emerson & Church, 2005.
- Pitman, Marc A. *Ask Without Fear: A Simple Guide to Connecting Donors with What Matters to Them Most.* Mechanicsburg, PA: Executive Books, 2007.
- Stanley, Thomas J. & William D. Danko. *The Millionaire Next Door.* New York, NY: Pocket Books, 1996.

Websites

- The Agitator: www.theagitator.net/
- The Association of Fundraising Professionals: www.afpnet.org/
- The Chronicle of Philanthropy: www.philanthropy.com/
- Council for Advancement and Support of Education: www.case.org/
- Donor Power Blog: www.donorpowerblog.com/
- Federal Election Commission: www.fec.gov/
- FirstGiving: www.firstgiving.com/
- The GivingUSA Foundation: www.aafrc.org/gusa/gusa_foundation.cfm
- GrantMakers Online: www.grantmakersonline.com/
- Growing Philanthropy in the United States: www.indiana.edu/~iunews/GrowingPhilanthropy.pdf
- GuideStar: www2.guidestar.org/
- Internal Revenue Service: www.irs.gov/
- Mal Warwick Associates: www.malwarwick.com/
- Open Secrets: www.opensecrets.org/
- Showcase of Fundraising Innovation and Inspiration (where I retrieved a number of these sites!): www.sofii.org/

Periodicals

- *The Chronicle of Philanthropy*
- *The Wall Street Journal*
- Your Local and State Newspapers

Example Appeals and Websites You Should Envy

This appendix will analyze excerpts from actual appeals and provide you with a sample that I have written for Betasab, an orphanage in Ethiopia for which I serve as the volunteer gift officer. In doing this, the hope is to get you thinking about writing your own appeals.

I am also including a major gift solicitation. I should note that the solicitation is written in my voice and might not resonate with your own. That is OK. You want the solicitation to sound authentic, so know that I am including this to give you an idea of how to structure a major gift solicitation.

More full length examples of actual appeals and solid websites can be found on SOFII's website (www.sofii.org). When you look at these examples, pay attention to how well and how succinctly these organizations make the case for philanthropic support, and how clearly they present the problem, the solution, the solution, and the ask. Don't just follow them blindly, though; approach them with a curious, but critical eye. No appeal is perfect, and no website is perfectly designed.

I'd also recommend signing up to receive e-mail updates from a number of non-profits that you personally support (or are interested in supporting but haven't done so yet) so that your inbox is inundated with online appeals. This will give you a robust data set that you can analyze to figure out what works, what doesn't work, what's inspiring, and what's just downright annoying.

At the end of this section, I'll give you a few websites of non-profits that you should take a look at, either because of the site layout or because of a compelling message that lives on the site.

Barack Obama's 2012 Campaign

Let's start with someone you've probably all heard of. Below is an e-mail I received back in September of 2011. The whole e-mail itself is quick and effective. The message goes on for more than one windowpane, so the reader has to scroll, which is something to keep in mind. This problem is more or less solved, however, because there is an ask halfway through the appeal—something for you to keep in mind if the person writing your appeal has a problem with concision. Let's take a look at a few elements of the e-mail.

The salutation is to me, an important little thing to note. It doesn't say "Dear Donor," or "Dear Supporter." It opens with my name.

Then the e-mail opens with an introduction. The person signing off on this letter is the Chief Operating Officer of Obama for America. Why is she writing us instead of the usual appeal from Joe Biden, Barack Obama, or Jim Messina (the campaign manager)? She says so immediately: "As chief operating officer of this campaign, I'm the person people come to when they want to spend the money you've donated." So we know why we're supposed to pay attention—we're about to learn how our money is being spent (a good stewardship step, if you're paying close attention).

The appeal definitely contains urgency:

> What we do before midnight on September 30th determines our budget until the end of this year. And what happens this year will set in motion the results on Election Day 2012. It's that simple.

I received this e-mail on September 23, and I'm being told that September 30 is the deadline for determining the campaign budget. That gives me less than a week to make up my mind. Two days before that, I received an e-mail with the subject line "Serious Deadline" from the campaign. That achieves the same sense of urgency that you need in effective appeals.

It closes with a gimmick, but an effective one: "you'll even be automatically entered for a chance to have dinner with President Obama." Of course, the odds of actually having dinner with the President are really small, but dangling the possibility could sway the on-the-fence donor.

The appeal also talks about its plan, its solution. It plans to open "offices in some battleground states right now, and laying the plans to open others across the country next year. The campaign has plans to be the biggest grassroots movement this country has ever seen."

The appeal's biggest weakness is the "problem" part of the letter, which is implicit, but a little diluted. This is the closest we get to hearing an explicit problem:

> Every team on the campaign has submitted their plans for the rest of this year—opening field offices, registering voters, building technology. And it all costs money.
>
> I can't say yes to everything…

I can't say that it's a terribly convincing problem. I know that opening an office costs money. And not being able to say yes to everything isn't a compelling reason for me to give. Are the Republicans opening more offices than you? The average reader needs something a little more meaty to be sufficiently inspired to click on that hyperlink.

All in all, though, it's a good message. The ask is for $15, and we are given a clear idea of what that $15 will do: open new field offices and provide those offices with the necessary supplies. We know that we'll be a part of this grassroots effort if we give, and we might even have dinner with the president.

Human Rights Campaign (HRC)

I'm going to present excerpts now from a 2010 appeal from the Human Rights Campaign, the oldest LGBTQ advocacy group in the US. The appeal was targeted at donors who had given to the organization previously, but had not in over a year (in fundraising lingo, the label applied can be "lapsed donors," or "LYBuNTS," an acronym for "Last Year But Not This Year").

In contrast to the Obama appeal, the HRC e-mail does a very good job of addressing the problem. They then include a link to a video that highlights how the HRC is addressing the problem. It's a shrewd way of keeping the appeal itself to one page, and giving folks something to click on other than a "Give" button or hyperlink (even if the video page also contains a giving form).

Without access to their analytics, I'm guessing that a fair amount of people actually clicked the link to the video (fair meaning anywhere from 20% to 50%). Let's take a look at what works here:

Again, the appeal is addressed directly to me. The first paragraph has an implicit introduction, but then dives *right into the problem*. Have a look.

> Dear Jeff—
>
> I spend most of my time on Capitol Hill, and lately I've noticed a clear intensification of right wing efforts. Emboldened by their win in Maine, **anti-LGBT groups aren't just trying to prevent new victories—they're trying to take away rights we've already secured.**[1]

That's a concern! Granted, it could be a platitude, as that's a pretty sweeping statement, but it certainly has my attention, and, if it contains any truth at all, it certainly is problematic if you support the work of the HRC.

The appeal later lists even more things that anti-LGBT groups are doing. Here is one of three bullet points that is included in the appeal:

- It's not just inflammatory words. They're spending money. Over the holidays, they blanketed the Washington, D.C. transit system with ads against marriage equality. In 2009 they spent **$1 million in New Jersey alone, and another $1.5 million in Maine**, on TV ads, flyers delivered directly to voters' mailboxes, and millions of automated "robo-calls."[2]

That's a ton of money! So not only is there an aggressive push in rhetoric, but large sums of cash are being spent on the endeavor.

Again, the solution is compiled into a video that you have to click to view, and that link also contains a giving form. Here is the language that HRC used to inspire people to click through:

---

[1] Emphasis in original.

[2] Emphasis in original.

> Watch the video, renew your HRC membership for 2010, and give us the resources we need to defeat them.

And later, there is a second request (also hyperlinked):

> Please, check out this short video – then help us take back the movement in 2010 by renewing your membership today.

In case the reader does *not* click on that link, there is still a nod to how HRC is part of the solution:

> **Your membership today will help fund a massive campaign to go head-to-head with groups like this,** from Capitol Hill to the doorsteps, town halls, and state legislatures where marriage equality is won.[3]

Preceding that second request to click on the link, there is a sense of urgency captured here:

> ...we need 2,010 people to pitch in before January 20th and help us hold our members of Congress accountable for what they have yet to do.

I received this e-mail on January 7, 2010, so that gives the HRC just 13 days to recruit 2,010 new donations. That's a tall order, but it does the job of giving the reader a clear deadline and a sense of haste. Urgency was also implicit in the bullet point that I included: just two weeks before, the anti-LGBT groups had spent a lot of money to get their message out.

It's a pretty solid appeal, with all of the elements necessary to make a convincing case for giving. And at the very bottom of the letter, after the Legislative Director's signature, there is still one more opportunity for readers to make a gift, in the form of a very large, blue "Renew" button that takes them to the giving page.

---

[3] Emphasis in original.

Betasab

And so we go from the president of the US, to one of the nation's largest LGBTQ advocacy groups, to a teeny-tiny orphanage in Ethiopia that has yet to get off the ground. Below is an e-mail that I personally crafted for Betasab, which is an orphanage in Ethiopia for which I am volunteering. I've also included the fact sheet to which I allude in the body of the e-mail. This appeal could also be sent as a hard copy if need be. I included this to give you an idea of something that you could send to people that you know personally. If I was sending to a stranger or mere acquaintance (which I will be doing), I would take out the personal note about what I've been up to this fall.

> Dear [informal salutation]:
>
> Greetings from New England. I hope that this note finds you well. It's a busy fall up here with work, running and martial arts.
>
> I'm writing to you today to let you know about an exciting project for which I am volunteering, and for which I am requesting your support. I am hard at work building awareness around an exciting new organization in Ethiopia, called Betasab, which means "family" in Amharic. This orphanage is directly addressing the challenges of poverty, AIDS, and orphaned children in Addis Ababa.
>
> The Betasab model will provide orphaned children with a stable home, a guaranteed education, a small bank account, coupled with practical skills and training, and frequent contact with mentors, local teachers, health, and mental health care providers. This model provides a long-term, sustainable solution to the deep, structural problems in Ethiopia of disease, unemployment, poverty, and the hundreds of thousands of children under the age of 18 who are orphans.
>
> Attached to this e-mail is an information sheet which provides you with a more in depth summary of Betasab's objectives, as well as funding opportunities for your consideration.
>
> Betasab relies almost exclusively on philanthropic support. We are hard at work building Betasab, and forging a movement of supporters here in the US to help lift this organization off the ground. Your gift is an investment in the future of a plagued nation. Your gift will directly and positively impact the lives of these orphans.

Please support us today as generously as you are able. You can either mail a check to the address below, or make a secure gift online at our website, which is www.betasab.org. Please know that you may always contact me via e-mail, or via phone, with questions of how you can get more involved, either as a leadership-level donor or as a volunteer.

You can be confident that a gift to Betasab makes a difference in these young people's lives. I thank you in advance for your support.

Sincerely:

Jeff Stauch

Volunteer Development Officer

jstauch@betasab.org

The text below is what I include as an attachment to the above e-mail.

Our objectives:

- A safe family environment: We hire and train the mothers and aunties; the children become brothers and sisters. Together they make a permanent family
- Stable homes including a main house that functions as a transitional house for new children and a meeting house for holidays and other special events and smaller houses, each with seven to ten children, a mother and an aunty
- Guaranteed education in local schools
- Support to pursue education and training to the child's maximum potential
- Means to a secure future including a small bank account in each child's name and practical skills and experiences
- A broader, supportive community
- Regular contact with local teachers, mentors, health and mental health providers
- Interactions with non-Ethiopian volunteers from Middlebury College and other American colleges and universities that will benefit the Ethiopian children and American students
- Sustainable community development including workshops and programming for both children and adults, as well as vocational education and support for the local community

- A focus on sustainability in all aspects of the project from small, local economic development to energy and technology sources and training

Your Opportunities for Philanthropic Engagement:[4]

- $ 500 would cover rent in the main house for 1 month
- $ 175 would send a child to school **for a year**
- $ 55 would buy meat for all the children for 1 month
- $ 25 would buy snacks for all the children for 1 month

Sponsorships: It costs almost $ 2,000 per year to support each child. To offset that cost, and most importantly, because we would like the children to form supportive relationships with a larger, caring community, we will offer sponsorships of $360 per year, per child. With the sponsorship, you will get photos and letters and updates of your child(ren), and we hope you will enjoy sending them letters, small gifts if you wish, and even visiting them if and when you ever get to Ethiopia. If you're interested in an initial sponsorship, please contact me at the address below.

A Major Solicitation

I'm now going to provide you with a major gift solicitation of $500,000. This type of solicitation would happen only after I had established a solid footing with John, and only after I had a good understanding of his interests and capacity.

As noted, this is written in my voice, but I wanted to provide you an idea of how you might go about structuring your written solicitations for significant contributions to your nonprofit. Some things to note:

- I made up a fund name for John, so that he can, as it were, imagine his name in lights.
- I request endowed and expendable support, to provide for short-term needs and long-term sustainability.
- I tell him that I am going to follow up in the next few weeks if I don't hear from him first.

---

[4] At the time of this writing, these figures are in the process of being adjusted, due to inflation.

Dear John:

Thank you so much for taking the time to meet with me during my trip to Franconia – and thanks for the delicious lunch! I hope that you found the conversation interesting and informative. If you left the meeting with questions or concerns, please do let me know. I would be happy to answer them.

In what follows, I am going to continue the dialogue that we in- itiated over lunch regarding a potential commitment to [college] in the mid-six figure range. I will present you with two ideas, which I am basing on what I understood to be your interests: a gift to endow a scholarship fund at [college], or a gift to establish an endowed internship fund here. I think both will hold appeal for you and both are areas for which there is great monetary need at the [college].

I. Scholarships at [college]: Ensuring Access for All

As I noted in our conversation in Franconia, financial aid is *the* big- gest fundraising priority for us here at [college]. It is one of our biggest expenditures each year, second only to the cost of class- room instruction (i.e. paying professors). Even full-paying students receive a "hidden" scholarship, thanks to our endowment. Whereas tuition at [college] is $40,000, the actual cost of educat- ing, feeding, and providing housing is closer to $65,000. That gap is filled through the endowment and from gifts from alumni, parents, and friends.

However, not everyone can afford to pay the full tuition. In fact, half of our students currently receive some form of financial aid. The average financial aid package here at [college] is **$20,000**. [College] is one hundred percent committed to making the unique, elite education here accessible to *all* qualified candidates, regardless of financial circumstances. A noble goal, to be sure, but one that requires significant funding, much of which will come from philanthropic support.

John, to this end, I would like you to consider a gift of **$500,000**, made over five years. This would entail setting up an endowed scholarship fund of $400,000 and providing expendable funding for financial aid as you build the endowed fund. In other words, you would provide $100,000 per year for five years, with $80,000 be- ing designated to set up your endowed scholarship fund, and $20,000 a year being used as an expendable scholarship.

Once fully endowed, [college] will be able to avail $20,000 each year from the *John D. Donor '77 Scholarship Fund* for a scholarship that would live on in perpetuity. That $20,000 is the average aid package for half of the students here at [college]. And the $20,000 that you would provide in expendable support while your fund builds to $400,000 would allow you to have an immediate impact on the life of a current student.

Based on your own narrative, John, I know that financial aid made your education at [college] possible, so I am hopeful that you might consider making that same opportunity a possibility for a student today.

II. Experiential Learning: Outside the Classroom Education

The other option that I believe might be of interest to you is establishing an endowed internship fund at [college]. Experiential learning opportunities are becoming ever more important to a student's education as the world becomes increasingly globalized. Competition for jobs is ever steeper, and many employers openly admit nowadays that the vast majority of their hires come out of their summer internship programs.

While some internships are paid, a good number of them, especially in the nonprofit and NGO world, are not, and there is *very high* demand for those types of opportunities here at [college]. The challenge is that many students cannot afford to have an unpaid position over the summer, so instead of pursuing these opportunities, they are forced to return to their hometowns to find a job which does much less to prepare them for life beyond college.

Currently, we are able to meet less than half of the financial requests for summer internship funding. Our goal is to be able to provide any student who wants to pursue an unpaid experiential learning opportunity with the funding they need for a summer. As I mentioned in our conversation, the average cost is $5,000.

John, if you were to make a gift of $500,000, then that would provide internship opportunities for four students who seek to pursue an outside-the-classroom learning experience over the summer. If you were to choose this option, again, it would be my hope that you would give $100,000 a year for five years, with $80,000 being set aside to establish the *John D. Donor '77 Internship Fund* and $20,000 a year being used as expendable, immediate use support to fund the internship experience for four students.

III. Next Steps

John, I acknowledge that I have put a lot in front of you. I wanted to provide you with a few options that I do think would be of interest to you. Please know that I am happy to answer any questions or address any concerns that might arise from what is contained in this e-mail. I can be reached by phone at 555-555-5555 or by e-mail. I will plan to follow up with you in a few weeks if I have not heard from you first.

Thank you so much, John, for all that you have already done to support [college]. I appreciate the fact that you are considering furthering your philanthropic relationship with your alma mater. I look forward to hearing from you.

With my kindest wishes:

Jeffrey David Stauch

Notable Websites

Here are a few websites for you to check out. Girl Effect's front page is a video that is a call to action. It's an incredibly well-done piece that you should sit through. Centre Point's website has a particularly solid layout. Before you have to scroll down, the tabs are actually labeled with the various elements of a good appeal: Home (who we are), The issue, The solution, What you can do (the ask). On the United Way Capital Area's site, donors can calculate out exactly what their gift is "worth" in terms of the impact is. Happy browsing!

- The Girl Effect: http://www.girleffect.org/video
- Centre Point: http://www.centrepoint.org.uk/
- The United Way Capital Area's Impact Calculator: http://www.unitedwaycapitalarea.org/give/impact_calculator.php

Funding Sources Beyond the Individual Donor

This appendix will provide you with resources to help you seek out funding from sources other than individual donors. There is some overlap from Appendix A. Please note that this list is by no means exhaustive.

I chose not to include individual foundations that give away money. There are simply too many to list. There are thousands of foundations out there, each with its own rules and regulations, some of which aren't even considering new grant applications at the moment. Also, their missions are often quite specific, so it doesn't make sense to list a number of foundations that don't apply to you. I did include links to government funding.

There are grant search engines, some of which are listed below. You'll often have to pay for these services. You can also do your own detective work via Google or your search engine of choice to see if you can find foundations on your own. However, I would recommend taking a trip to your local library and speaking to a reference librarian to help you navigate the sea of charitable trusts and foundations out there. They might even have access to the paid grant search engines. Research libraries on college and university campuses often do.

Here is a listing of resources to help you seek out those alternative funds:

- Center for Faith-based and Neighborhood Partnerships: www.hhs.gov/partnerships/
- Charity Navigator: www.charitynavigator.org/
- Federal Grants: www.federalgrants.com/
- Federal Grants Wire: www.federalgrantswire.com/
- The Foundation Center: foundationcenter.org/
- Fundsnet Services: www.fundsnetservices.com/
- The Giving USA Foundation: www.aafrc.org/gusa/resources.cfm
- Grantmakers Online: www.grantmakersonline.com/
- Grants.Gov: grants.gov/
- GrantVine: www.grantvine.net/
- GuideStar: www2.guidestar.org/

Index